NOW T

THAT I AM

GONE

a memoir by ALLAN MACDONELL

a barnacle book | rare bird books
los angeles, calif.

A Genuine Barnacle Book

A Barnacle Book | Rare Bird Books
453 South Spring Street, Suite 302
Los Angeles, CA 90013
rarebirdbooks.com

FIRST TRADE PAPERBACK ORIGINAL EDITION

Set in Dante
Printed in the United States

10 9 8 7 6 5 4 3 2 1

Publisher's Cataloging-in-Publication data
Names: MacDonell, Allan, auhtor.
Title: Now That I Am Gone: A Memoir Beyond Recall / Allan MacDonell
Description: First Trade Paperback Original Edition | A Barnacle Book |
New York, NY; Los Angeles, CA: Rare Bird Books, 2018.
Identifiers: ISBN 9781947856202
Subjects: LCSH MacDonell, Allan. | Music journalists—Biography. |
Journalists—United States—Biography. | Journalists—United States—Biography.
| Death. | Reincarnation. | BISAC BIOGRAPHY & AUTOBIOGRAPHY /
Personal Memoirs
Classification: LCC ML423 .M33 2018 | DDC 780.92—dc23

To Mom and Dad, for everything.

"Nobody's old in heaven. And nobody wears glasses.
God and Jesus light up heaven. It never gets dark.
It's always bright."

—Todd Burpo, *Heaven Is for Real*

CONTENTS

DEATH'S FOREWORD

FIVE STAGES OF SCHMALTZ

THERE'S A DOOR AT the end of a hall. It's marked private. But no one can keep me out of this club. The ranks of the dead, it turns out, are open to all comers. Everybody's a prospect. Rich and poor, smart and stupid, ugly and plain, wallflower, shrinking violet, late bloomer, apple of the eye, we all go sooner or later. Death appears to present itself as the ultimate common denominator. An extinguishing moment is the thing that unites us all.

Unfortunately, or maybe not so unfortunately, dying separates us in its universal process. Death's approach isolates us more completely than anything else that has come before it in this life. We may all be in this together, but you'll leave on your own, which is how some of us lived all along.

As a kid, as an adult, right up until the end of me hanging in here, I've displayed trivial variances. I scale toward oblivious—blind to so many obvious, crucial behavioral cues shared among the general populace. Still, I notice discrepancies between me and any of you who are not me. I unravel the mysteries of life a little slower than most of you do, or a little earlier, or not at all. Never right on pace. The rest of you and I, we've been this way all my life. Consequently, I'm not a joiner. I'll hang back. I'm not complaining. I've kept myself company.

But there's no turning back the fact that I've been born, spun into a cycle of life. The cycle includes a few nonelective twists. For instance, that one final mandatory and universal turn of human events. In the approach to death, we all become the other.

Rally around the gravely sick or hope-to-die initiate all you want. Shave your head in solidarity, but dying people don't fit in. Savvy party planners exclude the terminally ill from all popular festivities, until that time-honored time-ending gathering at which the expired "other" will be the center of attention, the guest of honor, and not present.

Now that I've passed on, left us, passed away, passed over, add euphemism to taste, now that I am dead, I have pledged the world's most inclusive fraternity. Membership has changed my life in several significant ways. Before I delve into all that, let's clear out a few common misconceptions regarding our last and eternal condition:

1. You won't be hearing from me again. This is it. I won't send down any messenger angels bearing cryptic instructional or inspirational dispatches from the great beyond.

2. Don't ask me for any favors. I haven't the heart to pass along messages to your sorely missed loved ones. My commitment to absolute nothing leaves me no time to track down the lost dogs of your childhood.

3. Nobody you know knows where I've gone. You will never meet a breathing soul who can tell you what I am about or what I am not about. No occupant of your planet or user of your Internet is positioned to share an informed opinion on what I am capable of or incapable of doing at my current place or non-place.

4. Everyone you meet cannot contact me. I am taking no calls.

5. I have no unfinished business. My work there, where you are, is done.

1

A FEW DEATHS I HAVE KNOWN
AND SOME I DREAMED

I N A WAY, THE end of individual existence does not come out of nowhere. Previews abound, like coming attractions for a movie you have no intention of seeing. The void ahead is introduced fairly early on, and you're face-to-face with it, now and again, from then on out. I'd been walking home from school, happy just to be doing something I was not supposed to do. I was following the bad example of a kid two or three years older than me. This was so long ago, neither one of us had even learned to say *fuck* yet.

I'd crested the top of the hill behind the parish house. A kid of seven could look up across the church road and farther out, above a cluster of evergreens that hid the house that sheltered my family, and his eyes would settle upon an ocean backdrop. Beyond where I lived, a steep descent of side streets bottomed out at train tracks, a pebbled shore, and the sea. The far-eyed kid on his way home from school could gaze upon a mild edge of the Pacific and follow that flat, blue-steel mirror to its outer limits, where it slices into the horizon. If that little boy stared into the big picture, he would see an infinite vista so sky blue that the wind took the blueness for a taunt and had smeared glowing streaks of cloud across it.

I wasn't looking toward the horizon. A white delivery van's tires hissed on the wet, black roadway. My companion and I stood safely off the pavement, innocent and still. The van's tires splashed through water left by the rain.

Our town was called White Rock, perched beside the sea outside Vancouver on the west coast of Canada. We stood on thick tufts of fat wild grass, a vibrant green testimony to rain being always in the forecast.

The van slowed at a cross street, and the kid, my mentor, made the first move. I was in action right behind him. We yanked clumps of grass out of the soft, wet earth. Clods of mud stuck to the twined roots. The delivery van idled at a stop sign. Without pausing to look both ways, my mentor and I ran into the road. We flung our green mud grenades at the back of the van. Two starbursts of filth exploded on the white paint.

Satisfaction! We scrambled into a roadside ditch, digging up more ammunition.

The truck skidded and swerved. The driver had mashed his brakes without considering the rain-slick steepness of the street. His rig spun half around and, to my eyes, looked as if it might slide sideways through the intersection, top the cross-street ridge, and tumble into the big ocean at the bottom of the drop.

"Allan, get away!" yelled my mentor. We ran.

"I'll fuck you buggers up!" The driver was out of the truck. He sounded angry and was in pursuit. I was galloping. I didn't stop to look at the driver. He sounded like an adult, and he'd spotted us.

My friend and I split up. I didn't want to run alone. Splitting up was the bigger kid's idea. I hesitated, and my friend threatened me with a face punch, so I took off on a tangent. I slid my scrawny limbs and jug head beneath hedges, through gateways and between bramble bushes. No grown man could follow in my tight squeezes.

As I moved farther from the point of ambush and closer to the house my family lived in, my terror turned to excitement and swelled to pride. I had done a bad thing and escaped the consequences. I kicked the gravel in our driveway. A huge grass stain smeared my dirty, wet pants. My feet stomped up the steps to the back porch, making the noise of a big, grown man, the kind of self-satisfied brute who flings back the screen door and slams open the storm door. My eager intention was to climb onto the kitchen counter, open the highest cabinets, reach to the top shelf, and eat brown sugar straight from the bag.

My mother sat working a pen and paper at the breakfast table. She wasn't supposed to be home. She worked days, for my father at his shop, a few blocks away in the opposite direction of school. She was slow to look up. I had no place to hide the grass stain on my pants.

My mother's blank and still face met mine straight on. I'd seen her angry. I'd never seen her look like this. She didn't even try to work up a smile for me. "Sit down," she said. "I have something to tell you."

Her topic, I recognized at age seven, would cause us both pain. In the pause while she found her voice, I concluded that she had seen me flinging mud and darting into the paths of moving vehicles. My reckless behavior, I presumed, had angered her.

"Your uncle Reg is dead," she said. My mother took a sigh. I guess those five words were the hard part. The rest flowed a lot easier, but not exactly comfortably.

On his way home the night before, Uncle Reg, married to my mom's sister, had missed a tunnel entrance with his 1961 Thunderbird. The car had been moving at a high velocity, so fast that Uncle Reg had been pronounced dead on the scene.

A cloud seemed to move away from across the sun. A bright sense of awe spread out through that kitchen. No sense of awe had ever been there before. I didn't recognize the change as something I knew the name of, but I was in awe of Uncle Reg. He had arrived somewhere no one else, as far as I knew, had ever been. There would be no coming back for Uncle Reg, never again, my mother explained, no return from being declared dead at the scene.

This was the first time any living thing had ever died in the entire world, as far as I knew. I sat across from my mother. My enthusiasm for plundering the brown sugar sank into the thick syrup of this grave event. Uncle Reg's death, I recognize now, was making an impression that would last a lifetime. From that moment on, not a day went by that I didn't think about dying.

Death is forever around. Keep half an eye open, and you see it coming all the time. It's in a truck making a slow left turn in a fast traffic intersection. It swims in the depths below and along the surface surrounding any ocean cruise. The fatal moment is piped through the air of every airplane flight.

All the old people on earth have something in common with all the other old people. They are much closer to the end than they are to the start. Old people seem to know all the tricks about dying. The elders are here to show the rest of us how to toddle along on our last legs. Maintaining some wisp of balance during that tight-roped home stretch requires craft, might even be an art. Step gingerly. Be forever aware that the next lurch forward may be the stumble that topples you off the ledge.

Gentleman Moe and Old Fred were two ancient gents who had befriended me upon entry to a secret fellowship I'd been court-ordered to join in my late twenties. Both Moe and Fred had failed out of Harvard in the same year, prior to World War II. I was thinking about degrees of separation in Fred's station wagon. This was back when I was approaching my mid-thirties, and Fred was still allowed to drive. We were headed for a hospital. I was going in for a medical procedure that calls for the patient to bring along a chauffeur. To pass time in the waiting room, I told Fred, speaking into his good ear: "When this is over, you'll be one of the few people we both know who has seen me high on drugs."

For half an hour, professionals shot me up with enough Demerol to remind me of why I always wanted more of that stuff. Afterward, Fred guided me in a wheelchair to the elevator bank. "Can you push the down button?" he said.

"The down button is a specialty of mine."

The steel doors tracked open, and Gentleman Moe stood within the elevator in his Guccis and cardigan, flashing his wry grin. He mimicked an elevator man, historically correct nuances only he and Old Fred would appreciate fully.

"Going down, gentlemen?" said Moe.

I took a few seconds to absorb the coincidence of this meeting. I looked at Fred. He seemed perfectly unperturbed to be facing Moe, and I worked out what had happened. I had died on that biopsy table. The anesthesiologist had given me too many drugs. My heart had fatally recoiled. I had passed over to what comes after. Here were Old Fred and Gentleman Moe to welcome me, to keep me oriented and to show me the ways of my new life, the fabled afterlife. My conclusion was certain and convincing for the space of three or four heartbeats, completely wrong on every beat after that.

"I volunteer here at the hospital every Tuesday," said Moe. He walked out into the sunlight beside Old Fred wheeling me in the chair, all of us just as alive as anyone could be. "If Allan wasn't so secretive, I could have taxied him here in the Jag," said Moe. He was ancient, but he drove in style.

Old Fred belted me into his station wagon and delivered me back to my place. Even then, we might have guessed he would exit first. When his big moment approached, Fred holed up in his apartment, an airy studio with a dappled patio crowded with plants. Old Fred's people gathered around. Glowing ladies from his meditation group, AA fellows aged from early twenties to late seventies, players from the chess club, and library cronies, we all circled the mattress, a rotating hospice of friends who planned to stay behind.

Fred had prepared a list of items needed from the market. Chip, a twenty-year-old chess prodigy, volunteered to run for supplies. "Pay attention to the brand of tissue," Fred said, not unkindly but with grave effort. "This is the brand that the tissues stand up and let you pluck them. My fingers are numb. I don't have a lot of time. I can't waste it digging for a piece of paper to blow my nose."

Imparting those directions cost the old man a day. He closed his eyes.

The room was sparse, the same as it had been in the years before the decades caught up with Fred. The bed was like a pallet, not quite a futon. There was a modest Buddhist altar on the floor and two photos on the wall, portraits: one of Guru Paramahansa Yogananda, the other of "our greatest American philosopher," E. B. White.

A few of us sat cross-legged on the carpets or squatted against the walls. Being with Fred created an "us," the us he was leaving. We caught ourselves staring out toward the patio and the plants thriving in the soft sun. I was comfortable not talking. I was comfortable not listening to the few words that were exchanged. We all tuned in on the give-and-take conversation of the dying man's breath.

Fred's chess friend came back and unpacked the sack of supplies. If I'd still smoked, this would have been a great time to go outside and have one.

"Oh, Chip, those are the wrong tissues. You have to go back," wheezed Fred, kindly. "You must go through the whole thing again. But better you than me." Fred laughed at his own joke, one of the last laughs he would have, a laugh that seemed to almost kill him, at Chip's expense.

HERE'S AN OLD DREAM: *I come awake behind the wheel of a vintage Ferrari on a winding Amalfi Coast cliff road south of Pompeii. I'm taking a curve faster than a local would. I'm crashing through the stacked-stone barrier and catching air, flying upward in defiance of physics and gravity, bursting into flames three hundred yards above the mild Mediterranean waves. The transmigration from this plane of existence into nothing else is instantaneous. No living thing is hurt, no ecological backlash, zero carbon smudge.*

TRINA AND I MET at home after work and left the house in a hurry. We took her car. We were on the way to see friends, a young couple that had married and moved out beyond the Valley to raise their impending family. We stopped at the last pizza place before the freeway entrance.

Trina wanted to wait out in the car while I dealt with the pizzas. I insisted she come in. Between us, we ordered half a dozen pizzas, with three configurations of toppings. The pizza guy had the nerve to ask Trina if she was a real redhead. The lift of his eyebrows and the dip of his eyes conveyed an insinuation that might have picked a fight on any other evening. I paid up and joined Trina, waiting beside the soda cooler.

"I don't really feel good about going over there," I said, which was something she already knew. "I guess we need to."

Like I said, she knew all this, so she ignored my saying it.

"The priest," she said, taking back her credit card, "did you call the priest?"

"I called the priest. He saw them at the hospital."

The wife looked at me in a way she did intermittently, a few times every year. She'd try to figure out how or why we had happened. For the moment, she gave up solving that mystery.

"It's weird," she said, "that we're the ones who are friends with the priest."

"Sure, that's what's weird about it; that's the weird thing."

I wedged the pizza boxes into the back seat and joined her in the car.

We drove out through the Valley without getting lost or speaking. That section of the journey was as strained as it needed to be. While she parallel parked the car, we quarreled, and we were silent walking up the driveway toward the well-lit house where our friendly married couple had dug in to raise the impending family.

I carried all six pizzas, silently resentful. Trina would not offer to carry two, unless I asked. Abruptly, she grabbed half the cargo from me. "If you need help, just speak up."

The sobbing started in the doorway, in the foyer, once we reached the fringes of everyone else. The mother of the couple handed me the picture of baby Henrietta. Her tiny foot prints. The baby our married friend had delivered knowing the baby was dead. The mother's hand landed on my arm, and I was crying, like I was at one with the rest of them. I sobbed and fielded a thought: *What reservoir of generosity have my friends tapped into that enables them to share this weight with us?* After that, I held my friend, the new non-mother, much tighter than I usually hold another person. She held me right back. No thoughts made it to the screen. The moment went on for more than a few minutes. I would never be more in the correct place doing the correct thing in my entire life.

I stepped aside, and my friend moved along. I sat on a chair in the living room, out of the way. A woman I'd seen plenty but had never spoken to engaged me in conversation. In these moments, we were all something like friends, but a little deeper than that. This woman asked if I knew Legs McNeil, if I was acquainted with Legs McNeil. She was well acquainted with Legs McNeil. She believed that Legs McNeil and I would get along, that we would be aligned souls. I admitted I knew the works of Legs McNeil. I concealed my doubts that Legs McNeil and I would get along. These doubts, in this place at such a time, it troubled me to have them.

Trina brought me some pizza. Her eyes were red and moist and free of all calculation.

"Henrietta will never even hear her name," I told my wife, as if it were something important that had just come to me.

"You can't know that." Trina wasn't arguing with me. She meant to give me a gentle reminder. "She probably has heard it."

I thought about something else, that Hemingway story: "For sale: baby shoes, never worn." I couldn't bring my mind to where I was and what I was doing. Back in the car with Trina, I gave her incorrect directions for the drive home. *Die pre-birth, like Henrietta,* is what I thought. *Handed straight off from the most carefree stretch of existence any human ever knows to whatever comes after the rest of it, without all the disappointment in between, without the joy and the receding, mocking echo that joy turns into, never knowing fear and the ways fear will diminish you.*

These thoughts were no real comfort. These thoughts invited you to hand back the unwieldy gift of grief that your friends had graciously shared with you. That disparaging voice was on me during the quiet, dark drive home with the wife, a drive so dark and quiet that I feared the same thoughts had occurred to her and that she could not dismiss them either.

ANOTHER DREAM: A SINUOUS woman I have never met comes into the hotel room. She smiles, and I feel the comfort of friends happy to have known one another for several easy years. I'd arrived at the suite about twenty minutes earlier. The sheets are fresh; the woman is fresh; the views and the soft winds coming in through the windows are fresh. Her scent matches the forest- and sea-perfumed breeze. We're having sex. She has come from a very highly recommended agency. I have never done this thing before, the paid intimacy. A thick envelope on the table contains a fat bonus to cover what is about to happen. The petite mort triggers the big one, and I leave her a little richer than before I came.

LITTLE MEG WAS FURIOUS: "Whitey had his dog put down." The dog's name was Carlita. "The fucker decided he couldn't handle the responsibility; so the fucker took her to the kill shelter." Little Meg drank from a bottled juice cleanse. "I would have taken Carlita. All he had to do was tell me. Now she's dead."

Whitey was one among a few dozen of us cleaving together like shipwreck survivors picked up by the same lifeboat. He was a big boy. He'd lived with hard men. We'd been plucked and spared, is what we all had in common, from a sea of misery. To drift any distance away on your own, even with a flotation device, seemed foolhardy, an invitation to catastrophe. Whitey had not let anyone know what he was planning.

"He won't answer the phone," complained Little Meg. "He won't discuss why he did it."

We gave it a day, and Whitey was discovered to have hung himself. Everyone knew right away the rumor was true, and none of us seemed to have seen it coming.

⁓✦⁓

DREAMING AGAIN: *I'M ON a park bench just off La Croisette. I've traveled first class to Cannes with a trusted friend of many years. We are on business, but it's impossible to keep pleasure from leaking in. Our work, personal, collaborative, has been screened to passionate acclaim. Bidding is competitive on foreign and domestic rights. The applause from the previous evening's standing ovation is still music in my ears; I assume it resounds in my friend's ears as well. The sun is red and huge and bleeding beyond its borders into the azure Mediterranean. For a moment, my orientation goes sideways. Is the sun rising from or setting into the sea? I lose sense of everywhere and pass from the embrace of my trusted friend deep into the center of a molten sphere.*

⁓✦⁓

DAVID WAS AN ACTOR I met in the lifeboat. He pulled me aside one night and tried to steer me around pitfalls in the path of my ambition. Even then I was beyond human intervention. With David's full name, you could look up a full stack of acting, screenwriting, and special thanks credits, all in the company of revered greats, all hitting a full stop by 1979. Fierce and funny were the split face of David's identity; *intractable* is the word that staged his career demise. Groomed by agents, producers, and studios, an investment, David had refused the lead role hand-selected to launch him, and the investors had let him slide. A formerly bright prospect, a once solid contender, after being off the sauce for twenty years, David bought a bottle of scotch for his last joke, taking the funny a little too fierce. He drank the scotch while disassembling a perfectly good vacuum cleaner. He inserted one end of the vacuum cleaner's hose into his car's tailpipe. He brought the other end of the hose into the car with him and attached it with silver tape. He let the car run in his sealed garage and sat drinking scotch inside of it. The wife who was leaving him found him.

The night we heard about it, I told Trina at dinner, "Neither one of them got out in time." We ate silently, maybe both of us wondering how we might avoid their mistake.

⌐

ONE FINAL DREAM: As an old man, I have found my way to the world's most comfortable bed. The morphine drip flows so fast and potent that dope is leaking out of my eyeballs. I don't know when the changeover happens. A staff member peels back the sheets, switches out the bedding. New hardware is wheeled in. Some lady, definitely not me, is settling into the bed with no intention of climbing out again.

⌐

WHILE I WAS AT work, a phone call came from my friend Al: "Summer shot herself."

Summer was our mutual friend Bobby's wife.

"Oh fuck, Al," I said. "Is she hurt bad?"

"She's dead, you moron."

"So she shot herself in the head?"

"Of course she shot herself in the head."

"You could have said so. You could have said, 'Summer shot herself in the head.' Oh fuck, how do I tell Trina?"

I stood up. I looked at the stacks of proofs and galleys and manuscript pages layered across my desk. I saw them all very clearly, but nothing else. I sat down and picked up the phone.

"Hi, honey," Trina said. "I'm super busy."

"Listen," I said. I listened for what words I might come up with. "Are you okay?"

"What do you mean, am I okay?"

"Summer shot herself to death."

That statement wasn't fully true, not yet. Summer's body was in Cedars-Sinai hospital; her pulse was attached. Cables and pumps exercised her lungs and heart. Trina dropped the painting she was hanging, left the gallery downtown, and was at Summer's bedside, beside Summer's mom and brother, when the power running all those pumps and cables was disengaged.

I went with Bobby, our friend, the widower, to the house where Summer did it. We stopped in to pick up some bauble the mother wanted to dress the body in.

"I need to use the bathroom," I said. I didn't want to, but we'd been drinking coffee and health shakes.

"Go ahead," said Bobby.

The lock was busted where he'd kicked in the door. Blood must have been everywhere, but it wasn't anywhere I looked.

Bobby drove Summer's BMW west to a spontaneous memorial in a Venice backyard. The gathering was tight, intimate, forty people deep. The turn to speak came to me. I sat silent, not knowing what I felt. Nothing shaped up to verbalize. I passed. I was the only one who passed. These people talked so glib and large. Didn't they realize what had happened? Did they appreciate the depths of the hole Summer had climbed into, so deep she could not climb back out? If they felt the remote tinge of what that felt like, how could they sit up in the sunshine and talk as if the world had not ended?

My car was the biggest and the blackest of anyone's we knew, a black-on-black Chevrolet Impala, so it was the funeral transit: me driving, Bobby in front, Roth and Al in the back. I parked the Impala in the lot of a Little Tokyo funeral home. Roth and Al eased out and slammed the back doors.

Bobby hung behind in the front. "Do you think Summer is better off now?" he asked. "Where she is?"

What can anyone possibly answer to that? No one knows anything, really, about what happens to people when they are cut off from the rest of us.

"If God is any good at all," I began, "if God is worth anything at all…"

But on that afternoon, who could bet on a God being worth anything good at all?

Time passed. People who want to help say it heals all things. The days, the good ones and the ones that were more memorable, trampled over me and marched into years, grinding me toward a particulate nonexistence. The suicides are never far away, always hovering just over my shoulder and just beyond the horizon out front. It's not exactly as if the suicides called out for me to join them. Also, they never warned me away from that thing they had done. To put it simply: all traps drop you into the other place. Everyone heads out through the same drain. The maze of circumstances and choices is an illusion to disguise the prompts. All comers funnel into the deep end.

From the start, I could have rested easy in the outflow, except flowing easy is not what I was after. I wanted to die really not wanting to die. I wanted to die wanting more. I had wanted to die with some sense that more was on the way.

MY LIFE AS IT PASSED BEFORE MY EYES

MY MOTHER IS THINKING of other things as I am born. Had she left some chore undone before leaving the married quarters for the infirmary? Would my father stand looking down into the kitchen sink and find some reason to be dissatisfied?

I slid out to suck in my first lungful of air. My mother was all a wonder. *Is he angry?*

Another time...

MY EIGHT-YEAR-OLD FRIENDS HAVE run off and left me in the woods.

For a while, I am the stumbling six-year-old lost among saplings, brambles, and stumps. But I'm lucky, as a youngster, half lucky. By good fortune alone, I emerge from the patchy brush, stepping clear of the parcel of trees on the opposite side from where I went in. I emerge onto a lane running parallel to the road I live on.

Coming out of the shadowed grove into the clouded open sky and the falling rain, I'm disoriented. I've never walked on this distant block, not without my mother's hand. I stare at landmarks that are recognized but not familiar. I pass by known signposts and feel no closer to where I belong. I approach a house that is identical to the house where I live. I walk up upon it from a perspective I've never known. The stone steps and the plank porch look familiar but seem strange. I am afraid.

My name is being called. I crouch down on the front porch. The door opens, and my worst fears are not realized. My mother clasps me to her like some valuable thing that had been feared lost forever but was only misplaced. A man, the age of my father, and a girl three years younger than me stand behind my mother. Who are these two people? They look so much like my father and my sister. I suspect they cannot be.

Another time....

THE TRAIN HAS BEEN crawling through California for what seems like weeks. The palm trees, exotic things we had never seen in Canada, have become tedious. When you're eight years old, five days passes like half a year. Sitting from dusk to sunrise with my forehead pressed to the window, the rails clicking below, the night gleaming beyond, desert horizons moving behind me with every blink I make. When I'm awake, I know I could be dreaming.

After forever getting nowhere, my mother shakes me into the now. "We're here," she says.

The interior of Union Station, Los Angeles, is cavernous and formal. It's a place beyond anywhere I have ever been. We could be lost in here for the rest of our lives. My mom carries the youngest girl, shielding my other sister and me. A man appears. He strides across the lobby toward our tight family grouping. I don't know this man who is so happy to see us.

He's right upon me. His hand lands on my shoulder. I recognize my father, and I tense up in the defensive posture.

He carries the youngest girl and leads the rest of us through the grand station. We clump together in the crowds and pass through the busy grand entranceway into the still, hot nighttime parking lot.

We cross a vast asphalt expanse, following my father's sure guidance, his unhesitant, wide stride, arriving at the Cadillac, the mythical car we'd been picturing since we'd heard about it so long ago, back before we were on the train. The '59, a glorious machine, it exceeds and magnifies all our hopes. Our entire stack of belongings fits into the trunk of that car.

"We could fit Allan in there too," observes my dad. "If he starts acting up."

The Coupe de Ville is four years old, not that I could have been expected to know its secondhand vintage. To me, the car's garish fins and pointed-bullet backlights make it more attractive than newer, tastefully ostentatious models.

I'm in the back of the Cadillac, my forehead placed upon the window glass. The roadway hisses below. The landmarks ahead move to the rear in the blink of an eye. The urban neon reflects and is doubled in the car's spotless windows. My father praises the miracles of the magical new land of California. I see lavish promises coming true all across the shiny, bright night.

Another time....

MY SKIN IS HOT in the sunshine and cool in the shadows, both at the same time. My girlfriend feels the same way I do. Being naked is like being in a whole new world. We're both almost ten, old enough to know that no one must ever find out about what we are doing. We've retreated to our hidden cardboard-box fort deep in an overgrown backyard between our two families' houses. Thick bushes stand all around us. My girlfriend and I can see out. The world cannot see in.

"My brother has hair," she says.

"I have hair."

She reaches out and points around my vibrating peg. "Here. He has hair here."

I forget how to say anything. I'm trying to make out what I see between her legs. She twists her thighs together.

"Do you know what he likes me to do?" she says. "I can show you."

Her face is very red. Her chest is crimson and mottled. She gasps for air and holds her breath. She might be crying. The shade in our retreat darkens. The breeze brings a chill and the voice of my girlfriend's mother calling her in for dinner.

Another time....

MY FATHER HAS MOVED his family again, and I am in another new school, Coronado Junior High, just in time for sixth grade. The neighborhood has a mean streak.

It's after lunch, late in the day, a reading class. Our teacher steps out, and I am pulled into a fight that comprises the entire classroom. Textbooks are being wielded as weapons. I'm slammed in the back, in the head, in the face. I relish the feeling of inclusion. The fight is everyone else fighting against me.

I'm sailing in midair across a worktable. My wind rushes out of me. I slide across the floor, come to my feet, and crash into some girl I really like. Her breath has been taken away, and she squeals in my face. I charge back in for more.

Another time....

FOR THE FIRST TIME, I have a bedroom of my own. I am in there dozing on the bedspread in the summer heat, deep into my imaginary relationship with Paula Short.

Black hair, brunette complexion, a physical development of secondary sexual characteristics that her peers would never catch up with, Paula has fallen victim to a sinewy, smooth-skinned sensuality in me. My perfect adolescent embrace compels her to flaunt the taboo against a high school senior being the girlfriend of a seventh grade boy.

"He looks younger than he is," she explains to three of her friends, "because he skipped second grade."

The three girls toss their ironed, lemon-bleached hair and tug their jean shorts up to expose their full thighs. They put their breasts to work animating their peasant blouses. They stare at me with a new respect and lewd curiosity.

My sisters have retreated to a distant air-conditioned portion of the house. I hear a TV, but can't tell what show is on.

Half asleep, squirming with my crotch pressed into the mattress edge in my preteen bedroom, I recall Paula as she had first materialized to me. It had been a hot day, like this one. We had met walking from the Foster Freeze and come back to my bedroom to dampen paper towels and dab away the ice cream trails that had dripped along Paula's neck and clavicles and cleavage. My sisters had been down in the far end of the house, where the air conditioner worked, watching TV.

Paula had sat on the bed and slid over to me. "I want to try anal sex," she said.

There was nothing new she could tell me about anal sex. I'd read up on it in a *Penthouse* magazine I'd found stuffed into a bag of golf clubs in a friend's garage.

"I think you would be good at anal sex!" I tell Paula.

"But I'm afraid."

"I'm not afraid," I say.

We'd been through this all before. The memory was recurrent. Still, as Paula and I started, I felt that this particular day in the stifling, breathless bedroom was different. Paula pulled off her shorts and backed into me. Sensations pooled inside me and quaked and breeched a point beyond where I could pull them back. No further effort was required from me.

My first orgasm rushed me to the bathroom. I mopped the residue with a wad of toilet paper, feeling alternating currents of revulsion and fascination, not at all like I would have felt wiping creamy drops of Foster Freeze from Paula's face, neck, and breasts.

Another time....

OUTSIDE IN THE FAMILY backyard, I hear the birds chattering. Sunlight streams up from the patio's white cement. The green of the lawn is a liquid dropping from the sky. The rose bushes are shifting wounds of scented color. Sweat runs down inside my shirt, and I understand the issues at stake and the negotiation points in the exchanges of the chattering birds. This is how I know the LSD has come on: the birds are making sense to me.

My father comes out into the backyard dressed for work. I'd been taking this acid and selling it for a few weeks, but taking it more than selling it. The batch was wholesome and clear and good-willed toward me. A shadow stops where I am and stays on me. Separate from the powers I've been given by the hallucinogen, I don't need to look up to see who stands there, looking down as if into a clogged sink.

"Can you look sharp?" says the old man, and my lysergic nervous system bypasses the flinch. *Who is this man? Who does he presume he is to me?*

His first appointment of the day has cancelled. He has an hour. He will teach me to drive the manual shifter in the 1947 Chevy that he's bought for my high school graduation, but intends to withhold from me because I will not walk in the procession.

I pursue a tangent on a parallel plane of consciousness. The physical me backs the Chevy out of the driveway, traverses a grid of side streets, and merges onto a four-lane artery. The clutch, the accelerator, the brake, the sliding lever, the gears meshing and transferring the power to the drive train; no conscious effort need be applied. My father is left with nothing to say except to praise me. He says nothing.

"I'm disappointed," he begins, "that you refuse to graduate. Your mother is very disappointed…"

My only difficulty is to veil my smirk and stuff my laugh.

Another time….

TOMMIE COMES OUT OF her parents' house but stops short of climbing into the '47 Chevy. She and three of her brothers' still live at home with their parents on a long barrio block off Valley Boulevard. We're about a mile or two west of the community college where we met.

Her hair, which when left free opens like a black halo spanning down to her lower back, is pulled tight behind her head. She wears hip-slipping jeans and platform pumps with block heels. Her eyes are brown and tight. Her lips are skeptical right here, but I've known them to be very sure of us. The first time I saw Tommie, taking the desk in front of me, wearing a baby blue cashmere pencil skirt, a thrift-store treasure, I had thought, *Everything would be better with this girl.*

I'm leaning on the Chevy, not to be cool or poised. I'm not sure I can stand up without support. "You said we would go for a drive," I say. Two of her brothers, both younger than us, I see them within the living room picture window. They're kneeling the wrong way over the back of a plastic-covered sofa to observe us.

A hill with no house on top is across the street from Tommie's house. She walks me up to the top of that hill. Her family's house seems tiny and far below. I notice that the structure is moving on its axis, twisting on its foundation. In a moment, it will be spinning toward us like something from *The Wizard of Oz.* We could be hurt. I say nothing about the danger.

"You need to not do angel dust anymore," she says.

I think I catch her meaning, but I cannot be sure. I'm askew from the night before. Some time after midnight the reality came to me that I might never come down. I had panicked. It's impossible to say exactly what happened. I know that I called Tommie on the phone, and that someone else had answered before I talked to her.

Her face glows like a cinnamon icon. She takes the tie out of her hair. It fans out wild and large and makes a kaleidoscope of the sun.

"I told Paco and Matty I had a bone to pick with you," she says. Paco and Matty are the brothers who are younger than her, the two who watch us from over the seat back of the sofa. She has two older brothers as well.

Her lips tickle my ear, and she whispers: "Paco said, 'You have a boner to pick with him is all you're going to pick.'"

Another time….

I'VE TRAVELED SOUTH HUNDREDS of miles, from San Francisco where I am dropping out of college, navigating the straight and dreary I-5 freeway through nighttime fog banks into the dawning haze of Pomona, California. The car had been driven and owned by a Boston greaser who lived in the dorm I was about to be evicted from.

"It'll be a smooth ride," he'd predicted. "A straight shot."

Caustic amphetamine powder had been snorted and joints of dirt weed rolled. About an hour in, our noses stopped bleeding. We realized we didn't like one another enough to be stuck in a car alone for the next six hours. Seventy miles later the vehicle had broken down.

The car limped into an isolated gas station between Los Banos and Coalinga, and the car's owner begged for use of the station's tools. We traded our dirt weed. The locals fired up and watched the Boston greaser elbow a temporary fix into the motor. The delay in the insect-plagued service station upset the timetable. I was dropped at a dark backhouse in Pomona a few hours too late for my homecoming reunion.

Chili, the girl who lived in the dark backhouse, didn't want to let me in. She opened the door but kept it on the chain. "Last time you weren't very nice to me," she said. Her face in the crack of the doorjamb looked more afraid than vindictive. It looked both ways. "I'm not safe being alone with you."

"You won't be alone with me. You'll be here too."

In the morning, it is Thanksgiving Day. My parents have not been told that I am in Southern California. Laid out stiff with eyes closed on a spare mattress in Chili's laundry room, I'm more wired than wakeful. All the time I've been away, the separation from my girlfriend has worn on me.

A knock at the street door alerts me. An empty kitchen and a vacant living room are between where I lie and the front porch. Sounds of Tommie walking fill that buffer zone. The door cracks open into the sliver of a room where I am laid out. I pretend I am asleep still. I'm peeking up along Tommie's crafty legs beyond her trim miniskirt and batik T to that godly black aura of hair. Tommie reels on her blocked platform shoes and clutches Chili.

She whispers: "Oh my God. He looks awful."

Another time....

IT WAS DURING ONE of those California downpours that are only endurable because you know the streets will dry up soon. Mudslides had swallowed houses whole on the lower slopes of the rich people's hillsides. The wealthy victims had escaped with the clothes on their backs and not even a decent pair of shoes. Entire super abundant families streamed down out of the heights and pooled at Kinney Shoes on Lincoln Boulevard in Venice.

Shoe shark Allan M— met these refugees at Kinney's door and guided them deeper into the sales floor. I sold them shoes, socks, products to care for the shoes, and sometimes a handbag to match. Customers and their kids clumped up around the displays, crowded, off kilter, off balance, unsure of what they wanted or were looking for, vulnerable, easy picking. I ran the floor, sending the sales crew in for quick kills.

The world was sort of mine right then, even though I was stuck selling shoes. I spotted a couple, a man and a woman, about my parents' age, unprepossessing, apologizing in their posture, like my parents. They added up to nothing. The couple had been together so long they cancelled one another out.

All the other salespeople rushed past this man and woman. I stopped. "I can help with whatever you need," I said. It's the first thing I said to all the customers.

The faded husband and wife both shrank back, the wife less so. "We're here to buy shoes for our son," she said.

"What are you looking for? Do you know his size?"

The man eye checked the woman. He spoke: "They need to be easy to put on and take off."

"It would be better if your son could try them on."

The wife had an idea: "Well, he's in the parking lot, in the car. Maybe we can take the shoes out there, for him to try on."

"Naturally, we would pay for the shoes first," said the husband. "We would only bring them back into the store if they were entirely unsuitable."

I was only allotted so much time and patience per transaction. "Why can't your son come in?"

They hesitated and seemed to decide the man should speak up: "He has a medical condition. He needs special treatment."

"If he'd like to come in, bring him in."

I cleared out three adjacent customer chairs for the kid and the parents. I checked for progress. Mom and Dad had a boy my age, twenty-one or twenty-two, flanked between them. He balked at the door. The big forehead, the gawky eyes, the lolling gaze and working mouth; I recognize this kid. Crowds have been unkind to him.

I put a hand on his sleeve, and I let his slow, grave eyes make up their mind about my face. His brain is defective. This many years along, and it still wants to believe some kind person will take charge of him. The son allows himself to be coaxed into the tumult of the store. Every motion and person frightens him, for good reasons. My face is safe, for no real reason. We shuffle him to the three empty chairs and place him in the middle one.

Seated between his parents, staring at his knees, the drooling boy's agitation is manageable. I measure his foot. I bring him a few boxes of shoes to choose from. I'm there on a knee on the floor. The kid can watch my face. He hasn't forgotten me. He tries on three pairs. He likes them all, but he doesn't want to stand up to walk through the milling customers to the mirror to see how the shoes look on his feet. I know what he means. The parents pick the most likely pair.

"Stay there," I tell the parents. I ring up their box behind the counter and bring them their change and the shoes in a bag.

"Let's go," I say. The boy takes my arm and looks at me like he's recognized someone. He's happy. We shuffle him through the streaming shoppers, out the door, and into the parking lot. Outside, the rain seems to be gone for good. Cars growl and squeal out on Lincoln Boulevard. The boy's slow eyes leave my face and drift warily toward the street sounds of motion and peril. I've accompanied this kid as far as I can go.

Another time....

TOMMIE AND I ARE outdoors in the dirt unprotected from the sun in the company of a nonverbal girl named Patti, not a friend of mine. Patti and Tommie met at Tommie's job. Patti is stolid blonde. Her flexed green eyes managed to be always looking at something else while accusing me of some unspecified infraction.

Patti has supplied psychoactive mushrooms. We'd stirred the organic hallucinogens into individual cartons of yogurt. We'd eaten our mixtures while driving from Hollywood in Patti's 1982 Honda CVCC out past the end of the San Fernando Valley to a canyon park on the outskirts of Chatsworth. We'd reached the stone-faced gateway to Charles Manson country. We've climbed a rock face and collapsed upon a flat space. The sky is a featureless distance.

"If we keep walking over these hills," says Patti, flat on her back, "we'll come out on Spahn Ranch. Do you know what happened there?"

The drug in the mushrooms is coming on. Structures are coming apart in the city grid to the south. The horizon is collapsing. The future is a haze of doom. None of us will survive. Patti becomes bestial and slithers from turf to gravel like a predatory reptile.

There's a tunnel, below us and to the right, dug into the hill we're sitting on. Train tracks extend from the tunnel. I'm looking into the eye of the tunnel. The opening seems alive like an orifice that can constrict and contract. A train barrels out of the hole, roaring, screeching, and belching smoke.

Tommie is shivering, belly down in the dirt. Her pelvis rocks. Five or six dudes stand in a cluster about twenty yards down the hill, watching us. They look like local dudes, not serious hikers, and they watch us in a seriously speculative way. Tommie throws up in the dirt. She sprawls prostrate in the dirt, squirming on the vomit.

"Get out of the dirt," I say. The racket of the train overpowers my declarative calm.

My wife looks at me like I'm a creep. Like I'm asking something unreasonable. The dudes watching us move closer. The ground is rich in improvised weaponry. I grit my teeth and force some words through them. "Get out of the dirt."

Patti slithers across the ground and writhes in the vomit dirt beside Tommie. The sound of the train recedes. The screeching and roar become remote. If I listen long enough, will I hear the sounds die out?

The dudes are far closer than I would have allowed them to be. "Hey, is this a private party?"

I look up in time to see the train's black smoke disappear into the dirty air.

Another time....

MAGAZINE PROOFS ARE STACKED on my desk. There is no focus in me. It's an hour until lunch, and I have a terrible feeling.

I shut my office door in Los Angeles and call a hospital in Canada, using a direct number. It rings in a room my youngest sister and I had driven up to visit the week before, driving twenty-two hours straight. My father had been sleeping in the room for days and usually picked up on the first ring. Six, seven rings later; someone I didn't know answered the phone, an employee, a nurse. I asked to speak to my mother, as a formality, or my father, as a practicality. The nurse on the other end put down the phone. I heard her walk away, and I knew what she would tell me when she came back. This is the day my mother died.

My boss saw my eyes coming toward him and cut me loose without exchanging a word. I left the office and drove in my 1967 Mustang toward the apartment I shared with a friend. It was a year and two weeks since I'd been drunk or drugged. Tommie had been gone half a year longer than that. The ride from where I worked to the place where I lived was rocky. Dealing with traffic kept the sobs at bay.

Loose ended is the state I was in. I called Peg, the latest girl who had said she didn't want to see me anymore. Peg was nice and had been in over her head with what had gone wrong with me. "It's probably best for you to be alone right now," she said.

I didn't want to be by myself, not really.

"I need to be outside," I said. My mother was not in her body anymore. She was somewhere outside. It had been about nine months since my mother was told she had leukemia. Outside was the last place she'd been; I felt sure of it.

"Well, come over if you'd like. Andrea is here. We've finished lunch."

Andrea is another girl who'd said she didn't want to see me anymore.

The Mustang was running as smooth as it ever would. Half an hour later, I was walking in on Peg and Andrea in Peg's living room. Peg presents beneath a dyed-black haircut in the form of an isosceles triangle. British, blonde Andrea has a shag cut like Rod Stewart's. Peg hugged me, and I hugged her back. My breaths were coming very deep. I was in love with the air in my lungs, for starters. Andrea hugged me, and I hugged her back.

"Sit down," said Peg. "We saved you something to eat."

Another time....

I'M HOLDING THE FRAMED high school portrait of this girl I'm with at her mom's place in Venice Beach. The apartment takes up the top half of a duplex half a block from the sand. Nautical windows line the front wall. If not for the photo, I might be looking out over traffic backed up at a Rose Avenue beachside parking lot.

The girl in the photo is unabashed, a beauty. The hair is straight black. The face is smooth, warm aquiline, enlivened by taunting eyes and teasing lips. The smile is an expression of apex symmetry. The girl, five or six years older than in the picture, watches me study her photo. She is alive and tall and standing close enough to touch me. The mom is not at home, and is not expected.

The tall girl with the black hair is my friend's girlfriend, this dude I know. Her name is Amira. Him, I picture as a vague outline. The guy has flown back to Arizona, perhaps for the week only. He has confided that he intends to try and reconcile with another girlfriend. "Going back there is a bad move," I'd told him.

With Amira beside me in the Mustang, cruising the 10 Freeway toward Venice Beach, windows down, her hair streaming free around her laughing, olive face, I thought again that my friend had made a bad move. The Mustang passed the high school of Amira's youth.

"Weed and sun, sex is fun," she sang. "We're the class of eighty-one."

We'd left her mother's place to walk on the shoreline. A dog ran up to us, preferring Amira's attention to the company of its owners. She tussled with the animal, batted its face, grabbed the ears, growled and wagged her tongue. We're both in our twenties. She's moving into that decade; I'm edging out of it.

The dog wandered off and we wandered farther along the seam of shore and sea. Bumping shoulders, pushing, tripping each other up, we fall in the sand. Full length and rolling, preventing one another from climbing back to our feet. My hand slides up inside her shirt, going in through the armhole, cupping a small, tight breast. The nipple stiffens from a mere brush of my thumb. Amira stops squirming and stares at me. She is at this very moment figuring something out.

"I'm not as surprised as I might seem," she says. She stands and takes my wrist and leads me. I follow her long sure strides and timeless sway of hip away from the water and toward the '67 Mustang.

Another time....

I'M IN MY PARKED car at night with my father. The confinement seems a little close and creepy. We're outside the apartment where my youngest sister lives with her wife, who is pregnant with their second child. My father and I have gone to dinner together.

I want to roll down my window, but he's gearing up for a conversation. The talk will unfold like an interrogation. I keep the window up to contain whatever forced admission the grilling brings out. My father is visiting from Canada. It's the first time he's been in the US since my mother's funeral, which was a few years past. He asks if I have anyone special in my life.

"No, not really like you mean."

At the funeral, I'd been placed to one side of him, my sister, the oldest one, to the other side. We were seated in a family section of the chapel, isolated to the side of the altar, cut off from view of the other attendees.

"Are you seeing anyone?" he asks in the car, as if I had not just answered. "Do you have anyone you're spending time with, going to movies?"

"No. I'm not getting out much."

A priest ran the funeral. I'd never seen him before. I guess he'd had two or three conversations in the hospital with my mother. He went on saying some things about her that he'd picked up during their talks. I can't tell you what he said. I couldn't have told you then. He had no right to be telling anyone about my mother. I blocked him out to keep from hating him. That was not the place or occasion for hating anybody.

In the car, my father has moved from interrogating to prying: "Is there any chance that you and Tommie will get back together? That split really disappointed your mother. She was…we were both surprised that Tommie would—"

"Tommie and I don't speak."

"I just mean, there must be some time—"

"We don't speak ever. We never speak."

Back at the funeral, my father must have been listening to the actual words coming out of the priest. Something broke. His front gave out. His head jerked and sobs wrenched out of him. My sister looked my way. Alarm vibrated behind her wide eyes. My father had been stiff and unyielding ever since we'd known him. Now it was his wife's funeral and he was crying. What could be so freakish and scary to my sister? And then I saw: my arm had gone out automatically, with no input from me, and wrapped itself along my father's shoulders. I returned my sister's look of alarm.

Back in the car, my father's composure is layered in. He digs again. "Is there anyone you even have an eye on?"

"No one."

His shoulders shudder. He breaks in with what he'd intended to say all along: "Your mother. I feel if I had been different, she would still be here. I can't help thinking that she got what she got from how I… That I gave it to her."

I'm not shocked that he could think such a thing. I gave my right arm a conscious command, and it went out to him. My limb lay inert and dead to me along his shoulders. "That's crazy," I say. "That's insanity talking."

Another time….

AT THE GLENDALE ANIMAL shelter, Amira and I walked on a concrete path laid down between facing rows of chain-link cages crowded with dogs. Every breed and mix of breeds was jammed in together, prancing, making noise, curled on the cement flooring. One compact dog is set off in a cage all its own, a little boxer.

Amira pauses: "I wonder why he's all by himself?"

We approach the fencing at the face of the boxer's pen. The animal makes a snap decision to lunge at us. Snarling, baring its teeth and slapping its jaws, the dog slams into the chain link and fails to cross the threshold of consideration as a potential companion for us.

We wander among the crowded pens, losing resolve. A skinny old guy in a municipal uniform strolls beside us as if by accident. He has the stooped demeanor of a man who knows he is not doing too well. I mean, he's working at the dog pound. How successful can he think he can be?

"Anyone you two would like to meet?"

"No, no one special." Amira gives him the smile. "We were only sort of looking."

"Did you see the little boxer?"

I assemble a contemplative face, not the same as thinking about what he has asked: "Not that I remember."

"Let me pull him. He's the sweetest thing. Never jumps. You know how some dogs jump up? This one is the most polite animal you've ever met."

As a courtesy, we agree to wait in a fenced meet-and-greet enclosure. The skinny man in the uniform produces a nylon lead and strides off.

Every dog in the shelter starts up a howl.

The skinny man walks toward us along the paved pathway between the two primary rows of cages. A boxer, fawn colored, small but chiseled, walks proudly and calmly on the man's nylon leash. The caged dogs to either side of this man and beast hurl themselves at the chain, snarling, growling, wailing. Every dog in the place wants to breech its gate and take a shot at the impervious boxer passing on the runway. The boxer disdains looking to the left or to the right. The animal moves in proud companionable step with the skinny man, a man who has been drinking since showing up for work.

The animal intuitively faces Amira and me and sits and looks up at us. His mouth hinges open, and he pants with self-satisfaction. I squat beside him. His face splits in a smile half the size of his head. His tongue hangs out the length of his jowls.

"This dog is more proud of himself than any living being I have ever met," I say.

"See? No jump in him," says the skinny guy.

I look up at the girlfriend.

"Oh my God," she says. "You're in love with that thing."

We drove from Glendale to West Hollywood with the dog. Parking was tight, as always. We found a spot a few blocks from the girlfriend's place. We turned the car off and marched, a couple with a pet, toward the 7-Eleven on Santa Monica Boulevard. Amira stepped in for supplies. I waited outside with our dog: muscular, compact, glossy, bright-eyed, tongue hanging.

A chemically enhanced couple in matching tank tops approached. I watched their admiration grow the closer they got to the dog on the end of my nylon cord.

"Oh, he's cute!"

"Can we pet him?"

"Sure."

The couple leaned forward. The animal's tongue reeled in and his mouth clapped shut. Hands reached out to rub his head. He lunged and snarled and bared his teeth. His jaws snapped together. A lot of space opened up between the coordinated couple and the dog and me.

"How long have you had that dog?" asked the guy in the tank top.

"A few hours."

"Then you don't really know what he's like," said the girl in the tank top.

The couple had been afraid. A feeling crept over me that was a lot like pleasure.

Amira slides the house key into the lock of her front door. The dog lifts his head. His black-masked face grins. He swings his tongue. I trip on a revelation: "This is the same boxer that attacked us when we tried to approach his cage. The cage he was in all alone, isolated."

Amira's light came on: "This is the dangerous one! This is that dog who wouldn't let us near him!"

"The dog knows we're talking about him."

We settle on the sofa and watch the dog pick a spot. He slides to the floor, looking up, mugging for us.

"We should call him Mugger," I suggest, unable to take my eyes off him. "Because he's mugging."

"And if you met him in a dark alley," Amira adds, staring at him, "and he told you to give him your watch, you'd hand it over."

We turn on the TV, and it partially distracts us from staring at our awesome animal. In a bit, we go to bed and have sex. Human carnality doesn't seem to bother the dog.

In the morning, Amira lolls in bed, singing out, "Mugger! Hi, Mugger!"

Who knows how long this has been going on? I'm awake, I realize. The girlfriend goes on talking in the dog's direction. His nails click on the hardwood floor. He's on the move. I'm pressed against the tight little bedroom's wall, with Amira between the walking dog and me. I can't see our new animal. I sense he's being patient and still, waiting respectfully for his new woman to roll out of bed.

I lift up onto my elbow and peek out over Amira's bare shoulder. I catch sight of the little boxer just as he sees me in the bed behind her. He'd forgotten I was there. He remembers who I am, and his subdued morning mood leaps directly to ecstasy. His body flips in the air, lands, and springs off the floor as if his legs are triggered coils.

"I think he likes you," says Amira, squirming close and moving under me.

Another time....

I WAS IN PARIS for work, maybe my second or third time in the city. My nerves were shot. There'd been a breakup with a girl, more than one. I experienced these things as final destinations not new beginnings. There hadn't been a start-up in a year. That dry year seemed to be the problem.

A quick inventory of my flat affect told me that an impartial observer, such as every pedestrian I passed on the streets, might think I was having a nervous breakdown. I had neglected to forward my hotel's address or phone number to the home office in California. For all my employer and staff knew, I was swinging dead from the exposed beams of some drafty, aromatic Saint-Germain garret.

I'm standing on a bridge that crosses the Seine, stooped, looking down into the river flow. *Here I am in my midthirties, savoring the eternal amusements of an adolescent.* Traffic runs behind me. A half folded map dangles in my hands. The map is only there to keep my fingers busy. I know exactly where I am. The water is like a lure, a deep, dire reality with a glittering illusion imprinted on top. You can be all reflective and alive on the surface, but the stream of oblivion is right under there.

Back on the bridge, an American couple broke into my river gazing.

"Hey, man, you look like you know this place," said the guy. He constricted the arm wrapped around his girl. "Can you tell us how to get to Notre Dame?"

They're younger than me, and probably better looking, at least in the way they look at it, the way they look at themselves. They're all wrapped up in one another. "You know Notre Dame is the big cathedral," said the girl. "Right?"

I pointed up river at the big cathedral. "That one? Right there?"

"Well, you have a nice day," said the girl.

"However you might choose to do that," added her guy.

I walked off the bridge and charted my course up toward the Luxembourg Gardens. The buildings, the shops, the trees claiming their sidewalk space, the pivoting vistas of the winding streets, and the sky so close and blustery and blue, none of this was lost on me. It was all secondary to the people, the people I saw but did not meet.

All sorts of characters and extras were trafficking the boulevards and *rues* by foot. I fell in with them. Tourists, locals, tradesmen, loiterers: everyone I'm seeing on the street will go home eventually. I picture living rooms and hotel rooms and hostels. I clutter my mind with uninvited visits into the shelters of others.

I have a place I go to too, I know, and all this speculation on lairs I will never lie in should crowd my place out of mind, but I see me when I'm at home: I'm alone in my domain. The dog, a compact boxer named Mugger, is in the bedroom, waiting. He's always happy to see me after any time apart. His happiness doesn't dispel the isolation from over here in France. There's no one else in that bedroom. I can't picture anyone else being at home in that room except the dog and me. I try to envision what a shared life would look like, how it would start. I work at imagining an attractive someone who sees me as a viable person stepping out of the anonymous passersby here in Paris. It would start with a smile. A hello. Who are you? How are you? Where would you like to go next?

So I'm a daydreamer, but my coordinates are set and my destination is easily located even in a state of mild distraction. That's the condition of me arriving at the Luxembourg Gardens, which is like a park from a well-ordered dream. Sculpted shrubbery, pebbled pathways, curving lawns; the wandering is pristine and easy. I happen upon two lines of chairs arranged along the length of a rectangular reflection pool. Quiet, relaxed men and women, youths and elders, fill every seat. Their eyes drift easily from the sky-topped water at their feet to a grouping of three statues at the head of the pool. The water is still, hardly a ripple in the perfect weather.

A chair opens up. I am the closest stroller to it, and I take the seat per the mutual agreement of every person present. I didn't know where I was; I was ignorant of the fact that this cloistered space was the Medici Fountain. I recognized civilization, the height of it. This anonymous group of French strangers had admitted me to its joint purpose. We are gathered in a shared moment of private reflection, tuning in to the stillness embodied by the fine marble figures reigning at the head of the pool: a youthful pair of larger-than-life gods lounges in a sensual sprawl. The girl, a nymph actually, Galatea, was closest to me. She reclined across young Acis's lap, belly, and breasts, fully nude. I'd seen that body. I'd held the image of it in warm, yielding flesh. Would I hold one like it again? Would I know when to let go? Or when to pull tight? A massive, jealous Cyclops lurks upon a ledge above the loving Galatea and Acis.

No one is speaking. All the chairs are taken. We have filled in the space. I am part of this collection, the collective. I am connected with the person to the left of me and the one to the right of me. The wavering bodies and faces in the pond, the individual seated directly across from me; no empty space exists between any of us.

Another time...

AGAIN, A RECENT ROMANTIC misadventure has left me off balance. I have my dog and my apartment and my job. I walk into a friend's kitchen unexpectedly and discover that the two girls I've been hitting on are hitting on one another. As a consolation gesture, they take me to a party down the block from their love nest at a hill-perched house overlooking the Silver Lake reservoir.

Trina, the woman who lives there, guides us on an initial tour through the party house, pointing out the best vistas. I'm tagging along, not catching the words Trina's tossing off. It's hard to listen. I'm too closely following the animated cadence of her artful, crimson mouth and the sharp inflections of heavy, real red hair as it falls across her beaming, knowing face. A teasing green eye seems to be playing hide and seek behind shifting locks of vivid red. The hostess pauses, pivoting on steep heels, and allows a moment to admire the bedroom views: the reservoir's depths outside the picture windows, Trina's tight form in a polka-dot dress reflected in that window glass. All I can say about the smile she fires off is that I wish it were aimed solely at me.

"Where's the ice?"

"Where do we put the ice?"

Trina turns toward the kitchen to answer the calls of her friends, her familiars, people who feel free to preempt her attention to address some demand obvious enough a stranger could figure it out.

A cluster of the hostess's closest friends centers on her dog, a brindle pit bull male. I sidle up to this group.

"My dog is a boxer," I say. "He's a lot like that dog."

"Oh, no. Your dog's not like this dog at all," replies one of the hostess's friends, the one named Mandy, the one perhaps called Big Mouth Mandy throughout grade school. "You don't understand this dog," says Mandy.

Mandy explains by turning her broad back and round shoulders to me.

I join my lesbian friends who have taken refuge on the back deck. From the back deck, by sheer coincidence, I can see the apartment building that had housed my most recent romantic misadventure. I had wanted to never stop seeing the girl. She lived there still, in the front upstairs apartment. Lights are on in her windows. Next door to that lost refuge, a 7-Eleven convenience store stands like the harsh glare of the day after.

The brindle pit bull gallops full circles around the backyard deck and rockets back into the house. My two friends smoke in silence, sitting in a single chair. Trina, the party hostess, passes through the back porch area. "Have any of you seen my dog?"

I give it a shot. "That handsome beast was here," I say. "He had the look of an animal in search of unguarded cold cuts."

"That's exactly what he looked like!" says one of my friends.

"I could see him thinking, *Cold cuts*," adds her girlfriend.

Trina says nothing. She walks her red hair and her tight figure and her polka-dot dress back into the house.

"Our hostess can't see you back here," says one of my friends.

"You need to come out in the light," says the other.

We are all three in the same shadows. My crushed heart is down in that building below, beaten and feeble in the flutter of 7-Eleven neon.

"I know what you're looking at down there," says one of my friends.

"You know I can't help myself," I say. "I'll never stop watching for that girl."

I mean the hostess, Trina.

Another time...

IT'S THE MIDDLE OF September inside a Catholic church on Sunset Boulevard. I'm adorned in the most flamboyant suit that has ever swathed me: an electric-blue silk sheen from Gucci. I'm flaunting this suit in the backstage area behind the altar and feeling out of place and overdressed. I am alone but not alone. Many people I know have arrived from near and far and are seated on the consumer-facing side of that church altar.

We have gathered for my wedding to Trina, a woman with a brindle pit bull. Any minute now, these assembled acquaintances and family members expect me to step out from behind the altar and participate. The priest is with me back there. I have a confession for him: "I really think I am doing the wrong thing here."

I'd slept the last few nights on the couch, and that had been okay with everyone. I'd been burned by the future wife's concoction of crisis conditions, by her contempt for boring details, by a commitment to the desires and needs of people other than me, by her discomfort at connecting cause and effect as it applied to her indulged impulses. I had noticed these traits from the start. Something like magnanimity but more like myopia had caused me to overlook them.

I'd observed from the bathroom window as she'd driven her undamaged car on the road below our house. I'd watched her trudge up toward the home we intended to share, her hair under wraps in a scarf. Moments later, she stumbled through the doorway—her red mane all wild and free—and wailed that her car had been broadsided on the freeway. Totaled. She collapsed to the floor, rolled to her back, and flailed an arm across her forehead. "Maybe you could show me some consideration for once." She wept out loud. "I barely escaped with my life."

In the church on Sunset, isolated in a room behind the altar, I clutched the priest by his hem. "You understand what I'm telling you, don't you?"

"You have my full sympathy," replied my clergyman. "Now sit down in that chair. You will stand up when I tell you to."

Another time....

TRINA WANTS A KID; she tells me it's time. This desire is not an ambush. We talked it out in the months before becoming engaged. Having a kid means much more to her than my reservations mean to me. We've been married a short time, long enough to feel we are committed equals. That feeling moves us to make spontaneous love on sunlit sheets. Afterward, all tender and pensive, we breathe mouth-to-mouth. This is our first time without a barrier. I presume the fetus has been planted. From here on out, our lives and our life together will be profoundly altered.

Afternoon air comes into the bedroom on a weak breeze and cools the sweat on my back. "I want something to eat," Trina says.

So do I. I've never been so hungry.

Another time....

TRINA'S PERIOD HAS BEEN arriving with the regularity of a full moon; so I drive my car west and arrive at the office of a Beverly Hills fertility doctor. I have an appointment to jerk off into a cup. The reception area is like a futuristic command deck of the Starship Insemination. A woman is seated at a control panel set in a polished and molded mahogany pod. She wears a metal communications headset that plays to the brushed aluminum highlights in the molding of her workstation. Her eyes continuously scan the area between her post and the elevators as if she is on sentry for incoming life forms.

Women wander and mix in an area that is either a waiting room or a gathering place for pre-gravid and postpartum patients to share strength and emotional support. Photographs of rich-looking women clutching newborn children array a bulletin board behind the point girl. Occasionally, these photos of moms and miracle kids include a male figure. That male figure in the pictures is always the famous Beverly Hills fertility doctor. The receptionist's eyes continue roving as she assesses me. "Do you have an appointment?"

"Yes. How do I say this? I'm here to leave a specimen. Some material. Genetic."

Now her eyes do stop. She looks at me as if I have just asked to masturbate on her face. She slaps a zip lock plastic bag onto the mahogany counter. The smack silences the room. All the women look my way. They know what I am about to do.

"Make sure you stop and write your name and date on the cup *prior* to providing your sample. Is that clear?" Her distaste is audible. I believe it would have showed up in a photograph as well.

"Yes. But where do I?"

She points in a direction that she is not looking. "That door, sir."

The door opens into a glaring little side room. The room has two doors, both hollow from the sound of it. Neither locks from inside. I've been offered no assisting materials. I'd anticipated a TV and some kind of DVD or video selection. The room contains a low credenza, two chairs, and a desk. I inspect the furniture, looking for discretely stored erotic media, putting off putting myself into the mood.

I've only myself to work with. I put an elbow into it. The ladylike voices of employees and patients sound clear through the two hollow doors. I hold some facial designator from the woman who had coldly tossed the cup at me. Her pictured flinch of disapproval works me over the spill. It doesn't feel very good.

Another time....

MUGGER HAD BEEN RESTLESS all night. He wouldn't settle onto his bed. He was wheezing and walking in the predawn. Luckily, I'd been fired from the magazine a month before. I'm not worried about my disturbed sleep. I'm available to call the vet in the morning.

They have no open appointments, not this week.

"I have a dog who's become very old," I say. "He's had a rough night."

"Bring him in right now."

He's in the car, too cramped to be stretched out in the backseat. I've had him back there riding behind me for more than a decade. He's always liked being in a car. According to his eyes and his tongue, he even likes it now, as much as he can like anything.

In the vet's waiting area, Mugger makes a move toward a fellow patient. It's the first time he's shown curiosity in quite some months, I realize.

"He's really cute," says the other dog's owner, a woman.

"Mr. M—? Do you want to bring Mugger into the back?"

The dog owner and I trade smiles. My smile lingers on as Mugger and I sit alone in a consultation room. We cozy up to one another. "How did you get so old?" I ask. "How did you ever get so old?"

He doesn't know.

The vet comes in. Her name is Kate. She'd been recommended about a year earlier, but I haven't had a chance to try her until now. She puts a stethoscope to Mugger's chest.

"This dog is done."

"Can I take him home? For like one farewell night."

"Sure. I can insert a needle into his lungs and draw out enough fluid so he can last until the morning. But you need to know that procedure will be for your benefit, not for his."

So I fall in love with this woman, right in that moment.

"I need to call someone to come down," I say, "to be here too."

"That's no problem. We have a phone right out at the desk."

"The thing is, I'm going to break down when I make that call."

She seems to like me better. "There's nothing wrong with that."

She guides the dog and me to a private phone in her personal office. I shut the door and break down. I call the wife and break down again. I hang up. Mugger and I sit cozy and resigned for less time than we would like to have remaining to us.

"Do you remember Amira?" I say.

Trina arrives with the new dog, Twiggy, a young, stocky black pit bull with an open white face. The vet explains in so many clear, unhurried words that she will give Mugger two injections. The first drug will relax him and make him comfortable. The second shot will send him off.

Trina shields Twiggy's eyes, and the vet gives Mugger the first drug. Years melt off of him. The vet places a cookie on the floor and leaves the room. The dog eats the cookie with no wincing. "He looks fine now," says Trina. "Can't we just keep him stoned like this?"

I see just how far my dog has gone beyond comfortable. He looks at me like we are old friends. His look says he feels happy to see me right now, and why have I been keeping this relief from him? I recognize just how ready he is to leave.

The vet comes back into the room. Mugger shows his last expression of mild curiosity as the vet slides in the final dose, and he is gone.

Another time....

THE BEVERLY HILLS FERTILITY doctor, specialist to the stars, regards me scornfully across his desk: "Are you asking me to give you a number?"

I had been badgering him about odds and percentages and the impact of life-event factors, starting with age, in the likelihood of a person, such as my wife sitting beside me, becoming pregnant. "I won't give you a number," says the doctor.

He looks at Trina, who is two surgeries in on the process, to communicate that I am being unreasonable. So I try reason on him: "But you concur that every one of those factors reduces the chances?"

"The chances of what?"

"Of conception and of carrying the baby to term. Both."

He bites the inside of his mouth. "Yes," he says. "That should be obvious."

Trina and I drive home without any words floating around or flung back and forth. We take the corkscrew ascent to our Hollywood Hills home, leaning one way and leaning another according to the pull of each successive climbing hairpin. Our headlights play across a street-facing wall and the locked iron gates that secure our patio from outside view.

The car is turned off, parked in the driveway. The engine ticks as it cools. The sun has set behind us, and we've scheduled no follow-up appointment for the Beverly Hills fertility doctor. The darkness fills in without comment.

13

WHAT I MISS THE MOST (AS IF I MISS ANYTHING)

Crows: I was a child with an idea. My driving notion was that this family that inhabited the house I lived in was not my family. I made this family unhappy. When this family was unhappy, its members tortured my real family. This false family held my real family captive in a section of our home that was closed off to me. The rains had dumped puddles like lakes in the sloping vacant lot behind our house. The man who had taken the place of my father had said angry words to the woman who operated in the guise of my mother. The angry words were prompted by my actions. I had eaten something without permission. The angry words were drowned out by the rushing stream at the bottom of the bluff, a wet torrent bucking and spilling over the banks of the creek. A cluster of large rocks was visible in the thrashing water. The drop from the bluff was direct to the cluster of rocks. It was a can't-miss drop. I marched in stride with my idea to a rough-hewn platform overlooking the gorge. Older kids dived from this platform in the summers. My body, I see with certainty, will land on the rocks, break, and wash away in the overflowing stream.

There was no wind, but the leaves in the trees around me came alive with a loud fluttering. The black leaves took flight amid a great cawing. Noisy black birds swooped between the target rocks far below and me. The crows know me. They know all about me. They know things about me that I don't know about me. The crows know that I am a wonder. They fly toward the sun-busted clouds lifting my wonder skyward with them.

I was always happy to hear crows call and see them fly.

The feeling of a new drug: Let's say you're sixteen years old. You've been smoking weed for a few years. You've been drinking for a few years. School has ceased to be of interest to you, and your teachers have ceased to be interested in you. The world talks to you in a monotone. Your vision is a blur of indistinct shapes shrouded in a haze-colored monochrome. Your vistas are horizon-free zones. Your future is starting now and stretching out forever. You squat on the balls of your feet in the strip of space between a suburban house that needs paint and a detached garage containing two cars that will not start. You have a theme song, "Everybody Knows This Is Nowhere" by Neil Young. You have a sense that you will never be any other place. A featureless adult figure sleeps within the house slouched in a drab plush chair in front of a dim TV set. An eighteen-year-old joins you in the nondescript strip of space. This older person squats and pulls a substance wrapped in flat tinfoil from the pocket of a faded camouflage surplus jacket. You are second in line to smoke or sniff up or swallow or inject the substance, a substance that has never visited your bloodstream before. The evening haze shatters under strikes from the light bolts of the stars and the slivered moon. You rise from squatting on your heels to heighten the rush, and you stand alert to a world of amplified pulse and washes of sensation. Happiness, don't be fooled, is fleeting. Satisfaction is gone in the moment you recognize it has arrived. The lift is fast fading. Those facts are all secondary lessons from what you learn in the instant of feeling the new drug.

I was always happy for the feeling of a new drug.

A naked girl talking on through the dead of night: Using drugs wasn't so hard to figure out. Maintaining a flat, unconcerned affect at home and grades in school were fairly simple. Girls were beyond my comprehension.

All I knew of them was an all-consuming yearning. My appetite for girls devoured whole hours as I fed it and fed from it. The hunger took me at any given moment. In class, in the drivers' education car, in bed, with my imagination and central nervous system in thrall, entire blocks of time dissolved whole. There is a world that is not my world. This is a world of sensory immersion. This is a world where people touch and are touched. Where is the bridge to that world? I flail and fail to find the break in the curtain. One night I cannot see my way home. My parents and my sisters are at a house that I cannot place myself within. I am as aimless as I have ever been, and I am more familiar with being this aimless than any kid should ever be. A girl who was in my freshman English class asks me to walk with her six blocks through the LSD stricken night to her house where her parents will not be. I shy from the walkway that leads to the front porch. She takes my hand and pulls me in. "Should you be at home?" she says. "Is someone there worrying about you?" She's naked beside me in a bed. "Hold me," she says. She is warming. The tension has left her limbs. She is easy and soft and malleable beside me. Her mouth is operating directly into my ear, a whisper, a shushing, a soft lively drone. "If I lived where you lived," she said, "I would worry about you." I doze and come awake. "You would be on my mind." I hear and feel the comfort of a naked girl talking away into the dead of the night.

I've always been happy to listen to a naked girl talking away into the dead of the night.

Wind moving through trees: Work demands are immediate and from all angles. My bosses, my coworkers, the customers, all at once making concerted and conflicting demands on my mind, on my time, on my physical presence. Nothing of mine is mine anymore. My hours have been sold out for a sum that makes me bitter. My lunch break is thirty minutes of circumscribed decompression. I'm in my car at the outskirts of a supermarket parking lot smoking Kool cigarettes with the windows rolled up. Food that has no taste is in my mouth. Chewing doesn't improve the food's prospects. My time out here is running down. There are hardly enough minutes left to smother myself in. Tonight my parents will be away. There will be a place, quiet and still and enclosed where the car can run while the radio plays. A line of trees borders the parking lot.

Their branches swing in the wind, waving like arms warning me from a washed out road, waving like arms beckoning me to a blanket and a meadow, waving and bending like a row of majestic personages bowing to me, welcoming my presence, fanning off any ill effects. I am touched that I am touched by the magic of watching wind in trees from a parked car on a work break.

I could always feel happy watching wind move through trees.

Record albums: As a preteen boy, awkwardness and shyness and being at a new school one more time put you on the outside looking for a way in. The other kids all know songs. They communicate with one another through snippets of lyrics, through bits of refrains. *"I've been waiting so long/to be where I'm going…" "Duh da da na duh duh duh…." "In the sunshine of your love…"* Learning the music, maybe that's the way in. During high school, kids break into groups based on esoteric musical tastes and knowledge. You scout around on the outskirts of these high-school subsets. They're Frank Zappa freaks and Captain Beafheart freaks. They're freaking to Dr. John the Night Tripper. You're freaking too. Still, mostly you're moving in the excluded territory between the cliques. Maybe if you know more about Led Zeppelin's antecedents than anyone else has bothered to learn, positive attention will come your way. Wrong again, but you do gain an appreciation for the Yardbirds, and you trace out the careers of that band's three celebrated guitarists: Clapton, Page, and Beck. You develop a habit of researching in the music magazines. You read every word of *Creem*, *Phonograph Record* magazine, even *Rolling Stone*. David Bowie arrives like an opening window to Lou Reed and Mott the Hoople and T Rex. You track down back catalogs for the Velvet Underground and the Stooges, the commercial failures that young disaffected teens of your ilk are finding throughout the land. You don't know those other kids exist. If you did, you'd still be alien from them. After high school, briefly in college, you suspect that if you can just enjoy artists in their pre-popularity phase, staying ahead of the mass audience, you will reduce the gap between you and everyone else. Roxy Music and Brian Eno and German druggists like Can and Amon Düül II weave sounds alien and comfortable. Punk rock arrives just as you reach legal drinking age, and those two concurrents make the most of one another. In the hangover, you gravitate to the historical highs of Motown, Stax, James Brown, and Funkadelic. As you age, the Internet arrives, and you immerse yourself in the study of precursors and offshoots. When nothing else has any real holding power on you, you hold records in your hands. Some of these discs are items you've been handling since you were fifteen. Your initials are scrawled on the labels in a cribbed Chicano font. You fill in records that you missed in your youth or had discarded as flippant during young adulthood. Some records came out when you were ten and fix you when you are fifty. You mine forgotten genres and passed-over time periods. You study fluctuating vintage vinyl markets. You chart garage sales. You covet and you acquire collections left behind by the departed loved ones of chance acquaintances. When you play your records, the songs echo within the places you need filled. Through all your strung-together alienated years, you have taken refuge in records. Playing them. Reading about them. Playing them. Looking for them. Playing them. Finding them. Playing them. Making new discoveries. Making rediscoveries. Playing them.

Playing records has made me happy all the livelong day.

A pleasure that will take some getting used to: The record stores seemed to have run out of things I was looking for. My life was a few years into a sea change. Riding the tide, I hooked up with a girlfriend who embodied every arousing trait I could of dreamed of. On a swell, she swayed above me, straight shouldered with perfect posture. I eased back, letting go, thinking something that turned out to be true: "This will take some getting used to."

I like embarking upon a pleasure that will take some getting used to.

Turning off the TV: You have been single for too long at too late an age. Your loneness is unbroken even by short periods of company. You have been employed steadily. You have your own apartment. You own a Sony Trinitron television. You'd had a pleasure that had taken some getting used to. Now you have put in many months getting used to not having that pleasure anymore. The remote control is in your hand. The channels click through in front of you. You sit propped on pillows at the head of your bed. The TV sits on a stand at the foot of your bed. Your dog is curled in the visitor's chair in the living room. Each click of the remote puts you further from other people. Each flip of focus from station to station on the Trinitron screen exposes another world you are not part of. Nothing on the TV is for you. You register and release news, sports, advertisements, bowdlerized movies, game shows, situation comedies in syndication; in other words, nothing. The next step is to turn on the VCR and insert a videotape of paid sexual performers shooting cum in a world even more alien and unreachable than the universe of regular televised programming. Hours have passed broken into many, many more minutes that bring you no closer to human contact. Laugh tracks and surges of strings and jingles and ham lipped dialogue. With each exhausting quarter hour cycle of channels, the morning is closer and will be blurrier. You can be released. You can escape the enclosure of this cathode fencing. You can shut down this buffer, this swaddle of avoidance. All it takes is your thumb turning off the TV.

I have never regretted turning off the TV.

The first cigarette after not having a cigarette: My temper has never been this short. I'm walking in circles in Venice, Italy, one of the world's most beautiful places to be lost and disoriented in. Beside me is a woman who like me has no previous history with Venice, Italy. I'm crazy about her. Every turn in the twisted interior of the sinking city brings us a new wonder. I can't believe how hungry I have become in such a short period of time. I'd started smoking cigarettes after having quit for eight years. This is the first foreign trip I've ever taken with a girl. It's the first time this woman and I have spent so many uninterrupted hours together. I'd re-quit cigarettes a few days before we'd embarked for Italy. We have been to Milan and Florence. We have eaten amazing meals and had exhaustive sex. We have marveled and wondered. We are turned around and lost trying to find a restaurant we'd lucked onto the day before. The girl switches direction. I picture my hands around her neck. I switch to follow her, and the patch pocket of my sport coat catches on a handrail and rips from the body of the garment. An opportunity arises where a mild shove will place this girl in a canal. I back off and step into a *tabacchi* to ask for directions, and I am unable to procure effective guidance. I buy a red pack of Marlboro and secrete it in my torn blazer pocket. Now the girl remembers that the restaurant is back the way we have come and hidden in a warren of walk paths and waterways through a low arch that she feels she will recognize when she sees it. I believe she is wrong. Wandering and course corrections prove she is wrong. Being wrong, evidently, is something to fight about. We eventually stand arguing in front of the restaurant. After a wait, we are seated. The meal does arrive and is satisfying. Afterward, we stop at a museum and the pictures stand in my way while we stroll back toward our hotel. All I want is privacy and a reclining position. We navigate narrow passageways clogged with drunken British tourists and pushy Germans on holiday. During all this, my fingers caress the red cigarette pack in the blazer's torn pocket. We reach our room. I head back down to the lobby to see if the proprietor has anyone on staff capable of mending my jacket pocket. Standing in the hotel doorway, watching locals and visitors trudge past in the close thoroughfare, I peel the cellophane from the pack of smokes. I slap the pack into the palm of my hand, withdraw a cigarette filter first, light up, and inhale. After not having smoked a cigarette for quite some time, I surrender to the first cigarette. This surrender grants my nerves a general amnesty. I exhale, and the fight goes out of me. I suck on the butt, a good long draw. I have all the time in the world, and it's all good time.

I was always pleased with the first cigarette after not having a cigarette.

Reading a book: A block of time is my own, and I know what to do with it. Objectives and schedules and timetables and commitments and accountability are all notions that can be freely dismissed. I have places to visit. I have characters to meet. I have people to be. The night advances, and I should be asleep. My eyes close against my wishes. I'm reading a book, and it's two hours later. I'm fighting off the dreams as I'm feeding them. I've been lifted to heights and light; I've been dropped to depths and darkness. I'm alone in a room that has a good light and one door, and that door is closed. On the other side of that door, a job is on hold, a woman wants more from me than I have given, an accounting is being prepared. I am in Point Dume with John Fante and his dog Stupid. I am bypassing the San Gabriel Valley on the 10 Freeway East with Joan Didion in a commandeered sports car. I'm in a downward spiral bar with Denis Johnson's Fuckhead. I am in a New York City townhouse with Patricia Highsmith, and her friends are not real friends. I am in Falconer prison. I am a dog of the South. I'm on the road. I'm answering prayers with some desolation angels and the devil in Big Sur. I have wise blood. I've

killed a mockingbird. I'm hearing the ballad of a sad café. Two hours have
passed since I visited the chair I am sitting in. I am being told stories of
God. I am reading a book.

Some of my life's best memories were lived in a book.

A snoring dog: I've been in bed for hours at a time with no sleep, no
companionship, no rest, and no anticipation of a release in dreams. The
wife is motionless beside me. If she is conscious, she is far from conscious
in context with me. Did we touch during the preceding week? I don't think
so. Maybe I was asleep, for a few moments, for an hour or two. I try to
control what I will think about in lieu of sleep. I attempt to manage the
images that will stream through my head. I try to picture someone, anyone,
whose proximity would sweeten the sour darkness. The wife is hiding her
breathing from me. My own breath is shallow and sly and passes within
my lungs undetected by me. I hear a sigh. I hear a lippy exhalation. I hear
a living thing at the foot of the bed dreaming out loud. I hear snatches of
whimper and yelping. I take comfort in the snoring of a dog.

I was always susceptible to the comfort of a snoring dog.

The time we went back to Florence: All human ties are severed. The
wife and I are having the talk. She suggests therapy and striving to work
it out. I suggest that it has worked out, that this severing of ties is how it
has worked out. I am her friend, she says, and she does not want to forget
that or to act in a way that is contrary to that fact. I must confess that
what I feel from her is far from defining our relationship as one of friends.
We have been cleanly and clearly and distantly broken apart. There is not
even an argument about how to deal with this rift. We can divide. We can
separate. There is one consideration. She has booked a holiday to Italy.
The airlines will allow us to cancel the tickets, yes. But the airline will not
refund. The tickets can be used at a later date. But we are contractually
obligated to travel with one another.

"Then let's go to Italy, and we'll come back and take next steps
from there."

"But," she asks, "how will we treat each other in Italy?"

"You said you are my friend," I say. "In Italy, we'll treat each other as
if we were friends."

We'll return home and divorce, but we will go out as friends, in honor of all the trips before. We've had a strong run, and we should exit in a way that is consistent with it. Florence is a place we have not been to in so many years that the last time we were there we had been together. On our first night of the return trip, crossing an empty marketplace, we stop to rub the hand-polished snout of a brass pig that promises luck. "Luck is something we're going to need," says the wife, defeated, surrendered, candid. We take photos of ourselves with the wife's phone camera. In front of the wedding cake Duomo. On the Ponte Vecchio bridge when it is dark and deserted. We walk along the banks of the Arno under moonlight. The structures on the riverbank are reflected in the water, precisely and with eerie movement, accurately reproduced to a depth of three stories. The underwater mirror world draws us down within ourselves, within one another. Back at the hotel, we take a bath squeezed together in the ancient tiny tub. The next night we are back together in that tight bathtub, and we're fucking just like we were fucking the first time we went to Florence.

I was happy on the return to Florence.

Prayer: Everything can be great. Many things can be out of whack and lacking. Some things can be good, and some things can be not so great. And a panic, an abiding and enduring sense of senselessness, will set up and slap you in your face. All effort is exposed as pointless and worse. Every intention is revealed as a flaw. Circumstances only count for so much. People can tell you things are not what you believe them to be. People can prescribe chemicals engineered to dull or divert these perceptions. But you're the victim of realizations that no human power can disprove. The problem is not circumstances. Things are the way things are. The trouble is you. You are wrong, not all wrong. You are only wrong enough to be beyond salvage. This realization is not accompanied by fear, and then fear arises from having no fear. You're in a bed facing the night or the morning, you're in a car driving to or driving from, you're behind a desk. Wherever you are, you are alone, and alone is all there is. You acknowledge a void, and you beseech it. You are praying, and you are not praying for anything at all. I'm asking for nothing, and I'm not expecting anything, and that makes all the difference.

I have never wasted any moment that was spent in prayer.

Floating: Age has been piling on. Cares and concerns and worries. My years of indispensability have been dispensed with. I've driven a scenic-free highway to the desert. The trip out to the empty wasteland seems emblematic. I've been on my own in Desert Hot Springs before. Going to the nowhere I know feels like the first step in moving to the nowhere I don't know. These thoughts and considerations calmly ebb as I float belly up to the black sky in the mineral pool at the Hope Springs motel in Desert Hot Springs. The nighttime stars and the summer heat simmer my skin where it breaks into the air from the water in the thermal pool. The stars reflect off the back of my eyelids. The heat reflects off the cement surrounding the pool. I sleep as I float in liquid bedding like I slept in the womb. I turn belly down in the water.

I am floating in the waters lapping against Hawaiian sands. My face has turned toward the coral in the shallows. Life leading to this Kauai vacation had me picturing a handful of Vicodin pills and drifting out beyond where I could swim back. I knew everything the world possibly had to offer me from here on out. I did not know that the sea salt would draw all conclusions and worry from me. I could not have known that the slideshow of swimming neon creatures would fill my mind with magical presence. I would not have believed it if I were not seeing it. Floating with the psychedelic fish showed me something I did not know. Suspended distinct and separate from my consequences and my plans, through the grace of a narrow supply of air coming in through my snorkel, I first suspected what I finally know now.

Floating has always made me happy.

The final thing I will miss: After a hard day's aching fatigue, rigorous bout of sex, some professional achievement, flat on the mattress under the flat ceiling, satisfaction bleeding into second-guessing and self-recrimination, the case against the self building on a solid foundation of failed expectations and unmet standards of achievement and disappointing behavior, global frustration giving way to a very specific ideation—and you're out, asleep.

That moment of falling into sleep is the last thing I will ever miss.

9

MY ON-DEMAND FUNERAL

MY FUNERAL PLANS PUT more requirements on Trina than she could balance in her mind all at once. My farewell soundtrack, it saddens me to report, was dropped in an attempt to preserve her equilibrium. A selection of suitable songs had been compiled months beforehand, listed by pen strokes in a spiral notebook during a carefree bygone morning, a cloudy coffee hour when the departed still doubted that he would ever be required to go away forever, certainly not on any day in his foreseeable future.

The progression of designated tunes had been paced to match the funeral moods as mourners arrived, settled in, took stock, reflected, and returned to the concerns of the living. This page of scrawled ballpoint directives had been torn from the departed's notebook, by his widow, photographed, and reproduced in the program to be handed out at the memorial service. The music itself will not be played; no explanation is included for its exclusion.

"Are you sure we shouldn't have added a footnote?" asks Trina. "To acknowledge that people won't be hearing his song choices?"

Trina sits in the backseat of a black town car parked at the base of the hill our house stands upon, about ten blocks from the church where we were married. The widow's compact, hourglass figure is cosseted between plush Mandy Gold and a natty youthful man in his fifties named Paul.

"Where did my sunglasses go?" asks Trina.

"They're right where you put them," observes compassionate, critical Gail Campbell sitting up front and keeping a narrow eye on the hired driver. Trina's wizened child's hand locates the outsize shades perched atop her head, like a barrette, holding brilliant red strands of hair in a frame around her lucent, pale face.

Buttoned-to-the-neck Gail and Mandy (in a top that's low-cut, sleeveless, expensive, somehow sloppy) have been supporting pillars during Trina's romantic collapses from early adulthood to her current sudden-onset widowhood. Paul, dressed in slacks of Belgian manufacture and a tailored-suede over shirt, is the widow's earliest confidante. Paul was Trina's go-to gay when she met her husband, now deceased.

"How would we explain not playing Allan's sad songs?" ponders Paul. "'Advisors to the widow have rejected the set list as overly maudlin.'"

Mandy inks on Trina's eyeliner and holds up a mirror. "Look in here, honey. What do you see?"

Trina locks dewdrop-green eyes with the mirror and admires, skeptically, a delicate synthesis of raw will and nurturing sensitivity in her gaze. She lingers on the lines that might mean wisdom and certainly mark age. Trina looks away. "It's so much better than I could have managed on my own," she says.

Gail, sitting up front with nothing to do, directs the driver to start the car and take a detour.

"You want me to drive aimlessly?" clarifies the driver.

"We don't want to roll up early," explains Gail. "This day will be long enough. No need to stretch it out."

"Chase just texted," says Trina. "She wants to meet us outside the church and walk in with you guys."

"*Driver!*" chimes in Paul. "If a virile woman in a mullet tries to flag us down, try not to hit her, but by all means speed away."

"Chase isn't so bad," says Trina, enervated by recent events, unable to summon much conviction. "She's been helping around the house a lot. Ever since it happened, you know. The dogs have not been welcoming."

"I'm picturing what people will be wearing at this event," says Paul. "Heavy ink, I expect. Do they still carry the wallet chains?"

As Paul wonders, people dressed just formal enough to be self-conscious about it arrive at the memorial venue—an actual Catholic chapel on Sunset Boulevard.

Nicolas Cockroach (not his real name) and a dark-haired, tastefully tattooed girl in her nubile middle thirties who everyone calls Pretty Marina have arrived early and claimed the pew up front directly closest to the parking lot entrance. Pretty Marina would have preferred to linger outside the vestibule and mingle among cars and sun and other early arrivals. She's sacrificing her networking instincts to Nicolas's social anxiety. Nicolas turns the memorial service program in his hands. He flips it faceup.

Marina asks: "Is it customary to pick a photo of the dead guy in sunglasses for these fliers?"

"Maybe Allan picked the shot beforehand," suggests Nicolas. "Maybe he wanted some privacy."

Curiosity seekers and actual friends file in from the sunny forenoon and cross in front of the cool, shadowed altar space. Everyone's making more of an impression than usual. Mourners and others, indistinguishable from one another in the aggregate, pass Nicolas Cockroach and fill the floor. Eye contact will be unavoidable in the near future, an encroaching moment that Nicolas Cockroach delays by opening and rereading the memorial leaflet. He can't resist sneaking a judging glance at the new arrivals.

"Oh please God, it's Colin Cowboy," he says, minimizing the movement of his lips.

Colin Cowboy is a guy you can count on to show up at a funeral in a black felt cowboy hat. Decked in a slim-tailored vest, creased Lee jeans, and a T-backed tweed jacket, chill Colin peers across the rim of his artfully incongruous aviator shades. He fingers a sculpted sideburn and scans for something plush and vulnerable.

"Don't bring him over here," pleads Nicolas Cockroach.

"Too late," whispers Marina. "Hello, Colin," she says at muted volume. "It's good to see you here."

"It's good to see you too, Marina." Colin's voice is a strained leak into the airy vault beneath the cathedral ceiling. His hands knuckle onto the pew front. "It's even good to see Nicolas Cockroach. But he doesn't feel the same way about seeing me. Is it my hat, Nicolas?"

"Ten gallons is at least nine gallons too much in a place like this," reckons Nicolas.

"I'm so sorry, Nicolas! I've offended your sense of Cockroach propriety. You of all people are a stickler!"

Colin pivots on his boot heels and allows the surging crowd to herd him forward.

"This is interesting," says Nicolas, tapping Marina's bare, illustrated arm, returning her attention to the program in his hands. "While mourners were arriving, Allan wanted 'Everybody's Got to Live' by Arthur Lee to play on a loop. The song's on Arthur Lee's solo album, *Vindicator*. I have a copy that's only slightly trashed. I can sing some of that. Do you want to hear a bit of that?"

"Only if you whisper sing."

"My harrowing vocal range only comes through at volume. The song's lyrics make the point that everyone must live, and that everyone must die as well. That should be playing right now. It would set a mood."

"I get the idea."

"'Siren Song' by Tim Buckley was supposed to play while we all settled in. That song, I've got two versions of on a Rhino compilation. Next up, 'All the Things' by The Byrds. That's from their *Untitled* album. In Allan's mind, it fit in somewhere during the tributes. I have clean original vinyl on that. The slow version of 'Forever Young' off Bob Dylan's *Planet Waves* would be the soundtrack to our silent reflections after the speeches. I've got it on CD. And he requested "Til I Die,' which you'll find on the Beach Boys' *Surf's Up*, to play during what is known as the procession, or walk out. *Surf's Up* was disappointing when it first came out. I've grown to appreciate it over the years."

"You know all these songs? That says more about you than you want known. Nerd."

"Yeah well the songs and their origins are all listed here in the program."

Moving against the push, Colin Cowboy returns to Nicolas and Marina's pew front and drops in on their conversation: "This set list should have been burned right along with the corpse."

"So it's not an open casket?" asks Marina.

"Seriously?" Nicolas Cockroach diverts Pretty Marina's attention forward. "How could it be an open casket?"

On a table at the front of the room, a thicket of green stalks and lavender flowers hedges a double-scale portrait of Allan from livelier days. Beside the portrait, a silver urn gleams like a cross between an artillery shell and a carafe by Le Corbusier.

"Now I see," Marina says. "I didn't recognize that thing for what it was."

Colin gives tattooed Marina a look of empathy and lechery. "I haven't had enough coffee to sit through this if it goes long."

"Do you suppose there will be speakers?" asks Marina.

"It's a memorial service for God's sake," hisses Nicolas Cockroach. "They rarely use mimes at these things. Oh, God save us. Here comes Boxer."

Tall, rangy, amiable Boxer is saying his hellos among shuffling acquaintances on all sides in the crush of arrivals. "Hello, Marina," Boxer says, a slow and considered talker. "Hello, Cockroach. It's good to see you here today."

"Marina wants to know if you think there'll be speakers," says Cockroach.

"I'm pretty sure there will be," Boxer replies.

"What can these speakers say?" demands Nicolas. "Is M—'s family here? You can't really talk about him with any specificity in front of his family. If they're here."

Colin Cowboy breaks in: "I understand that one of the speakers intends to play a game of 'What Would Allan Say?'"

"This is where I move along," says Boxer. He moves his slow, considered hellos deeper into the gathering.

Colin Cowboy leans into the pew. "How are you holding up?" he asks Marina.

"'What would Allan say?'" answers Nicolas Cockroach. "Pretty lame."

Colin Cowboy doesn't retreat. He deliberately cuts toward the opposite side of the chapel, seeking someone who might offer a softer landing.

"Why are you so stiff?" asks Pretty Marina. "Colin is just trying to be personable. He wants to be your friend."

"*He fucked my girlfriend*," whisper sings Nicolas. "After he was divorced, and after she stopped being my girlfriend."

"I get it. But you were a little hostile to Boxer, too."

"Should we talk about Boxer?" asks Cockroach. "Boxer's the kind of guy who women are comfortable around."

"True," replies Marina. "And you think he's the kind of a guy who has taken advantage of that fact."

"What? Did he miss you? Did he not take you to the Boxer mat?"

"Oh, we went to the mat. But he'd taken Rachel to the mat a week earlier, and she'd thought they were in love."

"Has Rachel spoken to you since?"

"Only to say she hopes I enjoyed sucking the tongue that tossed her salad." Marina has cracked herself up. Through her chuckles, she notices Cockroach not joining in. "You have nothing to say back to that, do you?" she says.

"*Who are these two predatory she wolves?*" whisper sings Nicolas Cockroach. "*And what have you done to make them hate you so?*"

Two women stand stone still within the church vestibule and do not like what they see. A trickle of latecomers divides and flows around this solid pair. Implacable in their early fifties, plush Mandy Gold and clocking Gail Campbell, adjuncts to the widow, stare hard at Marina and Nicolas. Buttoned-tight Gail strides, consciously bossy, to the front pew and takes charge: "You are in the wrong seats," she informs Marina and Cockroach. "You'll need to move."

"I didn't see any marking," says Cockroach. His manner could be interpreted as apologetic. He is also put out, literally, intuiting that he is in the process of being ejected from his seat.

"Of course you don't see a marking," blurts Mandy. She adjusts her bra. She has never found one that gives a full degree of containment and comfort. "It's understood at an event like this that the front seats on the side closest to the exit are reserved for family."

"These seats are set aside for the widow's party." Gail clamps her face shut. "Nothing further needs to be said."

Marina's eyes open a little wider than when she is being frank: "Widow's party? Isn't there a better way to say that?"

"You know what we mean," gusts Mandy. "If you had any sense of occasion, you wouldn't force us to say it twice."

Making every effort not to overtly slink, Cockroach and Marina sneak toward the chapel rear, looking sidelong for a pair of adjacent seats. Gail and Mandy drape jackets and sweaters across the front pew's bench back, reserving the row. The two women exit to the parking lot.

A priest, thin, glasses, a distracted and tolerant glaze topping his slack facial components, mounts the altar and stands quietly at the lectern. He is known among a few in the congregation as Father Terry. The white collar at his neck exerts its force. Silence unites the gathering.

Father Terry announces himself as the day's officiant. "Don't worry," he says, "there will be no mass. I predict this will be an atypical service. I have an intuition about these things. Still, we will follow the loose traditions.

"Almost twenty years ago, I married two people on this altar, right here: Allan, who we are here to remember today, and Trina, who I am almost certain will be here to remember him."

As if cued, the widow makes her entrance. A formidable five-foot-two redhead, she's close to a banner age that is never enumerated out loud; yet she's animated still by the mien of irrevocable youth. She materializes solo from the blinding sunlight—formfitting and flowing garments selectively disheveled and artfully disarrayed, sunglasses trembling at her stressed temples. She semi staggers on the marble floor. The assembly sounds a hushed intake of breath. Trina steadies her legs, tames her four-inch heels, and struggles forward. One hand supports her progress along the communion rail.

She stops at mid-altar, drops to a knee, and makes a sign of the cross. Rising back to her feet, she continues across the chapel front to a section of seating directly across the room from where Cockroach and Marina had been pushed out. A man and a woman in their midfifties stand from these side seats and embrace the widow. No one else at the show has met this man and woman.

"That guy must be Allan's brother," speculates Marina, standing against a wall at the very back of the chapel. "The handsome guy in the family."

"Might be," agrees Cockroach. "Cousin. Something."

Having waited for the widow's wake to calm, Mandy, Gail, and Paul enter cloaked in a bearing of solemnity. A sturdy woman clad in formal denim follows sheepishly. Her name is Chase. The widow's seconds file into the pew that Cockroach and Marina had been shooed away from. Chase enters this private section and is ignored by its other occupants. She sits, legs spread as if to air and coddle a bruised package.

Father Terry speaks up in his role as officiant: "I've lost my notes. But I remember that this is the spot where the first speaker is meant to come up. So if you know you're the first speaker, why not approach the lectern, and we'll start?"

Boxer rises, rangy and slow, and eases toward the pulpit. Marina darts her eyes at Cockroach. "No wonder he knew there would be speakers."

Boxer clenches the sides of the lectern. His head tilts forward and a wayward ringlet of hair drops onto his brow. "Allan hated fans," he begins. "Not the type that blow air—the type who blow guitar players. He rarely talked politics because, as you know, his views were not up for discussion."

Boxer extracts a pair of reading glasses from an inner pocket and attaches their stems to his ears. "Children annoyed and depressed Allan M—. Which is why he had none and none are here. He texted me on the subject, right after my wife delivered our first son."

Boxer adjusts the slide of the lenses on the slope of his nose. He focuses on a paper scrap in his hands. "This is the question Allan asked me, upon the birth of my child: 'Have you ever noticed how early you can tell a kid's going to be an asshole for its entire life? Sometimes you can see it coming before the parents have even fucked.' That's what he said." The crowd is reasonably certain that laughter has been prompted, only half sure that the prompt was funny enough for an outright chuckle. Scattered titters trickle through the pews.

Marina leans closer to Nicolas Cockroach than she generally would and puts her lips to his ear: "Those two bitches totally wolf-pussied us for those front-row seats."

Cockroach moves his mouth so close to Marina's ear that he is surprised he does not bite it. "We were cowed," he says, "literally."

"Cowed," repeats Marina. She laughs and her laugh is pushed back by a distinct *shush* from a woman holding up the piece of wall beside her. Marina and Cockroach size up the lady who has shushed them: She's a fresh, imposing forty, tall, thin, multi-blonde, with a short, artful haircut showing off the architectural underpinnings of her face. She is both of the assembly, and an aspiration, a figure of adult competence that many in the gathering will fall forever short of. Her shushing lips spread in a winner's smile that would be easy to linger on. Marina and Cockroach revert attention to Boxer.

"You might wonder whether I felt privileged," says Boxer, "or did I feel imposed upon, to be receiving messages from Allan. He didn't get close to a lot of people. He might occasionally give the appearance of being open, but he was very conscientious about remaining shut off.

"If you've read either one of his books, you learned that he was not shy about exposing his faults. He was also selectively secretive. His biggest secrets were his good points. I won't say virtues, because he hated people when they exaggerated.

"You know he liked his dogs... 'But even Hitler loved his dog,' you say. This may be true, but Allan really, really liked his dogs. He had a bunch of them. In succession, consecutively, not all at once, which would be called simultaneously or concurrently.

"His family, that is his sisters and their kids, some of whom are here today, he totally cared about those people. He enjoyed being around them, for hours at a time. But he always lived in different cities than they did. The dogs he lived with day in and day out. He even let them sleep in his bedroom.

"Of course, his wife, Trina, was also sleeping in that bedroom, for like twenty years, which many of you may find hard to comprehend. I won't even try to explain that. Maybe she will."

Boxer folds his cheat sheet. He returns his eyeglasses to an inner pocket. "At the end, Allan seemed like he was on the verge of feeling a little bit better. It's just sad that he wasn't given enough time to do that."

Slow and rangy, Boxer steps down and sinks into his seat.

"This must be where 'All the Things' was supposed to play," whispers Nicolas Cockroach. "It's a dirge, a lament; because all the things you need to cherish at the end of your life were squandered before you got there. I can hum it for you."

"Shush," declares the short-cropped, architectural woman at Marina's side.

At the chapel front, a farce of hesitation and uncertainty plays out between the departed's youngest sister and the departed's wife. Which one should stand and which should stay seated? The impetus switches back and forth. People are watching.

Father Terry assumes his officiant's tone. "I think we could easily hear from Trina, and then Allan's sister, whose name, I apologize, eludes me. Or the sister could just as easily speak first."

Marina pokes Cockroach. "Who's that lady hitting on Colin Cowboy?"

A turquoise-haired pixie elder has pinned Colin Cowboy beside her in a middle-row pew. Cartoonish and oblivious, speaking silently with gregarious lips and vocal hand gestures, to the casual observer she communicates a long history and clear familiarity, which Colin appears to be backing away from.

"That woman in the tight black slip?" says Cockroach. "Jesus, when you factor in that she's almost sixty, you have to admire her commitment to the oddball style of her youth. I'll bet she was still hot up into her forties. And, obviously, long beyond that for a sleaze like Colin. I've never seen that woman in my life."

Trina parts from Allan's sister in the pew. One foot at a time, she makes stately progress toward the podium. It's her moment. She bends time to suit her, and Marina moves along to the next topic: "My God, look at Trina's shoes. She always has the best shoes."

"Those *are* amazing shoes," agrees the tall woman with the short vari-blonde hair, the sophisticated shusher.

Front and center, Trina ascends the few steps and wavers upon the plane of the altar. Her fine, artisan's hands can't quite land on the sides of the lectern. She takes a long-suffering look around the auditorium. She removes her sunglasses, reconsiders, and replaces them.

"It's true he was good to the dogs," she says. "But he was always irritated. I loved him so much, and he was so limited in his ability to say or express that he loved me, or any of us. But he stuck in there. He always held something back, but he was always there."

Trina may intend to say more. She gives that impression. She pulls a sheet of paper from her sleeve, unfolds it, and searches her inner expanses of fortitude for the strength to go on. She refolds the sheet of paper and inserts it back into her sleeve. Her brows and mouth contract with a profound effort, and words come out: "I want to invite everyone to the after-party. 'After-party' is what he insisted we call it. He also wanted a pool party; so bring your suits. You'll have a chance to have your picture taken holding his ashes."

The widow steps down, stair by stair, from the altar stage.

"Will she crumble to the marble floor?" whispers Nicolas Cockroach. "Or ascend to the saints painted on the ceiling?"

The widow, with a look back at the departed's blood relatives, picks up the urn containing her gone husband and clutches it cross-armed to her breasts. She marches ramrod straight out into the sunshine.

Gail, Mandy, and Paul, the widow's three oldest friends, the only three people in the chapel not caught fully off guard by Trina's abrupt departure, rise as a nimble unit and follow her out into the parking lot sunlight. Mulish Chase is a little slow picking up and collecting herself. Still, she beats the general crush out of the venue.

Father Terry reclaims the podium. "I'm not sure what to conclude, other than that the planned presentation has been shortened. Would anyone here like to pray us out?"

The transient congregation has stood and is shuffling as a mass toward the daylight. An aged punk pixie cuts in front of Nicolas Cockroach and Marina, cutting so close that her black slip rustles across their clothes.

"Marina," pleads Nicolas, "will you join me in a verse from 'Forever Young'?"

Marina is unsure how the words will go, but she whisper harmonizes the song's title with Cockroach.

"You're singing right into my ear," complains the imp in the black slip.

Nicolas steps away from the turquoise-haired biddy. "I feel that Allan got off fairly easily there," he says to Marina, crowding her. "It's almost as if he'd written these reviews himself."

"Not quite," interjects Colin Cowboy. "He would have said some things differently."

"Like what, Colin?" demands the turquoise-haired woman in the black slip.

"I'm still trying to figure out how you know my name," says Colin. "But if Allan meant as much to you as you say he did, here's a voice you should recognize: 'I'm doomed. Life's awful. I need to get out of here.'" Colin slices a finger across his throat. "The same spiel he always wheeled out." Colin pushes forward and pops through the door scrum. "See you at the pool," he calls back.

Once beyond the fighting crush of the chapel exit, mourners filter into the parking lot sunshine and to their cars. The breathing is easier out here. Vehicles form a leisurely line for the motorcade out to the Valley. Nicolas Cockroach puts his car into gear. Marina clutches the handle of the passenger door. She is about to become a captive audience.

"Just to remove all doubt," Nicolas informs her, "Allan specified that this guy, your friend Colin Cowboy, should be barred."

"Barred from what?"

"Barred from attending any aspect of any funeral type event. For Allan."

Marina slides her seat belt across her chest in a way that she hopes might distract Nicolas Cockroach from his fixation with Colin Cowboy. "Dead people don't get to pick who comes to their funeral," she says. "That's one of the first things a person needs to face up to when they die."

Cockroach inserts his car into the auto stream. He appears to focus his agitated mulling on the bumper ahead of him. "Have you listened recently to Brian Wilson's sentiments in the song ''Til I Die'?"

"I find it suspect that all the songs Allan wanted, you have CliffsNotes on all the lyrics ready to go."

"Allan confided in me. He told me the songs he'd picked. About a month or two ago. He'd wanted me to sing them. This dude he worked with in the nineties was supposed to play guitar. So I prepared."

"Oh. You and Allan were tighter than I knew."

"We were as close as he was to anyone else who'll be at this party."

OUT IN THE VALLEY, though squealing and splashing is heard half a block away, the funeral party is contained in a backyard accessible through a side gate. Directly within the entrance—per dead man's stipulation—sits a self-service photo booth. The tall, variable-blonde woman who had held her architectural face in proper repose at the back of the church closes the side gate behind her and steps into the backyard. More than one hundred apparent hedonists have jammed into this suburban plot of lawn and patio, and had time to don pool-party attire, while she was still looking for parking. She sees two girls in cutoff shorts and bikini bras pull fully clothed Boxer into the photo booth. The girls and Boxer brandish a metallic container shaped like a giant bullet and say cheese. A photoflash lights them up.

The winning off-blonde moves deeper into the wake, angling through intersecting cliques toward the swimming pool and buffet tables. Between camera flashes, Boxer notices the tall woman's exquisite success profile

framed within precision-styled short hair. He scoots from the photo booth
and quickly matches pace with her. He moves to shake hands. "I spotted
you at the service," he admits. The bullet urn is gripped under his arm.
"I'm Donald."

"Robyn. I saw you, too, of course. You spoke well. And accurately."

"About Allan?" says Boxer. "How do you know enough about him to
fact-check me?"

"I was his boss for two years."

"No wonder we never met. Would you like to take a picture?"

"Is this how I prove I'm game?" taunts Robyn. "Take a snapshot with
you and a fill-in urn?"

"Oh, do not be deceived. This is the real urn. It's full."

"A little morbid?"

Colin, in cowboy boots, sheriff's hat, and a bikini bottom, inserts
himself between Robyn and Boxer. He lays a hand on the urn: "You're
kind of hogging up the guest of honor, Donald." Colin lifts his aviator
shades and treats Robyn to a close-contact leer. "Donald has a habit of
hogging up the good stuff."

Colin's free hand clutches pretty Marina by her tattooed wrist. Marina
snatches the bullet urn and clasps it to her bikini top. She allows Colin
to tug her toward the photo booth, where Colin barges into the queue,
directly under the nose of Nicolas Cockroach.

"Divorce seems to be taking its toll on Colin," observes Cockroach.

Pretty Marina pats Nicolas's arm, and she's pulled away from him,
deep into the photo booth.

Boxer plays his most winning smile toward Robyn. She drifts away,
cruising behind the cover of Mandy Gold and Gail Campbell who stand at
the shade line of a patio awning.

Overlooking the swimming pool, Mandy and Gail face the sunlight
glare. Mourners change clothes at the pool's edge, shedding extra coverings
donned for the formal ceremony, revealing hidden skin and unexpected
contours and private ink. "People are confronted with mortality," observes
Gail Campbell. "They can't process eternity. They kneejerk to sexualizing
the complexities of their conflicting urges."

"When you're young and a slut," agrees Mandy, "everything is a call
to semi-nudity."

In freshly donned cutoff shorts and a wide straw shade hat, Boxer ambles toward Gail and Mandy. "See what I'm saying?" says Gail. "This douche." She moves toward the food.

Mandy shifts her bulk to block Boxer. He extends a hand. Mandy crosses her arms.

"I'm one of Trina's oldest friends, Mandy Gold. So you were a friend of his?"

"The deceased?" answers Boxer. "Sort of."

"I wanted to like him more, but I was never comfortable with his eyes. They were always moving and staring."

"Staring at what?"

"At anything that might jiggle." Mandy adjusts her bra. "Anytime he looked at me, I thought, *Is my tit hanging out? Did my tit just jiggle?*"

Marina, heading to the pool, says, "That's one of the things I kind of liked about him."

Mullet-bearing Chase, edging up on the buffet tables, trailing Paul, reddens at the words *tit* and *jiggle*. Paul has traded his Belgian slacks for gabardine shorts, but retains his suede overshirt.

Paul and Robyn come face-to-face and introduce one another to their top-shelf teeth. "We put on the party as a way to say goodbye to Allan," confides Paul. Robyn reads irony in Paul's smile. "Also the party is a way to say goodbye to everyone who might miss him."

"I'm blown away by how many people have showed up for him," says Robyn.

"Can you tell how many are here for him?" asks Paul. "And how many are all about the free food, the spectacle, and a chance to gawk at the woman who carries on without him?"

"I had a limited professional acquaintance," Robyn concedes.

"I've been told you were the departed's boss!" points out Paul. "Bosses almost never see the true face of their employees."

Robyn shades her eyes as if a cloud had shifted: "You're hinting that I haven't seen what allies of the widow saw?"

"Correct," says Paul. "Of course, I do lean toward Trina's side of the aisle. All of us who were her oldest friends attended her wedding to Allan under protest."

"The narrative twists all sound very ensnaring," says Robyn.

"Please," begs Paul. "A wedding is just a social construct anyway. Fully reversible. We're just so happy to be present and available for the funeral."

Paul sees Chase gearing up to talk, and shows her the palm of his hand. That fails to stall her.

"They're memorializing his perv stare," says Chase. "That's what his friends are happy to remember him by."

Robyn thanks Paul for hosting the event. The buffet appears to offer diversion and nutritional solace. On closer inspection, the offerings have all been scooped out from bulk bins.

"It is a carb-heavy panoply," says Colin, breaking into Robyn's deliberations, shifting the load in his bikini bottom. "How close were you to Allan?"

"Medium close."

"Did you confide in him? Did he confide in you?"

"We did actually, now that I think about it. As much as people usually do at work."

"If it could bring him back, if it would have changed things so he would still be alive today, would you have confided in him more when you had the chance? Would you have been an intimate even?"

Robyn puts down her plate. There really is nothing to eat here.

"You're a stickler," says Colin. "When I pulled up to this bikini party funeral, I never dreamed I would be speaking to a stickler."

A distraught pixie, a few years beyond a ripe middle age, bumps Colin's cool side. She wears a black slip and has a drink in one hand. The drink is fresh and almost finished. "Colin," she says. "Have you remembered me yet?"

"I remember we spoke earlier," concedes Colin Cowboy. "And I know I need to find the bathroom."

Robyn stands stranded with the aged imp.

"I'm called Viva," says the old punk rocker, arranging the black slip to best advantage and twisting a rattail of turquoise hair. "I can't believe how pissed off it's made me to be here today."

"These are emotional occasions," agrees Robyn, cursed with the gift of reflexive commiseration.

"If it wouldn't destroy my makeup," Viva stammers, "I'd be crying like an old drunk." Viva's face sets. On the surface, she seems to hold a deep grievance. "All this 'celebration of life' makes me so angry."

"I'm Robyn," counters the former boss.

"He named me Viva. Allan did. In his second book, *The Punk Elegies*."

"That's why you're angry," concludes Robyn. "It must be difficult to have your private life exposed like that."

"Oh, I'm not bitter at him," says Viva. "We connected when the book came out, and we've been friends. I'm bitter at these people who obviously, to me at least, are not taking his departure seriously or hard enough."

Colin has circled back to the buffet and rounded up a cupful of celery sticks and baby carrots. Colin chews roughage, rubs a baby carrot on his bare, hairless chest and stares critically at the pixie in the black slip. "I'm starting to recognize you," he says. "But it's from almost forty years ago. There was never anybody named Viva back then."

"My name was never Viva in those days."

"Then why call yourself Viva now?" asks Colin.

"Clearly. The name Viva was attached to me by the man whose death we celebrate today— to protect my anonymity—if I so chose to protect it." The sagging pixie's flex and face dare anyone to challenge her.

"Wait a minute," says Colin, "aren't you the girl we used to call—"

"Don't say it!" warns the elderly punkette. "None of us are who we used to be. That includes you. So call me Viva."

Chase, cradling a carb-laden paper plate, breaks in: "Did I hear correctly? You were having a long-term affair with the ex? While he was still a married man?"

"I was closely connected to the departed, briefly, while we were in our early twenties. After the book came out, we did engage in a digital relationship."

Chase sees the entire problem at a glance: "And now you feel used by him?"

"Not used by him," says Viva, "unacknowledged by the rest of you."

Trina in her role as widow emerges from some private indoor sanctum and braves the backyard sun. The widow wears a tasteful and foxy black bikini and lace body veil that befits and defies her age. Swaying on floral platform sandals, clutching a chic, compact resort bag, she z-lines toward a chaise within the shade line. Her presence is suddenly the focal point of the event. The widow allows herself a controlled collapse into the lounge seat.

"My God," observes Robyn, "Trina's boobs are amazing."

"That's what everybody always says about her," fills in Marina. "Amazing boobs, startling hair, fabulous shoes."

Viva, slip dress bunched in her crevices, pushes past Chase and through the fawning ring of Paul, Mandy, and Gail. Viva seats herself on the chaise with Trina.

"I am so sorry for your loss," blurts Viva. She pushes her face right up into that space where Trina is forced to lean away to keep her lips from touching Viva's nose. "And," confides Viva, "I know exactly what you've lost."

"Oh," responds Trina. "You've lost someone too."

"We've both lost the same person," clarifies Viva, and then off Trina's look of confusion, clarifies further: "I knew him too. Not as long as you did, not by a long, long shot. But deeply, in a way that's not the same at all, but not completely different either. I am so sad for you, and for him, and I'm here for you both."

"Wait," says Trina, adjusting the focus. "Are you like a girlfriend from the distant past? A one-off thing? I hear what you're saying, but I look at you, and I can't be sure we're talking about the same man."

Stung, Viva rears back. She pulls a mobile phone from between her breasts. She thumbs aside a few photos, and presents the screen for Trina's viewing.

"These are photos of his penis," says Viva. "As you well know. He sent them to me in the past several months."

Trina glances away and scours the bottom of her resort bag.

"I don't blame you for trying to avoid looking," says Viva.

"I'm not avoiding anything, honey. I'm trying to find my glasses."

"You're *wearing* your glasses, *honey*."

Trina taps a finger to her face and verifies Viva's claim. She focuses on Viva's telephone view screen: "That penis is not my husband's, not by any stretch." Trina gathers her belongings. "I'm going back inside."

The widow rises slowly and surely and moves with dignity and grace and pride. Her trim and miraculous figure wavers toward the sanctum she had come from. Viva pops up from the bench seat, takes half a step to follow Trina, and is boxed in by Gail Campbell and Mandy Gold.

"It's time for you to leave," says Gail Campbell.

Robyn slides smoothly forward and puts a hand in Viva's pixie hair. "We were just about to be on our way," says the blonde. "Weren't we, babe?" She quiets, shields, and escorts Viva toward the street. The side gate latches behind them.

"I'm sorry I've put you through all this trouble," says Viva. Her tone means the opposite.

Behind the two departing guests, Gail taps spoon to goblet and summons the party's attention: "Everybody has to have at least one dance. It's mandatory. Part of the departed's codicil."

The deejay, somebody's cousin, no one I would have approved, steps up to an open laptop computer. Music I've never known bursts from speakers hung throughout the backyard. Gail, Mandy, and Paul take a seat as if making a joint statement. In the open space in front of the deejay, Chase hesitates, unable to fix on a potential dance partner.

Pretty Marina slow drags with Nicolas Cockroach and wonders aloud: "How much longer before I can leave without being rude?"

"The dude's dead. How rude can you be?"

Dancing in their bathing costumes, the party mourners feel abruptly silly and wrong to the occasion. Everyone stops all rhythmic motion and mills or sits, waiting for the beats to end. The mood settles toward the glum end of the spectrum. Colin corners Pretty Marina on a wicker loveseat. His body language speaks to locking down and monopolizing her. "Life is about the moment, about not letting down the opportunities of the moment," he says, passionately. "This is a truth my near-death experiences have taught me."

Nicolas Cockroach pulls up a folding lawn chair, places it head on to Colin and occupies it. "A near-death experience is not a death experience," Nicolas says. "Near death and death are not even in the same neighborhood."

"I hear what you're saying, Bud," says Colin, "and I could give you some credit for saying it. If you'd ever been—"

Pretty Marina says sweetly to Nicolas Cockroach: "Let's go take a picture together. We'll make a memory." Strolling to the photo booth, Marina puts a hand to Nicolas's elbow and forestalls any immediate denunciations of Colin. "Here we are," she says. "Sit right here beside me."

Nicolas Cockroach cozies his flank up to Marina's flank. He nuzzles the phallic urn containing the departed's ashes upon Marina's inked-in shoulder. "Colin was on the shit list," Cockroach confides, "not at the top, but certainly in the upper third."

What possible harm, wonders Marina, *could there be in saying something Nicolas wants to hear?* She says: "Colin's presence at the after party must be pure hell to Allan."

Nicolas's face switches on like a NiteLight. "Just hearing that, I feel so much better about today," he says.

Marina and Nicolas clamber out of the photo booth. He drops the streamlined urn with a clang on the seat behind them, and they recommit to the party. But there is no more party. Paul, Gail, and Mandy have set up a reverse welcoming line. Sun-kissed mourners are leaving in clusters.

"Goodbye, Chase," says Paul to staunch and mulish Chase. "It was so good of you to come."

"I'm just here to help," says Chase, locking her handsome, square jaw. She stops as if to join the reverse welcome line. "It's all about being available for T."

"Keep it moving, honey," says Paul. "Let's keep this area free."

Pretty Marina, walking toward Nicolas Cockroach's car, changes her mind. She reverts toward the party house and from a distance of ten feet calls goodbye to Nicolas. She waves Nicolas on toward his car.

Colin lingers in the backyard. He puts on a shirt and pants and makes motions to help with dismantling the photo booth and assist in the cleanup. He nominates himself to tag along to the after wake at the widow's place. With Pretty Marina as passenger and navigator, he drives his Porsche up narrow, corkscrew Hollywood Hills roads, arriving at the home that had been mine. For the first time, as far as I know, he approaches that domicile's threshold.

The dogs lie ready to spring in their crates downstairs. Their growls remain low throughout the arrival of a dozen female visitors and Paul. Last to arrive, Colin enters through the front door upstairs. Snarling howls burst out below. Discreetly seeking a bathroom, Colin ventures downstairs, toward the dog sounds, and into my office, the workspace from which two books, and so much less, emerged. Colin sees a wall of floor-to-ceiling shelving cubes jammed full of record albums, thousands of record albums. Cowboy's factoring eyes make plans for those records.

The dogs growl. Colin urinates and climbs the stairs back to the public floor. The gathering is breaking up already. A swarm of women busy themselves around the left-behind wife and are dispersed by the proprietary troika of Gail, Mandy, and Paul.

"Today's been a long haul for Trina," asserts Paul.

From dragging herself out of bed and discovering herself all alone, to dressing for a dreaded occasion while knowing full well that all eyes will be watching for her slightest misstep, to standing for inspection while talking at the funeral, to putting on the bikini and emerging at the after-party, to the picture of, putatively, her husband's prick showing up in the hands of another woman, also a pixie, also almost sixty: the difficult hours have been sufficient unto the widow's day.

Paul extends a hand to Trina. She grips his elbow and uses its leverage to rise from her chair. The widow halts at the head of the staircase to the house's lower level. Both hands fold as if for prayer on the stair railing. The dining room's gallery windows face west, opening to the canyons and lights of Hollywood's hills, granting views toward the dark, unseen ocean on the far, night-cloaked horizon. Trina's slit, sparkling green eyes reflect the moonlit canyon's gleaming.

My second and everlasting wife says: "He would have been so annoyed by all of you being here right now. But I know he would thank each one of you for stopping by. And he would mean it, almost always."

The guests observe the widow's figure and crimson mane descend into the privacy of the downstairs area. Gail, Mandy and Paul follow. Chase moves to start down the stairs, but stalls at a signal she cannot be sure she received from Paul.

Gail and Mandy leave Trina at the master bathroom and continue into the grand bedroom. The dogs—two white pit bulls, a bulky male and a slight female—bark and leap in their crates at the foot of the bed. Trina flows in from the bathroom. The dogs keep barking.

"I've just decided something," says Gail Campbell. She holds a robe toward Trina. "The dogs need to be taken off your hands for a bit, while you get your feet back under you."

"I couldn't ask you to take them in. As a pair, they can be too much."

"Yeah, I already thought of that. I have a friend in Sylmar who can hold onto one."

Trina and Gail stand surrendered in front of the dog crates in the downstairs bedroom. I had occupied this space, sleeping and waking, through three sets of dogs. It's called the master suite, and it has every comfort and convenience. The only thing missing is the master. Bulger and Bardot, the white pit bulls, know something's up. Something that cannot change back has moved forward.

"The dogs were first on the scene," says Trina. "After the body went empty."

She opens the crates. The dogs rush out, and Trina cannot meet the seeking, yearning animal eyes.

"They *are* good dogs," agrees Gail. "My God. The male really is a *big* boy!"

Bulger and Bardot, easy with Gail on their leashes and pinch collars, leave the house. Looking back into the light of the living room, their sad eyes alight upon Colin Cowboy, and gleams of suspicion flash. Chase is also keeping a skeptic's eye on the Cowboy. She brings in the ashtrays from the balcony deck and empties cold butts into a kitchen trash bag.

Colin moves his silent brooding mien to a seat at the kitchen table. He glowers and sighs as Marina washes coffee cups. Chase dries the cups at the kitchen sink and shelves them into kitchen cupboards, placed as correctly as she can judge.

Having waited out anyone with an interest in them, having waited out everyone but me, Pretty Marina and Colin Cowboy finally leave together. I need a break from this house, and I leave with them. Cowboy drives.

Colin has never been to Marina's place. He moves from kitchen to bathroom to bedroom, doing a bit of business in each, as if he'd been paying rent on the place. He wants the lights on; she wants the lights off. The lamp on the bed table stays lit; the overheads go dark. A single hand pins Marina's shoulder to the mattress and twists her chin so she sees Colin eye to eye. His smile spreads.

"They call coming a little death," he says. His free hand moves to her throat.

Marina squirms. She might be trying to writhe out from under him. She might be adjusting his depth within her. "Why don't they call dying the big come?" she asks.

For a while, it's as if Colin hasn't heard her. He's digging what he's doing, and her pelvis digs it right back at him, but he's chewing over what she said.

"I don't care what they don't call death," he says. "I call it, 'I'm fucking you, and the dead guy isn't fucking you.'"

Not until I go to sleep, Marina thinks, and she speeds this thing up.

Here is my favorite part of my funeral.

It comes as I'm pictured perching upon the headboard, at the edge of Marina's consciousness, teetering at the apex of heightened expectation, waiting for Colin to have his little death and for Marina to fake her tiny fatality and disconnect and sink back and come into her dreams.

5

ALL OF YOU I'VE LEFT BEHIND

R UTHIE AND MY FATHER are but two people among an entire planet's population, you included, who have outlasted me so far. Ruthie was my mother-in-law. As far as she's concerned, she still is my mother-in-law. She is ninety-three years old, and she continues to live in the spare bedroom, bathroom attached, off the kitchen in the home where I used to make my morning coffees and have my evening reveries. Bulger and Bardot, the white pit bull-type rescue dogs, keep her company until this day.

Ruthie has been away. She spent a couple of weeks as a guest in the San Jose duplex of her dead sister's daughter, June. Trina's cousin June is fifty-something, a registered nurse, a single mother of two teenager boys.

"Trina got rid of the dogs," Ruthie confides to June in San Jose. "Why did she get rid of the dogs?"

June is putting Ruthie's feet into socks. "No, Auntie Ruthie. The dogs went to stay with Trina's friend for a week or two, but only while Trina adjusts. Do you understand?"

"Oh," Ruthie says, sage and cunning and not following. "I see."

But anxiety is recurrent, more so than memory. Ruthie confides: "Did you know that Trina got rid of the dogs? Why would she get rid of the dogs?"

"You'll have to ask her, Auntie Ruthie. Put your foot in the shoe."

Throughout the San Jose rumple in the fabric of her fading life, Ruthie keeps a firm grip on the question of the dogs. If her daughter finds banishing the animals so easy, Ruthie might be cast out next.

Once Ruthie's two-week exile is up, and her Hollywood Hills residency is reestablished, and Bulger and Bardot are home again sniffing her clothes for crumbs of dropped food, the question of where the dogs have been is, like almost everything else, forgotten. Ruthie's daughter is back to work, and Allan, her daughter's husband, is spending much less time around the house.

"Did Allan enjoy your vacation?" Ruthie asks.

Trina wrests her mother from the toilet seat toward the low stool in the adjacent shower stall. "Mom," answers the wife, "there hasn't been any vacation."

Ruthie's elevation to the Hollywood Hills and her subsequent decline into utter dependence were both gradual. Her stays in the guestroom began as weekend visits. She was reaching her mid-eighties in those days, and she worried about being left alone with the interstellar aliens infesting her own home in the master-planned suburb of Mission Viejo.

I've said goodbye to Ruthie many, many times. Whenever I left the house to eat, to attend a meeting, to apply for work, to distract myself at the record store, I'd pause in the doorway of Ruthie's room off the kitchen. I would speak to her as she gazed into a classic black-and-white film on the big flat-screen TV: "Bye-bye, Ruthie. I'll see you in a little bit." Each goodbye in the past ten years might have been the first time or the last time, as far as Ruthie's memory can pinpoint it. Our final goodbye, the ultimate sendoff, even though I am already gone, the way Trina's mother looks at it, that farewell is still in the future.

"Did Allan enjoy his vacation?" she asks her daughter.

Trina stretches with the washcloth, reaching around to wipe down portions of her mother that she cannot see. "I don't know if he enjoyed it or not, Mom. I really can't say."

One thing Trina can say is that my stamp has been postmarked. The postmark will never be off my stamp again.

☜

I'd been sending postcards intended to uplift my father—well that's not entirely true. The post cards, mailed to the last-stop nursing facility that housed the failing old man of ninety-two, were intended in part for the benefit of my siblings. I sent cards every week, and my sisters felt less bad about the distance between my dad and me. The mailings were the wife's idea. But to give credit where credit is due, it was me who ended every Sunday evening until there were no more Sunday evenings by addressing a card to my father.

First, I would write out the name of the institution: Sunridge Place, on British Columbia's lush Vancouver Island, the island of my father's birth. I would pause, picturing the Sunridge. I saw a tree line. I saw a mass of clouds ranging from snow white to metal gray banked to the far side of the sun. I saw the chilly, choppy Pacific Ocean in every shade of turquoise and green at the bottom of the Sunridge's gentle, grassy seaward slope. The next line of the address specified that my old man was quartered in Begonia House. My father's Begonia House appeared nestled back from the sunny ridge in a copse of evergreens. The art direction of this deliberately off-kilter hut leaned heavily on trellised, flowering plants.

On Mondays, I mailed off the postcards. I visualized a ruddy postman walking through the Sunridge cottage setting. An eager, young Sunridge attendant with a cream and cherries complexion gaily announces, "Mail call!" The young attendant steps through glassed-in galleries and crosses manicured lawns. Alert, snoozing old folks soak in the sunshine. Trim, efficient women, in motion like sober versions of sports bar waitresses, cater to the charming whims of old folks. Cream-and-Cherries hand delivers my handcrafted missive to the old man. He is gallant and flirtatious in his thanks.

The wife and I hopped up from LA to Vancouver Island for our summer vacation, our last one as it turned out, and I packed my subliminal expectations. We rented a car as tourists in Victoria and drove north an hour or so in rain, to the town of Ladysmith. We exited the highway. An access road serviced the dampened reality of a down-market residential block rezoned for commercial group housing. We drove cautiously. The wife spotted the Sunridge Place address, and I parked in a drizzle of negated anticipation.

We walked from the car, paused to sign our names at the check-in desk, passed through the code-locked Sunridge Place security door. That was all uneventful and disheartening. We stepped into the Sunridge Place elevator and rode up one floor. We stepped out into a dreary dorm situation. The smell momentarily obscures your powers of observation. All you can make out for sure is that the ceiling is too low, the fluorescent lighting is too harsh, and you want to move backward onto that elevator and not forward into the community room. The old folk, all the residents, are seated in a large half circle. Individually, with each outward breath and any other emissions, they give off fusty, musty odors of advanced age. My old man's voice, I would know it anywhere, shouts: "Hey!" and "John!"

The elevator doors slide closed at my back, shutting the wife and me in with this crowd of mortal decay. John is not my name. My father grew up with a cousin named John. That was a long time ago. Back then, young Dad would have been unable to pick out the Dad of now from this ring of oldsters. But I see him. He's the one with ears like a chimpanzee, predatory blue eyes, and mouth hanging sideways.

"This is my son, Allan," he announces to the group. It's as if he had been expecting me.

"Your son who looks just like you," says the group leader.

The residents do a synchronized turn in their wheeled chairs and scrutinize the wife and me. We are intruders. None of the residents are happy to see us, with the possible exception of the resident we had come to see. The group leader is fifty years younger than the residents. "We were just having storytelling time," he explains to the wife and to me. His words come out like a rebuke. "Your dad was telling us how he liked to restore old cars. Chryslers, I think it was."

"They were Packards," I say.

One unpleasant truth about old people is they smell like piss. Maybe at first you don't notice it. Maybe the stench is too strong to register right away. Ruthie has brought so much adult-diaper seepage into our lives that Trina and I, as we administer to her, both shudder at the prospect of a drawn-out future.

When Ruthie first moved in, and her medication had stabilized the space invader visitations, I would sit on the couch beside her. Not often, but once in a while, we would watch TV together. More precisely, I would watch the tube at the same time as Ruthie watched it. The Turner Classic Movies channel was her preferred station. Most of the movies were old; some were true classics. It's during the superior films that I might sink down beside my mother-in-law on the couch. She wasn't attentive to my presence. But she wasn't ignoring me, so we would talk. Her increasing incontinence became a constant reminder of her presence in our home, and these impulsive chats diminished.

Persistently misplaced urine is not a huge problem, really, in the pantheon of troubles. Piss is only a fluid. With time and the bigger troubles that have been faced or will be faced comes perspective. You grow philosophical. Piss is close to nothing. You picture your minuscule impact on the cosmic priorities. Then you think: *This chair I am sitting in is saturated with urine.* My advice is just stand up and walk it off, even if walking it off requires you to take your father's wheelchair by the handles and propel him ahead of you. That beats soaking in the saturation you've been stewing in.

We walk the old man's chair out of the group setting. He yells: "Hello!"

The nearest attendant yells back: "Hello, Stuart."

An adult-proof seat belt secures my father in his wheelchair. He may be belted in for considerations of his own safety; he may be belted in for considerations of staff. Maybe both. The flowery "houses" of Sunridge Place designate four hallways that spoke off from the central elevator bank. Azalea, Begonia, Camellia, and Jasmine are mere hallways. No one had warned me there would be no cottages, but life has conditioned me to adjust quickly to disappointment.

My sister Joyce and I have been communicating through text messages. She is three years younger than I am, lives ten minutes from my father's residence facility, and shows her face there at least once every day. A text comes in from Joyce as I wheel the old man the length of Begonia house and back again. We pass open doors that line close facing walls. "It makes no difference whether or not you go to see him," reads Joyce's text. "He won't remember you were there."

I expect my father to fully fail the short-term recall quiz. Still, the immediate moments of him being with us, of sitting in our presence, will be noted down below his levels of memory and thought, lodging in a subsection under or separate from conscious awareness, in the basement where the lights are out but emotion and hunger and the base bodily functions huddle in opposite corners. I'm living proof that a person doesn't need to remember an incident for its effect to live on. His visit with the wife and me will lurk in my father's every remaining hour, unrecognized but potent, like childhood trauma.

One day, back when I would sit on the sofa with Ruthie in our Hollywood Hills TV room, while Natalie Wood gamboled across the flat screen in *Splendor in the Grass*, I turned to the old woman and asked: "Do you remember when Trina was a teen?"

"Trina is downstairs," said Trina's mom.

Actually, Trina was at a yoga class.

"Did Trina ever give you trouble when she was a teen?"

"No. No trouble really."

Her daughter's delinquency and obstinacy, the mother-daughter fist fight, the running away, the coming home with the blood of a drive-by splashed on her hippie peasant blouse, the shaved eyebrows, the blue hair, the stealing money, the priest's failed intervention, Ruthie's do-it-yourself homemade exorcism of her only daughter, all of these are no longer any more real to Ruthie than all of the other memories that have slipped away. The only pressing trouble, the actual difficulties that had led to Ruthie's Hollywood Hills residency, are all tied to the dementia and decline heralded by a plague of extraterrestrial aliens.

I'd heard and witnessed contentious exchanges between Ruthie and the space beings. I'd sat beside her in the emergency room. I'd charted the contraindicated struggles over the medications. I'd seen Ruthie descend within herself, drop so far inside that she could not use the toilet or clean herself afterward without the intervention of another human being, generally her daughter.

I roll my father on a whirlwind visit of the flowery hallways that spoke off from the Sunridge Place elevator bank. Azalea. Begonia. Camellia. Jasmine. "No daffy daffodil, right, Dad?"

"Have you been waiting here long?" he says.

The wife strolls beside us. I wheel the old man to the end of each flower spoke. We find nowhere we want to accept as a destination, not even as a temporary stopping point. We pass among my father's peers, feeble, old, and housed, parked or rolling in tight slow circles.

The old man, I recognize him as housing my father, reels off an unstrung string of pearls: "The drive is pleasant. Be careful along the coast, the way property values are. The place has changed. Have you seen your sister? They tell me the drive is still very pleasant. The names are all lost to me now. We had a nice visit, years and years ago. Does anyone need to use the bathroom?"

"No one needs to use the bathroom." I do, but not in this place.

"I remember it well," proclaims my father.

None of the old man's sounds or futility makes an impression on the other residents. Have they all heard so much of him that they've developed immunity to his flow? Or, like him, have they stopped noticing new information?

"Hello!" he yells. "Hello!"

The nearest attendant shouts out: "Hello, Stuart."

"Hello!" He catches his breath. "I'm dumb," he says.

The smart move, I decide, is to retreat to his room. Stuart's history is posted in words and photos and one chart on the wall within the doorway of his Begonia House unit. In passing, I read off his full birth name, the place name Ladysmith as the town where he was born, grew up on a Nanaimo dairy farm, Royal Canadian Air Force base police, Royal Canadian Mounted Police, moved to California with his wife. Became a realtor. Enjoyed restoring old cars. Three children.

Most of that history has been erased from my old man's face and conversation. I detect little trace of the past on him and only a slight trace of the roles he has played. The wheel of my father's chair catches on the doorway, and he yells, "Shit!"

"That's the dad I know."

Looking at him, talking to him, the feeling is that my father's "down below" is dissolving. The puzzle pieces of linked experiences and memories that fit together to assemble Stuart M— are unlocking from one another. The pieces drift off into some fluid space that they cannot return from, carried in a medium that has made them soluble, slowly spinning into some dissolving dimension where my father does not exist. The old man looks at me. He knows me. He doesn't know how I can be where I am. He calls out to Sunridge Place at large: "Is somebody dreaming here?"

His eagle eye, the probing lens of bygone years that had etched out who I've been in relation to him, the pinpoint gimlet that during those crucial years under its oversight carved its judgment into the personality he helped make for me, that intrusive eye is on a prowl. It releases me. I'm glad of that. Staff members move about the facility. The old man's piercing blue eye tracks them. He points to a passing attendant and whispers: "There's one."

The wife deflects, studying a collage of family photos in a frame hanging on the wall above my father's dresser. "Stuart," she asks, "do you know who all these people are?"

"They are Glenda's," he says, referring to his second and final dead wife, the one who is not my mother: "She had many people she loved who depended on her."

"Yes she did," says the wife. "That's wonderful."

"I hated that," says Dad. "I feel awful."

A female attendant walks past the old man's doorway. He points to her and leans forward, conspiratorial: "She's another one."

"Your son has something to say to you," says the wife. She and I had talked about my presumed need to speak seriously with my father. We had not reached agreement.

"I do have something to say to you," I say to my father, "at length, evocatively." I cannot stop myself from intoning, from acting a little grand, and being largely absurd. "It's just, now that we're here, maybe I would have been better off saying it a few years ago, like twenty years ago. Or maybe there is nothing to be gained from talking out the past." I indicate the close walls around us. "Maybe this is all for the best."

He looks me square in the face. To all appearances, he's fully focused on what I have said and is absorbed in its meaning. "Are you going out for the day?" he asks.

"Stuart," inquires my wife, "where would you like to go?"

My father replies without hesitation. "I just want to go home one of these days and stay there."

This desire for home is not something he's saying from memory. He's not saying anything from memory. There are no more outings for my father. He's as homebound and homeless as Ruthie.

Up in British Columbia, the wife mentions a local business venture attached to the hotel we're staying at. The old man waves both hands dismissively: "There's not much profit in it."

"The newspaper says it's a vibrant business."

"I'm not talking about being here," he says.

The wife takes a consoling tack: "Stuart, you have a lot of great memories."

"I used to have memories." He gives me a snappy wink, one that my wife cannot see. In the exact now, during that blink of an eye, the old man's as sharp as ever. The blink lasts for less than a second. The next second ticks off, and the first second is lost. No continuity connects that conscious wink to any of the split seconds that blink along after it.

Just as if my father is not present, the wife speaks to me about Joyce, my sister. "You don't find it strange that she's not here while we're here?"

"I know the way we grew up. I don't find it strange at all." If my sister were here, she'd produce talk to fill the spaces. The wife and I between us go quiet, fully quiet. Even the old man has run out of things to say. Truck tires are heard hissing on the wet highway a few hundred yards from the service exit to Sunridge Place.

Passing trucks are a sound from travels with my father. A ten-year-old beds down in a car next to the highway. Stuck where I am on the floor of the backseat, hearing all the transit, unable to turn over. My sisters side by side on the car seat itself, sleeping as still as two little corpses. The trucks pass so close that the car shakes, and I cannot hear the breathing of my sisters. Looking up at the crack at the top of the car window where air and mosquitoes come in, I'm picturing a passerby whose interest is intense and extreme.

"Is anyone there?" My father wheels himself, shuffling with his feet in his thick, Velcro clasp slippers, out into the hallway. I catch him on the approach to the community room and turn him around toward his unit.

His bed is the only place to sit. I stand with the wife. I look at the framed photos of my family. Most are from when my mother was alive and we were all actively related. The sofa, the curtains, the den, all things I recognize: My father is talking to me during a late evening in the early 1970s. I'm sixteen years old, stoned beyond my years, and I'm not paying attention. I'm the only person in the room, other than my father. We are in the TV room, the family den in the photos. I'm not fully present. I'm not half as stoned as I need to be. The old man talks about as much sense as he would talk forty and more years later in Sunridge Place. He's in his full powers, excoriating me for hurting the family by declining to walk across a stage with my high school graduating class. I watch Slade on Don Krishner's rock concert and attempt to blot out my father. Inside the TV, Slade hollers the words to "Mama Weer All Crazee Now." After a commercial interruption, pimp elegant Curtis Mayfield comes on. I concentrate on every detail of Curtis's suede fringe and every fatalistic nuance of "Freddie's Dead." How could I possibly have any attention left for the old man's maundering guilt slinging?

Back at the Sunridge, forty years on, the old man sputters: "Allan certainly looks good, doesn't he?"

"Yes, he does," says the wife.

"Thanks, Dad," I say, flat.

He'd gone through all his trouble. He'd tracked down a vintage automobile, a 1947 Chevrolet Fleetmaster. He'd had it painted maroon and refurbished with gangster whitewalls. He intended to present this car to me on the day of my graduation ceremony. Now, of course, all of my father's good intentions are for nothing. He was aggrieved, and he was grinding me with grievances, wearing on me. He was breaking through my forced distance. I had wayward emotions, deep pools of them, backed up. I habitually denied them any runoff, and my face was breaking apart. Water came out of it.

"Allan is certainly looking well, isn't he?"

"Thanks, Dad." I give his wheelchair a shove and guide it out into the hall at Sunridge Place. No sense in standing still in an enclosure like this, not if you can move. Standing still allows an enclosure like Sunridge Place to close in and capture you. The old man realizes we're rolling. The motion spooks him. "Is someone there?"

"It's your son," says the wife as if that should be reassuring. "He's pushing the chair."

We approach an unimpressed old woman planted in the middle of the hallway. She's unavoidable. I don't want to meet any residents head-on, not any more than they want to meet me. This one's name is Sandy.

"I'm stupid," my dad confides in passing.

Sandy replies as if she has tired of doing so: "Stuart, you're too hard on yourself."

He gives her the same wink he gave me. "I'm stupid, but I'm not as stupid as people who don't know they're stupid."

"I think he's done enough socialization for one round?"

The wife agrees. I wheel him back into the deeper isolation of his room. He presumes the wife and I have asked questions even though we have not. He throws out answers: "No, I don't have a condition. I just feel dumb."

My father fumbles at the belt holding him into his wheelchair. He intends to rise up. "Are you free to stay the night? There's plenty of room."

The wife and I are leaving this dying place. The old man doesn't know what happened fifteen minutes ago. Fifteen minutes from now he won't know what happened. But he knows right this moment that we intend to leave him behind. He senses our lives, fuller in his mind than they are in ours, moving off in all directions beyond these no-future walls. His idea is to flee the home with us. He doesn't understand that we are harboring an ancient specimen much like him, a female version, housed in the structure where we live.

～

I SIT AT THE dining room table across from Ruthie on a weekday morning. Her daughter has left for work. Ruthie and I are waiting for the car service that will take the old woman to senior daycare. "That's a nice outfit, Ruthie. You're looking sharp today."

Ruthie eyes me. She might not recognize me as someone she trusts. But she's proven that she does trust me. Ruthie kept the alien assaults secret for as long as she could handle the aggression. When the invasive tortures of the space people became too much to bear alone, she wrote and slipped notes to me detailing the alien threats and where their Orange County sea cave nest is located. She was terrified that the aliens had followed her from the Mission Viejo planned community to our home in chaotic Hollywood. We had welcomed her, and as repayment to our kindness, the extraterrestrial invaders had latched upon us as well. Those fears, never actually calmed or allayed, have subsided from the surface reality that Ruthie shows and shares with us. We haven't spoken of the alien invaders for years. The subject isn't one I'm eager to broach. "I don't know how to tell you this, Ruthie. Do you understand how lucky we are to have you living here?"

"Oh sure," she says. She laughs. She thinks I'm teasing or being mean. "You're so lucky."

"You don't know how grateful Trina feels that she is able to make up to you for the trouble she caused you when she was young. She regrets that she never gave you any grandchildren, except for the dogs. Taking care of you now, in a way, it gives her an opportunity to honor all the sacrifice you went through so that she can live the life she has today. She's less sad about things that happened when she was a kid and decisions she made. She and I have a better marriage because you've been living here all these years, Ruthie."

"Oh sure," Ruthie says. She slouches in the sun of the dining room's picture window. Bulger licks her hands. Bardot keeps her distance.

"This dog always comes to me," Ruthie says. She clutches his collar and rubs his head. "The other one never does. Can you tell them apart?" she asks.

"Bardot is smaller, and she has a brown spot on her tail."

"This dog always comes to me," she says.

Both dogs rush the front door, barking. The ride to the elder care is here.

Ruthie toddles on her walker out into our Hollywood Hills driveway. The car picking her up for adult daycare is parked waiting. I open the car backdoor and guide Ruthie into the backseat. She slumps to the car's floorboards, splayed out almost flat. My impulse is to shut the car door and let them drive off with her prone like that on the floor. I scoop my hands around her torso, turn my face aside and pull up. "Put your arms around my neck," I say, "and lift."

She grabs and holds. We raise her so she sits straight in the back-seat. "Oh my. How strong," she says. I buckle her in, and she's driven off happy.

<hr/>

THE WIFE AND I have come up to Canada, in part, for a break from Ruthie. Although she isn't a demanding person, with whims or unreasonable requests or nagging, her very existence hinges on exacting maintenance. On rainy Vancouver Island, the lost father persists in trying to open his seat belt to stand up from the wheelchair.

"I have to get out of this place," says the wife, "right now. It came over me suddenly, the odor of it. I don't know if you can understand."

"Oh, I can understand." Every smell contains tiny bits from a particulate stream of excreted waste. The wife moves off to alert an attendant that my father is trying to escape and run off with us.

"You know that even if we could take you, I couldn't take you," I tell him. He's giving me the bird of prey blue eye. "I've had people, professionals, over the years explain that you did the best you could, considering circumstances, what the times were, the trials of your own childhood. None of these professionals ever knew you. None of these people ever heard anything from me about you. They just presumed that I needed to be handed a healing platitude. I guess it's too late to wish that they hadn't been able to detect you without even being told about you. So really there is no way that you could be leaving with us today."

I'm unsure what I've just laid out. My father's killer blue eye seems to have taken it all in. He says: "What's your wife's name again?"

"Trina."

"Thank you. I remember it clearly."

Trina reappears, without an attendant.

"Hello!" Dad calls. "Hello!"

"They say we just have to leave him," she says. "That's the way it works here."

I wheel him to the community room, park him facing a wall, and walk without him toward the elevator bank. Propelling the chair with his slipper feet, the old guy follows in frantic pursuit. The elevator doors close behind us, shutting out the visuals and most smells. The sound slips in, "Hello! Hello!" My father's voice works down the empty elevator shaft toward us. I hear a lost child calling into the dark. It's like you calling out into a void yawning out in front of you, and hoping some familiar voice might call back from the space, that some familiar person might be out there where you fear there is only nothing; some person such as me, for instance.

Weeks and months go on at Sunridge Place. Nothing out of the ordinary happens. New people arrive, settle, and die. Then one afternoon, out of nowhere, spontaneously, unprompted, my father remembers for a moment to listen for me. "That's Allan," he says, cocking one crooked old big ear. "I just heard him come in."

My sister Joyce is in the room with my father to witness this. I haven't been around for a while. "I don't hear anything," Joyce says.

Put an ear to the wind, to the ground, to the tracks, to your pillow; I am not calling *Hello!* I said I would not, and I am not. Still, Ruthie hears my absence clearly. She can see me where I used to be as clearly as she could when I was there.

"Allan's vacation was certainly good for him," she says.

"Mother, there was no vacation."

The wife, an ex-wife now for half a year, for the rest of a lifetime, checks her mother's diaper. It's time for a change. "Allan is looking well," Ruthie tells her.

Absently, the ex-wife answers: "Yes, he really is."

6

THE DOGS CARRY ON

PEOPLE ARE ALWAYS STARING at my tongue or at my penis or at both. My pink parts are my burden. Prominent even during chill snaps, these organs weigh extra heavy when I'm lying in the sun. My white fur filters the solar energy to the pleasure sensors all along my hide. A flush of warmth expands my sensual contentment like a bladder. And that swell of joy pushes out the tongue and unsheathes the lipstick.

The short one almost backed out of adopting me because of my genital size. "We can't have a dog with a penis like that," said the short one. "It practically drags on the ground when he walks. He could use it as a plow."

The tall one ignored the short one's objection. I sensed with the intuition only a dog knows that the tall one secretly desired the attention my penis might capture. "Think of it as a conversation starter," is what he said.

"Good idea. Someday, someone who might give you a job will come over, and we can all sit around the coffee table and talk about the dog's dick."

"Bardot needs a friend," is what he answered. "You've spoiled her. She's a princess."

The short one grumbled. She agreed to bring me to their home for a weekend, to see how I worked out, like if I could fit my gigantic schlong in with their feng shui, and if Bardot would accept it. They brought me in leashed from the car and walked me through their place. It's up in the Hollywood Hills, decks out back, ocean views on a clear day, squirrels in the trees, great food doled out of deep cupboards, no cats, no kids. They took off the leash, and I scouted the place. An extremely old person was hunkered in a small room upstairs next to the kitchen. Bardot, the original dog, called this one the Birthgiver. The Birthgiver hardly spoke except to say the same things over and over. "How's my little baby Bulger? Where's my little baby Bardot? Very good dinner."

The old one had shaky hands, the kind of hands that drop entire forkfuls. Why should all this be Bardot's? I pitched my charm at the short one. My big boy eyes, the loopy grin, the waggy tail activated by the merest hint of affection from the short one's direction. And I curled, docile and content, at the feet of the Birthgiver. That's how it's done.

Bardot wasn't too happy about me barging in on her sweet setup. But it's a dog meet dog world. Bardot and I were matched fairly well, when you get all the way down to it. So what? That dog never stopped wishing she was the only thing covered in white fur on the premises. To her mind, there's not enough sun out on the back deck for the both of us.

The sun Bardot and I bask in now is the same sun it was when the tall one lounged out here with us. For his last year or two, he would be out here reclining in the tree shade, doing nothing. "Hey, Bardot," he would say. "Hey, Bulger. What should we do today?"

Bardot and I would squint at him through our sleepy eyes. The tall one just stared off at nothing. We watched the squirrels networking in the branches above, waiting for one to make a false move. "I can almost see the tall one still," says Bardot. "When I'm just on the tip of a nap, he takes form in the shade. I sense him in the shadows."

Bardot is echoing the kind of dreamy shit the short one says. "I see him in one of the lounge chairs," the short one tells her friends. "Then the wind comes in, and he moves; so it can't be him. He never moved just for the wind."

He did remain fairly still. I do recall that. "You don't remember him any clearer than I do," I tell Bardot.

"We should have known something was wrong," she says, "that it was serious."

If we were friends, Bardot and I, this is where I would heave to my feet, lumber over and lick her face. I would offer physical condolences. We are not friends, really. This thing with the tall one leaving has pushed us closer together, but we are still cohabitants, inadvertent intimates.

We were there on the deck when the tall one took the breeze. Bardot knew he was gone right away; I'll give her credit for that. The short one showed up, saw the tall one, kicked him to be sure, turned around three times, and made a phone call. She called us inside and put us in our cages, brusque in her manner but nothing outside the usual unusual. Some people we didn't know—never smelled or heard them before—were allowed in through the house and onto the back deck. When the strangers were gone, the short one sprang us from our cages.

After they took away the body is when life started getting weird. It was unnerving. At first we didn't know when to act normal and when to just shut it down. Bardot and I did a running nose and eye check of the deck area. Most traces of the tall one had been removed. Then we galloped up to the kitchen door, as we normally do, and the short one let us in. Bardot and I took up our treat-begging positions. Bardot had suggested we should hold off, but I was really in the mood for a treat so I bullied her into it. The short one took one look at us and burst out crying. No treats.

"Too soon," scolded Bardot, the sensitive pup.

The short one pulled herself together. For a moment, it looked like she'd toss treats out to us after all. No such luck. She walked away from the cupboard where the biscuits and jerky strips are stored. She locked herself away in the bathroom. The short one made sounds that came out through the closed bathroom door that I for one did not recognize as coming from a human being. I knew that all was lost. It was worse than I had thought. Bardot was no help in deciphering what these noises might mean. Bardot ran downstairs and hid in the closet like she does every Fourth of July. I slumped down against the bathroom door and clearly heard the short one say: "I can't look at them. I can't even look at them."

Bardot and I stayed out of sight for a few days, not that we had a choice. We were in our cages while the short one was awake. About a week after the tall one left, there was a party at the house. No one sounded happy about being there. People walked all over the upstairs. A few came downstairs. Bardot and I heard a lot of murmuring and no laughing. We were caged up through the whole thing.

Around dinnertime, Bardot and I were looking at one another in the backseat of a car we'd never been in. Some friend of the short one called Gail who we'd seen maybe five times in our lives drove the car. Gail wore thick dresses and had never interested the tall one. "You two are going to spend a little time somewhere else," this friend said to us, "while your mommy settles in."

"Here it comes again," said Bardot. "We're being sent to a new home."

"Maybe you're right," I said. "Or maybe we're being thrown away. You were thrown away before. We both always knew it could happen again."

Bardot's history is the basic rescue-pup tale of rejection, malnourishment, and mange. The short one and tall one had been feeding her like a princess for years, but that early neglect is so rarely fully outgrown. Bardot's a gimp for life. You can see tragedy in the wishbone bow of her back legs. My sad depths are hidden within the proud musculature of a fabulous physical specimen.

The villain in my abuse narrative was a kid, a child, ten years old and cruel and cunning. No one wants to hear it, but children can be just rotten. I've known many families who should thank the Lord their dogs can't press charges. Ask any veterinarian. Vets have all seen the evil that kids do. Still, I don't want to talk too badly about the family that kept us for those weeks while the short one settled down. The family did take us in, after all, Bardot and me both at the same time.

"It's so good these dogs are able to stay together in a time like this," said the one in the thick dress, Gail, when she dropped us off. "The shock of being there when he… I mean, these babies have been disrupted enough."

If only we could have told her different. I was dying for a break from Bardot slinking around in my shadow, and Bardot longed every day for an only-dog situation. The way I heard it, these people who boarded us had given up having dogs when they started having babies. "Now that the kids are bigger, we want to think about reintroducing animals into the household. These two pups here are actually doing us a favor! We'll see how a dog or two might fit in; won't we, kids?"

The boy was the older one. He liked to poke a stick into Bardot's crate. He tried that routine with me, and I jawed the stick out of his hand quick enough so it hurt him. This is where Bardot was lucky she had me to look out for her. While she was asleep, the kid caught her in the side of the face with his sharpened stick. He almost sliced out her eye. "Bardot!" I caught her attention: "Don't you dare snap at this little prick. Never put a child in its place. You won't make it back to the pack."

Of course the kid blamed me for the wound. He told his dumb mom that I'd bitten Bardot.

"Well, Bulger, we'll just need to keep you locked up, won't we?" said the mom.

So Bardot and I held out. It wasn't so tough. We got used to being in the new place. One day not long after that, the short one's essence came into the room where we were caged, and she followed the scent. She wasn't crying, but that was a remarkable thing about her.

"I knew she was here," said Bardot. "I heard her car. I didn't want to mention it in case someone else was driving it."

When we got leashed up and out to the curb, the short one turned out to be driving a different car. Back home, the smells weren't the same, or so it seemed to Bardot. She started complaining while we were out in the driveway, a little neurotic about it. She complained again while the short one unlatched the gate to the front patio. Bardot complained once more while the front door was being unlocked.

"How many times do I need to tell you?" she said. "The smells don't add up."

"You don't need to tell me even once. I'm a dog. I have a nose for these things."

The short one pushed open the door to the house. "Oh, God, it stinks in here," she said.

"See?" said Bardot. "Even a person can smell it."

The short one barged into the Birthgiver's room. "Mom, I asked if you had to go to the bathroom before I left, and you said no. Now here you are; you've gone to the bathroom."

"The new smell is the Birthgiver," I told Bardot. "The Birthgiver has a richer bouquet than last time we saw her."

"It's not the Birthgiver I'm smelling," insisted Bardot.

I have a sensitive nose as well, as dogs do, but the changes in nose play meant not much to me, and I told Bardot so.

"My sensibilities are more sensitive," she retorted. "That's why the short one calls me Delicato."

"Used to call you."

The short one had used only our proper names since the tall one left. The pet names, it became clear, were meant for the tall one's enjoyment, not for ours.

The neighbors had a dog next door, a bit of a chatterbox, and a flirt. The first few weeks after Bardot and I were back home, if I was running along the fence with the dog next door, I tried to do it when I thought the short one wouldn't see or hear. Around the short one, I tried to be appropriately somber. "You're different," said the dog next door. "You've changed."

"I don't want the short one to think I am insensitive and frolicking when I should be moping and mourning. She already calls me Brute. Well, she used to call me Brute, back when the tall one was around to hear it."

"You know, Bulger, that tall one who used to lie around back there with you and Bardot and almost never move? I overheard something from my people that you might be interested in."

A small, decent voice inside told me to move away. "What was that?"

"Your short one was ready to leave your tall one when the tall one left first."

"I don't think so. I would have known. The short one would have told Bardot. There would have been someone else. To fill in for the tall one."

"There is someone else, is what I'm hearing."

Some people, humans I'm talking about, might protest that animals shouldn't tell stories. Maybe. I can't speak for every animal, but dogs talk among ourselves, and we're in a position to see things about people that no human sees. People don't hide things from us that they'll hide from each other. None of this is any reason to dwell on the liar next door. It's not her fault, really. A dog can only be as honest as the people it lives with. I stopped running around with this dog after that exchange.

Sleep and squirrels remained constants, unchanged by the tall one's departure. The short one was changed, very changed, but she was making an effort to change back. A woman named Chase who walked and sat like a man dropped by three or four times on her own. The short one would put a gate up at the top of the stairs. I'd perch there, level with the room where the people ate. I'd listen to the chatter of the visit and relay information down to Bardot cowering at the bottom of the stairs.

"This Chase is making a move," I said. "She wants in."

Chase always said the same thing on her way out: "I should join you and the dogs, Treeny, on one of your hikes. Up into Griffith Park."

Eventually, the short one took Bardot and me to the park, on our leashes, to walk us together in the company of Chase. The walk is a time-honored activity out in public where people are free to come up and speak to one another. Chase held Bardot's leash while the short one wrangled me from the backseat of the car. A pair of strange women crossed our path.

"Are those pit bulls?" asked one of the women.

"Are they siblings?" asked the other.

"Yes," said the short one.

"Yes and no," said Chase. She stepped up between the short one and the questioners, but the short one was hurrying me back into the car, rushing from the questions. We're both white, Bardot and I; so everyone assumes we must be related, which is logical, since all white humans are related.

Chase yanked the metal prongs around Bardot's neck and pulled her backward, shoving her toward the car. "But we just got here," said Bardot, setting her feet. "We haven't even walked." Chase gave Bardot's collar a nasty yank, and Bardot went with her knee-jerk aggressive response. Bardot tasted Chase's hand.

"Holy cripes," said Chase. "She bit me."

"That's the way the breed is," said one of the strange women.

"Bardot, I can't believe you've done this," scolded the short one. "Bad girl. Bad, bad girl. But it's just a nip, isn't it?"

"There's blood here, Trina."

"That breed is all the same," said that same strange woman.

I didn't know how much longer I could hold out before making my feelings known. Finally, the car started, and we were on the move. The tall one, the one who's not coming back, was always more specific in his answers to people who couldn't mind their own business. He would explain that Bardot and I were both obtained from the same pit bull rescue organization, but a year apart. If you look closely, he would say a little sarcastically, Bardot and I are probably not even the same breed. He would contrast Bardot's tapered nose to my mug snout. He would point out the mismatch of Bardot's slender frame and my solid muscle. He would indicate the spot of brown fur at the base of Bardot's tail. I am an animal with a lot of bulldog. Bardot is some wholly different willowy, feline, kind of thing. The tall one always found these distinctions worth making.

Still, let's not diminish the short one: she is the human who saved us from a kill shelter sendoff in the first place. I'm certain it was the short one's idea on both occasions to bring a dog into the house, even though she did balk before clearing the hurdle of my disproportionate penis.

Here's what gnaws on me now that the tall one is gone: The activities and cues from the short one are muted. She alternately smothers us with affection and neglects us. Like, as soon as Chase had left after the canceled walk, the short one let Bardot out of her doghouse and plied her with treats and affection. Maybe the short one always did it that way. Hot, cold and not present. When the tall one was here, he filled in the empty places.

The short one kept catching herself talking to the tall one out loud. Usually, once she saw us within earshot, she clammed up. Once in a while, she just tore into it: "You're not any less useful to me now than you were then. You don't contribute any less."

Sometimes the short one talked directly to us about the tall one. Other times she phoned some person and chatted through the details. Here's something she said in an unguarded moment on the phone: "Paul, can I tell you what really kills me about him being dead? I hardly miss him anymore than I did when he was here." Sometimes she talked to everyone at once. "And now it's about the way he kept his money," she said forcefully into the phone. "Not that there was much of his left. He had it in six different accounts. Nothing is up to date. Nothing has a current administrator. Do you hear this, Bulger? Can you take this in, Bardot?"

In the sense that Bardot and I were kept up-to-date and informed, it was better the short one was the survivor and not the tall one. The tall one would have been far more tight-lipped. Bardot and I would have been forced to rely on one another and on our uncanny understanding of human behavior and motives.

The short one busied herself around the house and around the Birthgiver. She stood with her fists on her hips, staring at the tall one's filing cabinet. "Let's get down to business," she said. She used a big screwdriver to unlock the drawers and dug in. Bardot and I sat close like cats, watching. "Bank accounts," said the short one. "Brokerage accounts... Money market funds... And what's this deep in the bottom of the bottom drawer? All wrapped up in an oversized manila envelope? It feels like Polaroid photos."

The short one cleared all the emotion off her face. She opened the envelope and extracted a handful of pictures. She slid through the pictures one by one, and she sat down right there in the closet. She looked at Bardot and at me. Don't ask me how, but I knew the word *whimsy* and I knew the word *fatalistic*. Her look combined the two.

The short one down-stayed Bardot and me in the closet, side-by-side, at eye level. "Let me confide in you," she said. "I've found photos. Naked photos. I'm not in them. Your father is in them. He's naked with someone from before he met me. Evidently, this is someone he never completely gave up, not like he completely gave up on me, and on you two."

The short one took to the phone. She waited for someone to answer. "I knew it," she said. "Remember that chick? I mean the neon-haired one who came out of nowhere and ambushed the funeral. She behaved horribly. Well, it turns out she really did know him. They had a definite connection. I can't tell you how I know, but I am certain."

She stood holding the phone motionless at the side of her head. At first, she paid attention to something I couldn't hear. She drifted off. Her face shut down. She was seeing and hearing things no one else can guess. "Okay," she said, "that's enough, Gail. I obviously called the wrong person."

Almost as though that call had never happened, guests of the widow, Chase, Gail, and two trippy, highly flexible friends, came over to practice yoga. Gail spoke to the short one about the state of the dogs in front of us as though we were pieces of furniture. "They're lethargic," said Gail, critically.

"They're waiting for him to come home," said the short one, defensively.

"You're romanticizing," said stern Gail.

"They talk about us like we're not even in the room," said Bardot.

"There was a dog in Japan," said a trippy yoga friend. "This dog went to the subway station to wait for her master every day for a year. The master had, you know, passed on."

"I've heard that fable," said our short one. "I've even seen the statue in Tokyo with Allan."

"They're real, you know," said the trippy yoga friend. "There was this other dog in America. The American dog visited a dead soldier's grave every day. I think it was after Operation Desert Storm."

Bardot and I went off downstairs to gnaw things over. The short one and her friends hardly noticed we had gone. Bardot sat, tilted her head and stared up at the tall one's wall of records. "Am I cuter than that dog in Japan?"

"I don't know what charade that Tokyo dog was playing, Bardot. What do you think about that American dog? The one at the hero's grave?"

"An addict," said Bardot, "for attention."

While Bardot and I were downstairs, the yoga humans upstairs decided a road trip should be taken to a Central Coast beach town that we—me, Bardot, and our people—had driven to and frolicked at as a unit, when the tall one was intact. That's how Bardot and I ended up closed in with the short one and Chase in the short one's car.

The short one put something, a metallic cylinder that looked like a thermos, on the back seat between Bardot and me. Chase sat a little antsy in the front passenger's seat. She eyed Bardot from around the lenses of her skull-hugging shades. "Some cars," Chase said, "have a chain-link barrier between the front seat and the rear compartment where the dogs ride."

The short one handed a device to Chase. "Plug in the iPod, will you?"

"How about since you're doing the driving, I man the radio?"

"I have a play list on the iPod. Allan put one together every trip we took up here. It was always the same stuff. One of three Bowie albums and Tom Petty's greatest hits, something noisy from Miles Davis and Grant Green *Alive!*"

"You want to hear the same thing again and again?" asked Chase.

"We used to joke about that on the drive," said the short one. She was remembering a moment. She was having a feeling, a feeling she liked.

"Yeah, that's pretty funny," said Chase, as if she knew better. "That's a pretty good joke."

The short one smiled to herself and to Bardot and to me. Except for being so sad, she might have let go with a laugh. "'When we're old, we can move up to Cayucos and work as dog walkers.' That's one he always said. When we first started going up there, he'd talk about hitting a jackpot and buying one of those houses that's right down on the beach.

A couple of years later, we joked about putting a bid on a place across the highway. Later, he downgraded to the trailer park at the north end of the town. Last year, he drove around pointing out spots where we could sleep overnight in the car." The short one had started out jovial. At the end of that memory, she was not joking. "He was making a lot of money when we met." The short one kept her eyes on the road, not on Chase. "I mistook him for someone with material ambitions."

Bardot and I had been keeping our eyes on Chase. We were not taken by surprise when she said: "Maybe he was someone with ambitions. But they were selfish ambitions."

The short one turned up the music and digested Chase's point of view, wordlessly, as the sun stared them both down.

Going for long drives is not my strongest dog skill. With every curve of the highway and abrupt lane change the thermos-like object on the backseat rolled between Bardot and me, banging into our flanks. I am susceptible to carsickness and drowsiness; so to keep from barfing on the short one's impractical leather upholstery, I asked Bardot to keep watch on the mannish lady, and I took refuge in deep, deep sleep. The next time I awoke, we were coasting down the Cayucos off-ramp from northbound Highway One. The dark had halfway moved in.

"You missed it," said Bardot. "The short one started talking again, and this Chase player doesn't even know what she said wrong."

"So what was it? What did Chase say wrong?"

Bardot put on her little superior smirk. "Snoozers are losers."

The short one hit a curb pulling into the motel, the one we'd stayed at a dozen times with the tall one crabbing along. "Chase," she said, "why don't you go check in, and I'll hit the grocery store for essentials."

Chase left the car and turned back as if to protest. The short one reversed out and pulled away. We backtracked about half a mile and parked next to a public access beach path. Bardot and I followed on our leashes out onto wet grass and a damp cinder track, sniffing in the sea breeze and blinking in the dark light. We were given a chance to pee on a sticky pair of scrub bushes. After that, neither one of us pulled or lagged. It was a silent agreement. We hadn't needed to be told to heel.

The short one headed to a wooden observation deck with benches and railings perched on a rocky outcrop. The tide pooled up on both sides of the outcrop. Inrushing swells broke below on both sides of the decking. We stared down at the nightlight magnified in the froth. Vivid color streaks were disappearing from the sky. The stars and moon lurked close by. "This is where your dad and I sent Twiggy and Oscar to sea," said the short one. "It's not as if they're waiting for him out there. It's not like anyone is ever reunited. But this might be a nice place for him to drift out…"

The short one squatted on the floorboards of the deck and embraced Bardot and me around our necks. She pulled us close to her so that my face and Bardot's face were less than a tongue length away. I shot a lick over to Bardot, and Bardot twisted her neck to put some distance between us. "It's like Chase doesn't stop to think that I have his ashes in the car with us," complained the short one. "She's been so helpful. She wants to be there for me. But she just opens her mouth and blurts. It's like her mind can't keep facts straight. We've made the trip up here to let his ashes loose."

Later in the evening, the short one and the ones she calls Gail and Mandy and Paul engaged in a verbal push and pull in a parking lot in front of a restaurant. Bardot and I were kept in the car for most of the word scrimmage and missed the details and the shadings. We did see clearly that Chase's attempt to speak up was shot down. The people quarreling outside the cracked car windows were all people who had been confined to the outskirts when the tall one was present. Since the tall one went away, these people were at the house all the time. They placed their opinions in every discussion and decision the short one made.

One stray woman, dressed as if she was ready for bed, stepped out from a dim side street and inserted herself into the arguing pack. The others united in attacking her. The stray woman lashed back, and they all quieted down and entered the restaurant as a group. After the humans had eaten, the stray woman was sent off on her own. Bardot and I were taken for a moonlight walk on the beach, with just the short one and Chase, who was acting extra mannish.

The short one and Chase were clearly talking to one another, but not about whatever they had on their separate or shared minds, and Chase changed all that: "Your friends are cool and everything," she said. "It would be even cooler if they would accept me. It doesn't matter to me if they like me or not, but they could at least have the common courtesy to pretend to like me. Otherwise, it's not like they're insulting me. They're insulting you."

"Of course my friends like you," said the short one.

"They don't act like it," protested Chase. She deepened her voice. It was deeply aggrieved. "You'd never know they like me from the way they keep so distant from me."

"Oh, don't be silly. Of course they keep distant. You're a newcomer. They hardly know you."

"That's just what I mean! Bardot! Come here!"

I've noticed that when humans are seized by fury, they never see it coming. I see it, and Bardot saw it coming too. That's why Bardot was slinking away from Chase. Bad move. Chase hunched her shoulders and swung both arms with all the weight and velocity she could muster. The force of all that leverage snapped into the ring of steel prongs circling Bardot's neck. The little dog jerked into the air. As Bardot flew, Chase howled: "Pay attention to me!"

Bardot came back to ground on all four paws and sprang, jaws open. She clapped her teeth shut on the hammy inside of Chase's thigh.

"Goddamit! You little bitch!" Chase flung the leash from her, put her hand to her thick leg, kicked at Bardot, missed, and landed in the sand.

"Fuck!" said Chase. "I'm bleeding."

"You can't just pull the dog's collar like that," the short one said. "You can't just take your anger out on a defenseless animal."

The mannish lady threw up. She was sick throughout the night. When the morning came, none of us in that Cayucos motel room had any real sleep to shake off. The ride home was four hours of silence with everybody thinking things over, especially the short one.

"The short one is thinking things over," said Bardot.

"Like I don't know."

"I think I did the right thing biting the mannish lady."

"Wait," said the short one, late in the drive. "Are the ashes back there with the dogs? Chase, do you see the ashes back there?"

"What ashes?" said Chase.

"Don't play dumb. My husband's ashes. The reason we even started this trip."

The mannish one twisted in her seat and glowered back at Bardot and at me. She climbed up on her knees, and Bardot cringed away from the face on her. Chase looked like she'd stepped on a bee, but was trying to hide that she was stung. "They're in the trunk," she said.

"You're sure?"

"I saw them in there this morning. After I walked to get the car. When I put in your bags."

"I don't remember putting the urn in the trunk."

"Would you rather have it rolling around in the back seat?"

Chase put plugs on a white wire into her ears, closed her eyes, and rocked her head as if she was hearing sounds the rest of us could not hear. The plugs stayed in her ears for the rest of the ride home and also as she got out of the car, slammed into her own car without looking back and drove off.

We sat parked in the driveway. I was about ready to fall asleep again. "I guess it's just us now," said the short one. "Just us. Let's go into the house."

We were alone now, the four of us—Birthgiver, short one, Bardot and me—through the rainy days and on until it was sunny all the time again. Of course, the dark season always came back, and the coolness became too cool if the windows were left open at night.

As dogs, our metabolisms work faster than humans. We process loss faster, and Bardot and I were both ready to move on years sooner than the widow was. Being dogs as we are, we also grew older faster and in a more devastating manner than the short one did. Maybe she noticed when I lost a step on my fly up the stairway. One day I jumped and missed that second step. That stumble, recurring under controlled conditions, changed how I did things.

In the middle of when I started hobbling is when the Birthgiver emptied out. Some men came and took away what the Birthgiver left behind, and the short one settled into the Birthgiver's sofa like she'd just dropped a big sack of groceries she'd carried all the way up the hill. She sat there with her head back looking at the ceiling. Her face might float up into it. She started filling sections of her lungs that had been doing nothing. She walked around the house, room by room, not touching anything. "This is mine," she said. "This is mine too."

From here, time jumps forward. The years bring you so much you don't remember, folded in with all the details of the decline that the days never let you forget. The short one has returned to the sunshine. We are out on the deck behind the house. Bardot and I lie in the shade. Squirrels, maybe descendants of the squirrels Bardot and I used to chase, slink through the trees and skitter across the railings of the deck, just a few yards from our noses. Bardot and I are curiosities to the squirrels, almost immobile, but big and of a threat breed.

The short one drinks lemonade with an in-between character she calls Paul. "You're still playing the widow part," says Paul. "But you seem all better. Somewhat elderly though; as if you've let a few years slip by."

"Primarily, I'm annoyed and disappointed. That my choice of partner didn't work out better."

"Just because he alienated your closest friends, withheld affection, ate up your childbearing years, became unemployable, plundered your retirement accounts, and held you up to public humiliation in his thinly veiled fictions? Is that really reason enough to wish you'd done better?"

"Paul, I'm talking about the fact that he died. How am I supposed to have any faith in any future choice? If I submit to some light romantic advance, how do I know it won't lead to the same profound letdown?"

"You're not remotely talking like yourself. Have you been seeing a therapist?"

"We've been having such a pleasant afternoon. Why would you ask that?"

"The vocabulary. The way you put together those sentences."

This is too much for me, and I drag myself off to piss, although not as far off as when I was younger.

"Do you think Bardot has started to limp?" the short one asks Paul, resuming conversation.

"She's been staggering for a couple of years. If I were you, I'd be more worried about the one with the big dick. It looks like he just peed out a splash of grenadine."

The short one steps over me and inspects the marking I've left. "Oh no," she says to Paul. To me, she says: "Brute, are you feeling a little under the weather? Do you want to come inside? I have steak from last night."

Bardot can't help herself. She stagger trots over to the marking and puts her snout in for a sniff. Her ears pin back, and then she tries to act nonchalant. Maybe she loves me after all. She wants to shield me from the facts. Her discriminating nose and delicate sensibility can't hide the significance of the scent she's picked up. Of course, I know full well that blood shouldn't be coming out of my wang. A chunk of last night's steak won't remedy what's wrong inside me. It's a dog's life, but a dog's life is short. Time is limited, that's a passing reality all good dogs know.

That night, when no one is home except the three of us who live there, the widow pulls out a step stool and takes down a box behind her shoes. She sits on the side of the bed and sifts through photos of her departed husband, of the Birthgiver as a young person, of a very still baby she calls Henrietta. "Look, Bulger, look, Bardot: see her tiny foot prints? Baby Henrietta's feet never touched the ground."

The widow lets the photos drop. She clasps a pillow and sobs. The sobbing is deeper and goes on longer than it has before. I would jump up on the bed with the short one, not that I've been invited, but my joints are not the fluid interworkings of sinew, muscle, and bone they once were. I place my face up near her pillow, close enough that my tongue almost reaches her mouth. I flick that tongue again and again.

The short one laughs, and her face clears. She pulls me up onto the bed, which is agonizing, and she clasps me. She has never allowed me on the bed. Only Bardot has been on the bed. The short one's arms are so tight, the embrace would hurt except it's her. "Oh, Bulger," she says, she sighs. It's the gentle her, the soft her, the dreamy, optimistic her of before. "Old Brute," she says. "You are not long at all for this world, my good old boy."

I am dazzled by the short one's smile and by the diamond tears on her lashes. I think I know what she's hoping to tell me. So does Bardot, lying low on the floor beside the bed. Bardot and I, our intuition is all animal, but we grasp the slippery insight and emotion the short one is trying to pass across. She wants me to look for the tall one, but it's something she could never put into words without feeling foolish. Bardot gives off one bitten weep in the background and turns away.

I'm able to keep eye contact with our human. My smile might be wavering. It hasn't been what it once was. There's no reason to believe that the short one notices that I have faltered. "Thank God," she says, "you can't understand a word I'm saying."

7

THE LEGACY OF MY WORK

PEOPLE LOOK AROUND WHEN they know the end is here. Their tissue-paper skulls swivel on their matchstick necks. Bugging eyes burn beneath a hot urgency that had been a cool brow just forty-eight hours ago. All it takes is a two-day downswing. The patient is looking up in a way the patient has never looked up before. What is the poor expiring thing peering at? Is some frightful specter creeping across the ceiling?

First off, the poor expiring thing is not looking *at* anything. The poor thing is looking *for* something. I know this from experience. The poor thing is searching itself. The poor thing asks: *What do I leave behind? May I please be shown something I did that was worth doing?*

Often families gather around. Descendants swoop in, flush with the bloom of life. Their faces are cringing evidence that some corrupted vestige of the dying progenitor lives on. Picture the tight, awkward mob summoned by the announcement of your nearing date of departure. These people are your kids. They've come to pay glum respects. You are still breathing. Your eyes open. The premature mourners, hugely inconvenienced, discretely wish they were someplace else. There is some crying, not for you. This shifty vigil is also an occasion to divvy up the material leftovers. Though you who are nearly gone haven't left yet, the negotiations over your estate descend naturally into bickering. That's where the weeping comes in.

There you loll, on the deathbed. A full spectrum of your sad genetically transferred personality traits looms over you. You are immobile. You cannot escape the teary drizzle raining down from the open-mouthed pantheon of your creations. This pensive overhang is how you must have looked to them when you stood gawking down into their cribs. Bending over that baby bedding, or years later with those grown babies bent over you, you might reproach yourself: *Look at what I have produced!*

But I'm making all this up. The final gathering of the clan is a pre-death dissatisfaction I can only imagine. In real life, I used a condom. Or the woman was on the pill or had inserted an IUD or we disengaged in time. This fiction of myself with kids has only spooled out because I am alone in a car and my mind seeks swaddling.

One ultimate problem arises from having no children. As you creep up on the end, you're robbed of the diversion of reconciling with estranged offspring. You have no distractions from facing your stark realities and embracing them. While stressing in heavy traffic along the Cahuenga Pass, I was forced to swallow the choking fact that I will live on only through my art, like Emily Dickinson or Edgar Allan Poe, but leaving behind inferior material. Two motorists with minor dents blocked an active transit lane. Adjusting my rearview mirrors, I edited *art* out of the phrase "will live on through my art" and substituted the word *content*. In other words, I slathered dismay on top of disappointment. That *art* signifier disregarded my later years crapping out targeted copy for Internet media start-ups. Some fine sentences, too many to count maybe, had been crafted out of nothing and later deactivated in a series of bursting digital bubbles. I was thinking all this, of course, because I was driving in my car with no other person in the car. That's when morbid reflection melts your face like sun glare on a windshield.

I wasn't completely alone, not like I've become now. The big boy dog, Bulger, was stretched across the backseat panting and motionless. We are on a rush-hour run to the emergency veterinarian, a run we should have made the night before. I didn't want to think about what might go wrong at the vet; so I jumped into the flow of things that had gone wrong with me. I'd failed to take in the dog yesterday. That had gone wrong. Twenty-four hours earlier, I'd magically thought, *Maybe Bulger will recover on his own power.* Like how I always hoped a car would repair itself. Now I was afraid my car wouldn't make it to the vet and back, because of all I'd done wrong. The car, a big, four-door Chevrolet with a black-on-black color scheme and blacked-out windows, had kept itself running for almost twenty years. The big white dog gave a wretch in the backseat: the start of a death rattle? His tongue was curled back and dry; his gums were pale.

About a month after Trina and I married, I'd paid cash for the black-on-black Chevrolet and drove it straight home from the dealer's lot. The car, the 1996 Chevy Impala Super Sport, had been a reward to myself while I was writing at the magazines. Magazines are close to my heart, sad for them. Storing anything in the vicinity of my heart places it a few weak beats closer to extinction. The Impala had outlived the magazine job and its warranty. A few thousand more miles, and it would outrun me.

I find great parking at the veterinarian hospital, and the dog tries and fails to muster the will to walk. Magazines are textbook lessons in what it is to be ephemeral, especially the magazines I worked on. I carry the big dog into the emergency waiting room. He's huge and he's helpless. I picture *Hustler* magazines, *Barely Legals*, *Leg Worlds*, and *Taboos* being cleared out from under unmade beds and tossed into waste receptacles of all kinds. The recycle bin, pulp returning to pulp, is the best end-case scenario for magazine work. The veterinarian is a no-nonsense woman. Bulger looks at her as though she is his last hope. The vet believes the boy is afflicted in one of two ways.

"One: snakebite," she says.

"Like a rattlesnake?"

"Precisely." She runs her hands all over the dog, brushing back his fur and peering at his skin.

I worry out loud: "We live in the hills. He goes out into the yard. It's brushy. I've never seen any snakes there, but I can picture them."

She presses her hands at the top of Bulger's jaw, under his ears. "I don't see any puncture wounds." She exposes his pale gums. "I do see lividity. So possibility two: rat poison."

"How do you determine if it is rat poison?"

"We'll give him vitamin K. If he responds, we'll know it was rat poison."

"And what is the response we'll be looking for?"

"If he doesn't die."

In the car, totally alone now, watching the heat gauge rise toward the red, I'm scolding myself. Why didn't I write more books? There's an obligation here to phone Trina and tell her what the vet has said. That would mean talking about the pie pan. My books are far from eternal. For starters, there are only two: *Prisoner of X* (Feral House, 2006) and *Punk Elegies* (Rare Bird, 2015). They'll sit on a few hundred meager shelves until two people move in together, and the couple's shelving yards contract. The discussions are inevitable. "Honey, we have only so much room. If we keep that *Prisoner of X*, we'll need to dump the Ron Jeremy bio or the Linda Lovelace *Ordeal*."

At home, the day before all this, is the day we should have taken Bulger to seek emergency medical attention. We didn't, due to worries about my car, the vehicle connecting me to my bygone prosperity. The intervening years had been kind enough, but every twist of the Impala's ignition might be its last.

A pie pan no one from my house has ever seen before gleams in the courtyard, and the male dog is lethargic. Panting. Won't eat. Puked water. The pan has been licked clean. Bulger's breath is putrid. His leg swells. "If the swelling hasn't gone down tomorrow," I volunteered, "we'll do something." Trina showered Ruthie, dressed the old thing in pajamas, and put her to bed. We put ourselves to bed. In the morning, Ruthie is guided from bed and dressed and fed without Bulger underfoot. Bardot, the slight girl dog, vogues for our attention. Bulger does not barge in. He has always muscled in. T and I move off to our outside days.

I'm home in time for Ruthie's drop off from adult daycare. I walk her and her walker into the house. Bulger elects not to rise to his feet and lick hello or to sniff for spilled food on the mother-in-law's pants. Bulger's bad leg is twice the size of the unaffected one. I take a photo and send it as an image text to Trina. She responds immediately. All the way from her gallery in downtown LA, she can see: "That's not a sprain. That's a hematoma."

How does she know a word like *hematoma*?

"He's bleeding in there," she clarifies, "in the leg."

So he must be bleeding in his organs too. I trundled the big ailing animal into the big ailing car and transported him to the vet, where I left him in uncertain condition. I headed home knowing for sure only that something unsettling is happening. It will keep me awake. It will be a long night of the heavy soul, and the big dog will not be there to comfort me. The wife comes home from late-night yoga, and the call comes in from the emergency vet soon after. Ruthie is almost ready for bed.

"Your dog was poisoned a day or two ago," says the serious woman, Bulger's last hope for a savior.

Trina, wiping her mother, hears my side of the conversation: "Okay. I see. Right. I see. That's all I can ask for."

I hang up. "What did they say?" asks Trina.

"The prognosis is touch and go. No one's making any promises."

"Who was that on the phone?" asks Ruthie. "Where is Bulger?"

Life and death are all a big joke until your dog gets sick. Then you're on your own, you and your questions. For instance: *What have I ever done worth doing?* We have the tools, if we are willing, to make the deepest, most scouring personal assessments. Trina puts herself to bed, and I start the night looking for evidence of my lasting self on the Internet. I follow the dead-end leads—legacy links to news-and-opinion articles I'd typed up on gun violence and narcissism, the 1967 borders, Reagan, Gorbachev, Reykjavik, Fall Out Boy's viral dick pic, months upon months of lighter stuff and heavier fare, ground out daily for a succession of online employers and posted to my byline, all relegated to error page oblivion by site shutdowns. No sense looking for me in all of that.

I bypass any search results linking to online commentators' opinions of my best efforts, a morgue of dismissive hatchet work that will apparently live forever. Seeking sanctuary, I click into the Goodreads site, a safe-place platform for pop-literature nerds where I have deposited a trove of thumbnail book reviews, readily locatable to any curious party with Web access and nothing better to search for.

The first Goodreads book review I ever wrote was a burst of studied modesty awarding the full five-stars top rating to my own book *Prisoner of X*. The reviews I've written of other people's books are stingier with the stars, and the commentary on the first few is skeletal. My entire reflection upon reading John Berryman's collected poetry is to wish that

Berryman's novel *Recovery* had not been left unfinished due to the author's suicide. Scanning forward, I discover myself to be a big wisher. A review or two down the line, I wish Roberto Bolaño had lived to produce another apocalyptic behemoth in the vein of *2666*. Shuddering sounds come to me from upstairs. I wish I were hearing the big dog; immediately I know better.

Ruthie is on the move in the kitchen, clumping around without her walker. I go up and steer her back toward her couch. "Where is Bulger?" she asks. Bardot makes a pass through Ruthie's room, looking for dropped crumbs in her tracks. The old one kicks toward Bardot. "Is that Bulger?"

"No, Ruthie, that's Bardot." I like to be as honest as I can be. "Bulger's at the pet hospital. We took him in for a checkup."

Trina's mom is ninety-three years old. She's had diabetes since her forties. A creeping dementia started at eighty, and Alzheimer's showed up about ten years ago. She stops just before the sofa and drills me with a clear eye to eye. "I hope Bulger is okay," she says. An unspoken "or else" hangs in the air, and her old ass drops down onto the sofa cushions. Ruthie and the Brute make a good couple. The old woman likes Bulger, and the big, powerful bulldog watches out for her. If he fails to pull through, the balance will be thrown off.

I make it back downstairs and put in a call to the overnight vet, oddly expecting her to extend some reason for optimism. "We have administered the vitamin K, and Bulger did take some water on his own," she reports. "He threw it up right away, but the fact that he took any water, we interpret as a good sign."

But, I want to ask, *is there any clear sign, without need of interpretation, that points toward a positive outcome?* I already know the answer to this question. I've been living it since age twelve. I don't want to endure the hem and haw of the vet deciding if she should lie to me. I don't want to picture my ailing Bulger panting in a life-or-death stasis in the care of a liar or of someone who refuses me the dignity of lying. I authorize the vet to pull blood work as she sees fit and ring off politely.

It's harder now to scramble my attention on a social media platform. I am a man whose dog is beyond human care, and no one will ever know me. Halfhearted, I click around the Goodreads site, taking a roundabout route back to my collected literary critiques, unasked for criticism, uncompensated, over-punctuated. Under my desk, on top of my shoes,

Bardot sleeps, and the night drags on. I read forward, seconding my own opinions on James Kelman's *How Late It Was, How Late*, Charles Portis's *Dog of the South*, Leslie Marmon Silko's *Almanac of the Dead*, Patti Smith's *Just Kids*. Dozens of books had escaped my mind: *The Driver's Seat*, *The Comedians*. Oh, shit! I'd used *dessert* for *desert* while bragging about having read Bolaño's *Savage Detectives*.

I fix that typo, for the benefit of no one, and I move on, following twisted strings of complex interlocking sentences that set up ponderous climaxes, all mine: *"The Lone Ranger and Tonto Fistfight in Heaven* will read like home to any reader who has ever felt misplaced and dismissed and seen the rays of grace glinting from unlikely, seemingly hopeless places."

Is a ray of grace to be seen in me trying to parrot Nobel laureate Herta Müller? *"The Appointment* is not some cheap tale of one woman's valiant struggle against a corrupt, dysfunctional, petty, and totalitarian system and her inspirational escape to victory. *The Appointment*'s power is in escaping the notion that escape exists." Do I share Müller's wisdom? Do I reflect it? Am I all wrong? There is no mistaking the vibrations of the cell phone as it crawls across my desktop. Bardot is awake and alert and in my lap nosing at the skittering device. I answer it.

Bulger's blood is bad. The rat poison, the veterinarian is now sure that the animal has ingested poison, has impaired the blood's natural self-restorative qualities. "The effect is only temporary," the vet says. "He's a young and healthy dog, very strong. He should have several good years left. But if we don't change out the dog's blood, there's a far greater chance that the impairment to self-restoration will be permanent."

"You mean, a far greater chance that he might die?"

"That's one way to put it."

"Of course, go ahead with the transfusion," I said. The vet fulfilled her obligation of informing me how much the blood and labor would cost and that it was no guarantee of continued survival.

The hour was still and dark. Trina slept in a different room. How she could be unconscious at a time like this, I failed to understand. The money to replace this big dog's blood had to come from somewhere. There was little chance of bleeding it out of me. We were too deep into the early morning to break Trina's slumber with an inconclusive and costly update. I turned back to my computer. I dipped again into my web of tangled exposition, into the thought strings of what so many people had taken the opportunity to never read. Bardot left me, loping into the bedroom and toward the slumbering wife.

What a lot of words I had churned with no lasting profit. Start with the stack of scripts and treatments cranked out chasing the carrot on a scythe that's always there to lop your head if you pop up within the Hollywood circumference. Take a look in the closet beside this desk. Hard copies of working drafts and final passes are bricked up halfway to the ceiling. These blocks of printed matter form a commemorative wall to development, redevelopment, producers' notes, agent input, talent brainstorming, and, eventually, the inability to have your phone call taken or returned.

The appeal of Goodreads is that any sentences typed into the template are guaranteed to make it up onto the screen. I tried so hard to put my best angle forward: "It's dangerous to read *The Easter Parade* past a certain age, after accumulating a certain quantity of disappointments in circumstances and self. I failed to protect myself from the realization that some creeping horror might make itself known to me at any time, anywhere. In fact, that creep and I, *The Easter Parade* forces me to admit, are old acquaintances."

I am the writer adjacent, positioning myself as a confederate or colleague to someone I'd never met. Here I am, trying to bask in brilliance not my own, to be lit from within by a light at my side. I had presumed that some vital Richard Yates essence was flowing into me the same way some donor dog's hemoglobin was siphoning into Bulger's veins. I was an idiot. Or maybe I was actually quite bright. My reviews were amplifying truths that needed to be said a little louder. Unless I had absolutely no idea what Yates or anyone else was getting at. I hardly knew what voice to listen to. Was I fronting or flinching? I couldn't take the risk of answering my own questions. Allow me to lift a line from Roberto Bolaño's *The Insufferable Gaucho*: "If you're going to say what you want to say, you're going to hear what you don't want to hear."

In the approach to dawn, my head spoke to me from several conflicting directions, in a mess of dialects, all opposing me, scolding, weighing me down with heavy reproach. I dipped into my chair and sank into sleep. The grinding cell phone pulled me up from a dream of recriminating circumstances into a waking reality, and the chorus of acrimony rose and pitched against me. I had let my beloved pup slip into critical condition because I resisted jeopardizing my mode of transportation.

This incoming call, I knew, was the emergency vet. Who else would phone when still darkness wrapped the new day? Summoned by the phone's first shake, Bardot stood at my flank and Trina appeared at my shoulder. I picked up and croaked out a hello.

"The worst seems to be over," the vet said. I made arrangements to pick up the big boy later that day and reassured Trina standing in her pajamas.

"He's okay," she said. "Something went right. What do you say to that?"

"I'm glad after all," I said, "that Roberto Bolaño is dead."

"What are you even talking about?"

"Bolaño is gone. He is forever beyond stumbling upon Goodreads and happening upon me saying what I wanted to say as if he and I had said it together, and then him responding with a reply that I don't want to hear."

"You have been awake too long." She says this with certainty and understanding and no sympathy.

I go to bed. It's like the wife and I are sleeping in shifts. I slither to her side of the mattress. She has warmed it and put in a dent. I wrap myself tight in her share of the covers. It doesn't help. No sleep descends; none is on the way. Bardot's breathing comes soft and steady from the floor at the end of the bed, and I take no solace in it. The steady rising sun crosses the bedroom, pushing toward noon. My eyes opened to what might be projected on the ceiling's clean slate, but they focused on cobwebs in the corners.

I drove the waning car out to the Valley to pick up Bulger. The cashier put a tab on my credit card. They allowed the dog to see me. His nose remembered my scent, and his body wagged, overjoyed to have me take him from this place of stress and death and deliver him unto the sleepy comforts of home. He clambered down the stairs and settled into his dog bed cushions.

I took an action I don't believe in. I called the cops. "My dog was poisoned," I say. "I want to report it." The cops give me time to hang up while my call is passed around the Hollywood substation until some officer agrees to field it. Earlier in my lifetime, I'd been held captive at the Hollywood substation overnight. A few years prior to that captivity, cops at the station had been busted for running a burglary ring. Home-delivery hookers had also been on the menu. The primary witness against the police, a prostitute, ended up murdered in a motel room, stabbed about a thousand times in her back. The cop who had stepped forward to testify, the blue voice for institutional justice, drove dead-on at fatal velocity into a pylon on a stretch of closed freeway. I knew all this about my neighborhood police force, and still I called these cops.

"How do you know your dog was poisoned?"

"The vet said he was poisoned."

"And how would the vet know?"

"Because the vet gave the dog the antidote to the poison, and the dog recovered."

"You mean your dog is not even dead?"

"Only because I spent three grand."

"Look, I really don't know what you expect. Am I supposed to write this up?"

"Well, I thought maybe there had been other incidents of dog poisoning. If there had been, then you would want to know. To track them."

"Okay. Thanks for that opportunity."

The interaction had been disappointing and satisfactory. I had called mainly to place my name on a suspect list, as insurance to reel in my own behavior. I had a notion that I could discover who had placed that pie pan into the courtyard and tried to murder my dog. I wanted to not do some rash thing based on that notion. Not doing some rash thing seemed to be the most reasonable decision I could make.

Having alerted the cops to the menace on their beat, I checked on Bardot, I checked on Bulger. I put on an ironed shirt and expensive shoes. I went out to the garage and strapped myself into the black-on-black Chevrolet. I started up the car and considered what I was about to do. Some career pieces had snapped into place. I'd met some friends who had friends on the job at a fancy entertainment company where creative aspirations were hatched as movies. I had drafted a motion picture treatment about Cold War journalist I. F. Stone. The story hinged on battles for justice, social progress, and several democratic virtues that perhaps do not exist, such as freedom of thought. I. F. Stone is the guy who said the only fight worth fighting is the fight you can't win, a logic that spoke to me. Once the car had warmed up, I went ahead and opened the garage door.

I motored to the office of this movie person, this shot caller friend of a friend who had agreed to review my extensive notes on the life and times of I. F. Stone. Nagged by guarded hope, I parked myself in the reception area outside this development executive's office. A slender, mixed-race girl perched like a prize behind a polished wood desk. She's young enough to be my daughter's too young friend, except I have no daughter. The girl comes out from behind the desk. She leans over me and clasps her hands one in the other. Solicitous is how I would describe her aspect. The start time for my meeting with the movie person, she takes pains to inform me, is bumped. I choose to interpret this inconvenience as a good sign. My man is in demand. Important developments need his personal attention. When he signs up for the I. F. Stone project, that fire and passion will burn for a higher good!

Space is an interesting thing to contemplate, an infinite, as far as we are able to comprehend. I stare off into it. I stare as though this is something I could do forever. Soon enough, my stomach grumbles and my foot cramps. I'm back from space and I'm checking my watch. The new start time that the old start time had been bumped to has passed. My impulse is to stand and approach the desk and request an update from the girl who might be my daughter's inappropriately younger friend. I assemble myself to stand, but I hadn't needed to. The young woman comes out from behind her desk, moving in her heels and pencil skirt like a modern day geisha. She takes a seat beside me and twists so we are face to face. Her face so close to mine is a mix of consolation prize and condolence card. She hopes I will understand. She feels awful, and her boss feels worse, but the start time for our meeting is bumped again.

I'm antsy. An email arrives on my telephone from the development executive as I wait for him in the lobby of his office. "This Cold War stuff is all old news," reads the development executive's email. "We've seen all this blacklist witch hunt blah blah before. There is no continued relevance."

By this stage in my life, I know how things work. The world should have no surprises for me. Expertise informs my perspective, and

I'm willing to offer it for the enlightenment of others: Fuck other people. To keep hope alive, hold it tight and close. Sunlight, air, space; that kills it.

Trina came home, fed Bulger his first post-poison meal, and roused me. "I'm not judging you," she said. "I can't find fault in the fact. But did you retreat to bed for the entire day? You are solidly of this earth," she said, "and you have buried all ambition, all striving and expectation."

"Thank you for reserving your criticism," I said. "I have been emotionally flat, true. But not unhappy until a neighbor poisoned my dog."

"You can't accept everything sitting down," she said.

"I don't want to," I assured her. "I prefer to lie down for it."

"There's something we can do," she said. "I have an idea. I need you to write it out."

What Trina needed from me took about an hour. I finished it, and she and I took a walk in the neighborhood. It was dinnertime. The roads up through the ridge we lived on are as twisted as anything else in life. We knock on doors along both sides of the roadway to the right of our house, interrupting households at table. We return to our point of departure. We knock on doors along both sides of the roadway to the left.

People answer our knocks, and I show pictures of Bulger's hematoma leg on my cell phone. I've printed up fliers: BEWARE reads the top headline. DOG POISONER fills in the bottom headline. Between the headlines, terse copy details the emotional and financial expense Trina and I had suffered as a result of a neighbor sliding a piece of poisoned meat under the courtyard gate rather than ringing the doorbell and communicating their grievance to us.

I bullet point this information at full voice on the front porches of every house within earshot of Bulger's loudest barking. Bits of spit fly from my lips. Delivering my spiel to familiar faces and some we have only seen drive past our gate, I assure each neighbor that I am taking no further action, but only because my dog has survived the attack.

"If he had died, I could not be responsible for my actions."

"The whole neighborhood was complaining about that dog's barking," says one neighbor. "We were all talking about it."

"One of you fuckers should have mentioned it to me."

When we've finished the circuit, a real victory has been won. We've let all occupants of eight houses in every direction know that I am insane.

My neighbors have let me know that they are grouped against me. I rest with the satisfaction of having planned some undertaking and seen it through to the finish.

My dog was still there, I realized in the following weeks, and so was I. The alive-again dog chased squirrels around the railings of our backyard deck. Sitting shielded from the sun, out there with the burly boy dog and delicate Bardot, I plotted a stealth project in my head. From this point on, I worked only in secret. I initiated new, private endeavors that made modest promises to me as they took shape in my mind. I determined to draft my masterpiece. This was back when I existed. Keeping nothing written down kept my outline for this culminating work impervious to the shivs of jealous haters, and to the reasoned dissection of serious critics. Secrecy provided some consolation…less than I might have hoped for. But consolation at that juncture, come on. Do you think consolation makes any difference in the face of what comes next? But I'm ahead of myself. I was keeping a baffling number of intricate moving pieces straight in my mind. The creative impulse can unleash all manner of exacting processes.

"Is it a book? Another book?" asks Trina. "I always said you had another book in you."

"You've never said anything like that, but thanks for the article of faith."

"I'm looking for a sense that you're working on something. I worry if you're not working on something."

"At my age, you know, I can hardly remember my social security number," I tell my wife. "But the pieces are falling into place."

We are on the coastal highway to Cayucos for a beach weekend with the dogs. Bulger, the survivor, is vivid with happiness in the back of the car! Bardot is back there too. She scowls along her slender nose, irritated by Bulger's ecstatic, gaping jaws. Ruthie sits upright between the two dogs, swaying in a separate world to the music of Tom Petty and Grant Green. She would prefer Benny Goodman.

I am driving and squinting. From the passenger seat, Trina checks her phone and tells me that her mom's Mission Viejo house has just received an offer $30,000 over what T had prepared to settle for.

"Our luck," she guesses, "is about to change. For the better. Our luck already has changed for the better."

We check into a shoreline motel in the small seaside town of Cayucos. Trina installs Ruthie in her adjacent room, attends to the old woman's bathroom break, and sets her up to sun on the beach, wrapped in a blanket on an ocean-facing lounge chair. We leash up the dogs and pass a good clump of time walking south along the shoreline, turning around and walking back north. The stinging breeze, the booming waves, the stacked formations of rock and cloud, the pelicans circling in the radiant sky and piercing the sea surface mirror, all of it should suggest that a bigger world is going on outside what's in your mind, but it doesn't always. The night before, I had tallied up all of the likes given to my Goodreads reviews. What would it have taken to break one hundred? I meditate on being here and gone, like any one of these receding waves seeping back into the sand.

Trina walked ahead. An orange rayon scarf billows behind her. She tosses a green tennis ball forward and follows after as Bardot chases the ball in the foamy ocean's edge. Bulger, constrained on a leash at my side, lunges in stifled pursuit every time the ball flies.

"It's your own fault," I remind the big dog. "You're too strong. You're too fast. You are a force unto yourself and cannot be trusted to coexist peaceably among lesser living things, such as every other dog on this beach."

We march onto a crowded stretch of sand directly in front of the clustered motels and pizza stands. Loitering teens, families with infants, and out-of-shape mopes have staked out towel-size domains. Behind them, blanketed in her lounge chair, Ruthie is easy to spot. The families and young bodies keep a respectful distance from the ancient woman; it's as if they don't want to catch what she's got, and why would they?

From the shoreline, Trina waves to her mother. There's no response. Jumping and swinging both arms above her head, my wife's gesticulations escalate from eager to wild to desperate. The dogs—hyper by association—pull. Bulger snaps at Bardot. Perhaps Trina is reliving a summer episode from her childhood, when she was a lost toddler on the sand. "Mom!" She's shouting, attracting attention up and down the beach. "Mom, here! Mom, here!"

Bulger doesn't know what kind of game is being played out. Trina takes off her orange scarf and waves it above her head like the iridescent tail of a land-bound kite. People point toward us. Ripples of curiosity flow all the way back to Ruthie. Maybe the old mother recognizes her middle-age daughter gesturing in distress at the waterline; maybe Ruthie's only joining in the general movement: she raises her hand and waves back at the flailing figure outlined in the brilliant sun.

At that instant, Bulger bolts and one steel link snaps in the prong collar circling his neck. Suddenly, I am holding a dead lead. The live end lies empty in the sand. Bulger springs and bounds, weaving through and leaping over the ranks of beachgoers lounging in the expanse of sand separating him from his friend and companion, the Birthgiver. The dog could so easily have been dead, murdered by a serving of rat poison, and here he goes gamboling without care or opposition in the blustery California sun.

Moms and dads and frantic dog owners all along Bulger's erratic path clutch their children and animals to their breasts, protective and petrified. The marauding brute's speed is impossible to track. His lunges and head feints, so quick, are seen in retrospect. Maybe an instant and a half passes, and he sits still and calm at Ruthie's side, oblivious to the pockets of panic in his wake.

I hustle with an empty leash toward Bulger sit-staying at the mother-in-law's side, and a large, florid woman blocks my way. Blood pools in the palm of her hand, and a Yorkshire terrier lies motionless on its back at her feet. The woman is a shrieker, I realize. She's been shrieking since Bulger broke free. Her shrieking had attracted the big dog to her and to her tiny puppy. "Your dog is a killer," she shrieks. "I'm bitten! Your dog is a killer breed!"

She holds her bleeding hand up to my face, but her Yorkie has flipped to its feet and yips heartily, and I move twenty yards beyond her. People are on their cell phones, taking photos and calling for backup.

"That breed is a killer," the woman shrieks.

Glancing back, I see Trina and Bardot, all apologetic and admitting nothing, approach the bleeding woman. I leash up Bulger and keep walking. Halfway to the motel, I hear sirens coming in. Three local delinquents, a girl and two boys, hang out in front of the liquor mart, smoking cigarettes. "Nice dog," says one of the boys.

An ambulance kills its siren and continues on the way I have come. Animal Control will be called, this I know, and local police will be summoned as well. Bulger will be seized, interred at a high-kill shelter, put down. Appeals will be useless. My dog had survived the rat poison and now his days are numbered anyway, with this day's number being very close to the final digit.

I pack up our things and stow them in the car trunk, and I lie on the bed in the motel room, above the covers, fully dressed, staring at the ceiling. Red tinged shadows creep into the room, heavier with each degree of the sun's descent. Trina stands beside the bed. The dogs sit beside the bed. I sense that everything will always be this way: unbearable.

"Put your mom in the car," I tell Trina, immobile. "We need to make a run for it. Cops will come and take Bulger. They'll put him in quarantine and he'll never make it out alive. He'll be doomed."

"Maybe he'll be doomed," agrees Trina, "but not today. That lady's own dog bit her. It went nuts when Bulger ran by. The ambulance was total overkill. You should see her hand. They put it like in a cast. She's staying at this same motel, which I guess could be awkward."

I picture the bitten lady, her hand professionally and elaborately bandaged, pointing a splinted finger at Bulger and at me.

"Don't you want to go outside?" says Trina. "We've come all this way, and I'm spending all this money. Doesn't it seem pointless to just stay here in the room?"

"Why is existence so grim?" I ask.

My wife moves to turn on the lights. "I do so much for you," she says. "Must you always say things to hurt me?"

With a flip of the light switch, the shadows are gone. The night is shunted to the outside. Everything is bright and clear. I sit up. I'm still able to eat. We might as well go for dinner.

"What I meant to say," I say, "is what an amazing opportunity you've given me to see things turning out for the best, in the end!"

"You act all pessimistic," observes the wife, "and doomed. But I think you've finally found a project that will work for you, with the new thing you're doing. You just won't admit that this time is different."

There are many things I could answer to this. Where to start? How to finish? "I hope you're right," I say. "I believe you are."

"What the fuck now." Trina double checks her phone and tosses it onto the bed in disgust. "That offer on my mom's house just dropped out."

8

SPEAKING ILL OF ME WHEN I'M DEAD

Lanky Donald Boxer lucks into street parking on Sunset directly in front of Intelligentsia Coffee. The table he likes at Café Stella is open. The preferred perch is a four-seat setup deep inside the covered patio, cool and discrete within a cloak of shadow. Boxer takes the corner chair and assumes a vantage of the full dining area. Café patrons walking in from the Sunset Boulevard curb and persons of interest at the tables and in the queue at Intelligentsia Coffee next door all fall under veiled surveillance. Lanky Boxer can see out; the objects of his benign watch cannot see in. He notes three or four prospects in line at Intelligentsia. They'll be standing in his viewfinder for a quarter of an hour. The Café Stella waitress he likes best asks, "Just you today?"

"I'm expecting company."

"Too bad."

Here company comes; Robyn. Tall, thin, with short feminine hair, striding on four-hundred-dollar heels and in contoured Japanese denim, Robyn peers into the Café Stella shadows. She can't see Boxer, but she exhibits a reasonable certainty of where he sits in there. This woman had been M—'s boss, the last boss he'd had, if Boxer remembers correctly. He stands to greet her and does a math exercise. She is clearly fifteen years younger than M— could ever have been.

"Thanks for agreeing to meet me," Robyn says. "Let's sit?"

"After you."

The waitress is tableside before they've fully scraped their chairs forward. Boxer orders while thinking of M—'s après-funeral swim party. An old punk rock chick, near retirement age, had inflicted a disturbance on the gathering. Robyn, the woman poised across from him now, had been instrumental in containing the damage. She'd brought grace to calamity and calm to chaos and she exhibits great natural style. There's something else about this woman.

"I've been lobbying the *LA Times*," she says, "with no real measure of success."

"Lobbying for what?"

"So they'll run an obituary on Allan."

A spill of cream is beaded on the tabletop next to Boxer's coffee cup. He puts his finger on it: *That's what it is about this woman. She's a stickler for propriety.* "I'm just wondering," he says out loud, "what argument you gave the *Times* for running a eulogy on this guy."

"Oh, come on. You know his history. He was unique to this town. He played a part in a political moment that was centered here and had impact on the national scale. And he was a founding participant in a 1970s cultural upheaval that is still reverberating worldwide today."

"Well, you've certainly put in time talking to him. I mean, listening to his version of things."

Robyn laughs with ironic subtlety that complements Boxer's subtle sarcasm. Robyn is younger than Boxer, perhaps by five years. Still, Boxer feels as though he is the child being talked to by the adult. She says: "I'm here to ask you to collaborate on creating the obituary. You spoke so well at the service. I think of you as the funeral talker."

"Do I seem, what's the word, *funereal* to you?" Boxer enunciates *funereal* deliberately, slowing down to one syllable at a time, cautious of the word's pronunciation.

Robyn is patient and soft: "You brought a lot of life to your talk. But not too much life, you know, considering what the event was. That's why I think you're perfect for this."

Being told he is perfect for something is a strong start for Boxer. It's not enough to close the deal. In a sense, Boxer the funeral talker feels that he has contributed enough already to the departed's legacy. He hedges. "I didn't really feel fully comfortable with giving that speech. We'd been acquainted for years. Still, I never really knew the dude all that well."

"But he confided in you. You were close enough for that?"

"He did confide. I wasn't so in love with the kind of shit he confided either." Boxer checks his phone. He dashes off a quick text message. When he finishes, Robyn is ready for him.

"I'm not asking for a love letter," she says.

Boxer looks away from her and watches his phone vibrate. He lets the call go to voice mail. Robyn's eyes have not released him, and he meets them: "Isn't the obituary something the wife should be doing? Have you cleared it with her?"

"My intuition says the wife is not into it."

"Your intuition should be a cue, right?" As he talks, Boxer's eyes wander off from Robyn. He scans the dining area and scopes a perimeter out into the sunlit tables and waiting line at Intelligentsia Coffee. "If the wife doesn't want an announcement in the newspaper, if the family, the wife being pretty much the family, doesn't want it, and it's a little late in the day in the first place, shouldn't that about close the book on it?"

Boxer's roving gaze sees something he would rather have not seen.

"The wife isn't the one who died," insists Robyn. "The book is still wide open on this."

Boxer stiffens. What he has not wanted to see is approaching. It talks, in a stressed, upper-register male voice: "Gee, Donald, it's so unlike you to be found sitting here at the lurking table."

"Hello, Colin. You running into me really is a sour coincidence."

Robyn scrutinizes Colin. She sees a hyper, thin, natty, and bitten man of Allan M—'s age. He concentrates on her.

"I recognize you," says Colin. "I'm trying to call up from where."

Boxer makes the introductions. "You were both at M—'s sendoff. You probably saw one another there."

Colin moves up to the table and pulls up a chair between Boxer and Robyn. He takes a long, thoughtful draw on his cup of Intelligentsia coffee to go.

"So, Colin," summarizes Robyn. She notices that his fingernails are freshly manicured and lacquered. "You knew both Donald and Allan."

"Another sour coincidence," mocks Colin. "I was a long-term acquaintance of dead Allan M—. And until recently I was a long-term friend of Donald Boxer."

"Colin and I haven't been talking," offers Boxer. "I say this in the form of a disclaimer."

"We're not speaking directly to one another. But there has been some communication through second parties."

"Which," says Robyn, "I hope will not be what's expected of me here."

"Let me reassure you," says Boxer, "if Colin leaves, that won't happen at all."

"But, Robyn, why should I leave?" says Colin. "I've known the departed the longest, from when he failed as a punk rocker. He is the agenda for you two meeting today?"

The ensuing silence is uncomfortable, but less so than the talking. Still, Robyn breaks it: "This confluence of Allan's friends at this particular café table must mean something, am I right?"

"No, Colin being here is not in any way a miracle," says Boxer, "not by any interpretation. In fact, Colin showing up isn't really that big a stretch of a coincidence."

"This is a huge city," argues Robyn. "The chances that two—"

"Boxer's right," says Colin. "Us meeting here is not a coincidence. It's this place—actually these two adjacent places. There's this whole circle of sort of skeevy acquaintances who know each other from lurking here."

"Six more dudes who knew M— by sight or by name will cruise through Intelligentsia in the next half hour," Boxer predicts. "The fact that we're all here at this one moment doesn't mean anything about M— having a meaningful circle of connections. Believe me on that."

Robyn unwraps a smile that harbors zero trace of irony anywhere in its corners. "My goal for today was to recruit one long-term friend of Allan's to help me get his obituary published. Now I intend to recruit the two of you."

"There won't be an obituary for this guy," says Colin. "What did he ever do that a reporter should be taken off of a real story?"

"Not the editorial type. The classified ad type, the one where you pay."

"How much is that going to cost?" asks Boxer, immediately embarrassed to be asking. "I'll put in, that's not the question. I don't want to spend anything crazy."

"I will pay to place it," says Robyn. "All I'm asking from you is to write down a few nice things we can say about him."

The two long-term acquaintances, Boxer and Colin, meet one another's eyes for the first time this day. They nod, in agreement, and put themselves at Robyn's service.

"That's fine," says Robyn. "Let's begin."

Boxer's phone shudders on the tabletop. He picks it up and speaks into it: "Honey, I can't talk right now. Yes, I can listen, but only for a limited time. I'm attempting to draft out an obituary. It's a long story."

Boxer goes on listening, and Colin places a call.

"I don't know that restaurant," says Colin into his phone. "I'd prefer to have the dinner at a restaurant I know. Look, this is an important meeting. Do I want to go to an open house on Sunday? Listen! Why don't you ask me closer to Sunday? Why don't you ask me after I've qualified for the loan? I'd like to think I can trust you to find a restaurant that is known to me."

Colin slaps his phone facedown onto the table. Boxer has wrapped up his call. Robyn smiles.

Boxer concentrates. "Well, let's see. He liked his dogs."

Colin concentrates. "He worked at *Hustler* magazine, but that was a long time ago."

"You know he wrote a book about *Hustler*, right? He didn't say a lot of nice things about himself in it."

"And then he had that other book, the punk junkie one, and he didn't say a lot of nice things about himself there either."

"I've read the books," says Robyn.

"Then you see that he had ample opportunities to say nice things about himself," argues Colin, "and he didn't. And now we're supposed to go against his inferred intentions?"

A guy in a gray-streaked ponytail and wraparound sunglasses takes a seat a few tables away and salutes Boxer and Colin. They ignore him.

Robyn sighs. "Nice is not a prerequisite. Let's just stick to facts. Do you know where he went to school? What was he interested in? Did he do any volunteer work?" Blank faces left and right. "There was the music, right? Didn't he love music?"

"Oh, he liked music all right," agrees Boxer. "He loved records."

"He loved scamming people out of their records. Did he ever hit you up for your records? He hit us up for our records. Maybe he went after your dead parent or absent sibling's records?"

Robyn is showing the effort it takes to be patient and poised and positive. "And he liked coffee?" she says. "Can we say he liked coffee?"

"Exactly!" chimes Colin. "And eyesight. He liked having eyesight."

Boxer's phone shudders back into play. "It's my wife," he says. "I really should take this. Just to preserve the peace."

"You know, Donald," interjects Colin, "if you could keep your wife from talking shit about me to my ex-girlfriend, it would be easier for me to look at you like someone I could work with."

"I'm not asking you to look at me as anything. In fact, don't look at me. I'm asking you to not look at me. I want no thought of me anywhere in your mind." Boxer stills his phone and types in a text message.

"As revealed earlier, Robyn," explains Colin, "Donald and I haven't been speaking to one another. So now that he and I are directly communicating again, the day isn't a total failure, if you look at it in a certain way."

"I can contribute Allan's work history," says Robyn.

Boxer turns his phone facedown. "Good idea! We'll put in a URL for his LinkedIn page."

"I'll personalize the work history," says Robyn. "I'll give it context."

"If you think it might be valuable to look at his debt profile and credit card data," offers Colin, "I can put my assistant on assembling a report."

"That assistant of yours is a total affectation," clarifies Boxer. "That's exactly the kind of thing Dahlia was talking to Lauren about. You threw this huge piss fit like my wife was slandering you, when in fact—"

"Lauren says you and Dahlia are making plans for a vacation in Spain."

"What, really is the point of travel plans—"

"Oh, nothing, but isn't a vacation to Spain exactly what Lauren and I were planning when we broke up?"

"When she broke it off with you."

"Irrelevant. The germane point here is that you and Dahlia can't even come up with a vacation destination without ripping me off in some way."

"Don't be a fool. Dahlia was on a shoot in Barcelona for two weeks last winter. She's wanted to go back ever since."

"It's a mystery to me how she ever completed any task. She was so busy poison-talking my affections for the woman I'd been living with for two and a half months."

"Wait!" interjects Robyn. "If I want to find out what Allan was working on for the past two years, whom do I ask?"

Colin stares off into a distance. He is tempted to snap out a harsh, cutting reply. Boxer fields it: "You know that nobody was current with this guy at the end there, right?"

"Well that's all the more reason we should do this," says Robyn. "Now that it's too late."

Colin comes back from the far-off, imaginary distance. "Do you see the girl waiting in line at Intelligentsia with the fleece yoga pants and no underwear? And then three back in line, there's a girl with fleece yoga *shorts* and no underwear. If this is a natural progression, then next we should expect—"

"What we should expect, Colin, is for Lauren to stop in at the bar here for a drink and confirm why she moved—"

"Donald, first off, I've gone back to my family—"

"That makes your kid such a lucky boy."

Robyn, for the first time since she's walked toward Café Stella, gives mixed indications of impatience and offense. She gathers her belongings and places cash on the table. "My time is up for today," she says evenly. "I hate to, but I'm leaving."

Colin watches her walk out, more overtly than Boxer does, and delivers the summation behind her back: "That woman is a stickler for propriety."

"So, Colin, I guess you'll be moving along now?" suggests Boxer. He waves for his favorite waitress.

"I'll stick around to make sure you're covered on the check."

The wraparound sunglasses and gray-streaked ponytail moves up from a nearby table and takes Robyn's chair. "I couldn't help overhearing—"

"Yes you could have," says Colin.

"Not really. Some of those exchanges were fairly intense."

"You're slouching, Wiseman," points out Boxer.

"You know, I was wondering myself," says Wiseman, speaking up without straightening up, "wondering about the obituary for M—. I mean, I was wondering when it would be out and if it would be in the *Times* and the *Weekly*, or only in the *Times* or only in the *Weekly*, and that made me wonder, *Am I fucking high? Did I just smoke a shot glass of hash oil?* You two, let me be the first to congratulate you on your heroic actions."

"Heroic?" says Colin.

"Heroic for taking on a doomed task. This shit is going nowhere, and you both know it."

"I really love our waitress," says Boxer. "Where in fuck is she?"

"Oh, you're cute when you're bashful," observes Wiseman. "It is so goddamn valiant of you two to take this on, to collaborate on M—'s wordage. Beyond the call of duty, surely."

"It's not what I would call a duty," Boxer defers. "I mean, you know."

"Beyond the call of friendship then."

"No, it's squarely within the call of friendship," says Boxer.

"Sure," agrees Wiseman, "it's something he would have done for you… if you'd been friends, maybe. Realistically, he never did shit for anyone. You don't care a shit about him any more than he would care a shit about you if he was in your place and you were in his. You fuckers just care about that chick."

"Point taken," says Colin. "Once you're dead, you really do find out who your true friends aren't."

"Your true friends will definitely not be Wiseman," says Boxer. Colin laughs. He and his old pal Boxer are on the same side again. Colin laughs once more. He puts enough edge on the second one to send Wiseman away from the table.

About a week later, Colin is on his way home from filing a motion at LA Superior Courthouse. He stops in at Boxer's Highland Park recording studio. "I'm just here to pay a visit," Colin says. "If you're not in the middle of anything."

"I've been trying to think of a reason to stop what I was doing."

"You know that woman, Robyn? I've been feeling a little bad about what happened. We embarrassed ourselves in front of her."

"Yeah, I've had that on my mind."

"Do you think she was fucking M—?" wonders Colin. "Is that why she needs to see his name in the paper?"

"I don't know," says Boxer. "If she'd been fucking him, wouldn't he have seemed a little happier?"

Colin digests that. "It's all so sad," he observes. "How hard could it be to write an obituary?"

As is typical, both men have their phones in their hands. They do a web search for *obituary*. Boxer adjusts the distance of his phone from his face, squints and reads: "'Joanie Blondel of Canoga Park, California, entered into rest on Saturday at the West Valley Convalescent Hospital.'"

"That hospital has a very loose definition of *convalescent*."

"'Born August eighteen, 1939, in the town of Yountville, California, Joanie married the late Robert Blondel on June sixteen, 1962. Together they raised three children. Joanie worked in the customer-relations department of Sears Roebuck for twenty-three years. She enjoyed needlework and walking puppies at the West Valley Animal Shelter.'"

"My God. Joanie Blondel sounds like such a drag," says Colin.

"'Memorials may be made in Joanie's name to Boxer Rescue Los Angeles.'"

"I found a better one," says Colin. "Isn't it kind of pointless to post one of these when the funeral has already happened?"

"Just read it."

"'Born on February fifth, 1952, in Spokane, Washington, John Jay Morris passed into God's loving arms Saturday at six a.m. The eldest of two sons, John fought in combat during the Vietnam War and later studied forensics sciences at the University of California, Los Angeles and had a long career in personal security for some of the highest-profile celebrities and business people in the motion picture industry. John was patient, kind, loyal, and humble. He leaves behind a legacy of love, faith, and admiration.'"

"I heard about this guy!" says Colin. "Isn't he the one who shot himself in the head while he had the movie producer in the back of his car?"

"That is him! Was him. Now I'm getting a feeling for how this is done."

"So," begins Boxer, "'Allan M—, born about a hundred years ago in some typhus-ridden Canadian logging camp, was called to answer to his maker on whatever the fuck date it was in the emergency room at Cedars Sinai Hospital.'"

Colin picks up the thread: "'At the time of his departure, Allan was surrounded by puzzled operating room techs trying to determine where he'd put his insurance card.'"

"'He was the son of a couple of hard-working Canadian bacon farmers,'" continues Boxer, "'who moved the family to California to escape the seasonal depressive disorder of their homeland. Allan temporarily cheered up and eventually married native Los Angeleno Trina Derrick.' When do you think that was? They were both probably almost forty when that happened."

"'Allan enjoyed accumulating vinyl records, long walks with his dogs, and pontificating about anything he thought he knew more about than you did.'"

"He had a badass car."

"He always had a badass car. 'He pursued a vocation as a writer, working at a notorious pornographic magazine empire, publishing two books, and stacking up a pile of screenplays read by even less people than the two books.'"

"'He is survived by a wife, two dogs.' And there's that niece who is around, and I guess her mother is his sister? Also, the niece may have siblings. We would need to find that out."

"In conclusion, 'Allan M— was a lesson in humility, generosity, unconditional love, tolerance, patience, putting a happy face on things, and being extremely handsome and personable.'"

"Can we do this," asked Boxer, "without reverting to satire?"

Donald and Colin looked into their phones for that answer. Donald came up first: "'Allan M— was a dude who hung out for a while, made some friends, irritated some other people, drifted away from all of them, and now he's dead. He liked eating good food and going on vacation. Some of the people who knew him, through being family or whatever, are still alive.'"

"And the next step is to track down those people and find out how old they are and where they live?" asks Colin. "I can't believe I thought I could be bothered with this."

"Come on, Colin. All we can do is idealize him. Maybe that'll be enough to make the stickler lady happy."

"I'm fighting an intense temptation to abandon the effort."

"I don't see you fighting anything," says Boxer. "It *is* more work than it looks like. I'll give you that."

A few days later, back at Café Stella, Robyn joins Boxer and Colin at the lurker table. A picture comes clear to her. "You did like Allan, didn't you, Colin?"

"I liked him okay," says Colin, "but I won't invest a lot of effort arguing with anyone who didn't."

The wraparound sunglasses, the gray-streaked ponytail, the knowing smirk, and candy-ass shuffle; Robyn is conscious of having been peripherally aware of this person. He has now approached and taken the fourth seat at the Café Stella lurker table without being invited to do so. He says: "M— was the kind of guy who any kind of shitty thing you could think of a person doing, well, he wasn't necessarily the guy who did all those shitty things."

"Thank you, Wiseman," says Colin. "The toilets are around that corner there."

"And the only reason he wasn't that guy," insists Wiseman, "is he really didn't have the nerve. It's not like he had some kind of moral or ethical objections that stopped him from fucking—"

"When was the last time you talked to him?" asks Robyn.

Wiseman slides down his wraparound shades and tilts his eyeballs as if their misalignment conveys something words cannot. "I saw him around here all the time," he says.

"And when did you last talk?"

"I never really talked to that guy." Wisemen pushes his wraparound shades back up the slope of his nose. "We didn't like talking to each other."

"And now you're free to move along to the men's room," says Robyn.

"Like I said," Boxer informs Robyn when they are again alone with Colin, "no one was current with M— at the time he died."

"I sense you're trying to manage my expectations," says Robyn, "about what you wrote for him."

"In truth," Boxer admits, "we didn't come up with much."

Colin slides an iPad across the table. "We have it on my tablet."

Robyn puts on a pair of glasses and reads. Robyn takes off her glasses, cases them up, and slots the case in her purse. "I thought we might spend some time going over your draft sentence by sentence," she says. "That won't take long, will it?"

🦗

IN HER HOME, WITH her child napping in an adjoining room, with her husband preparing a late lunch in the distant kitchen, at a desk in the couple's shared office, in sight of a portrait of her uncle Charles, Robyn sat in front of a computer screen and sought a portal to resolution on the Internet.

"What's on my mind?" she typed. "A human form named Allan M— who is no more. This page is not my first pick as a platform, but the newspapers have turned me down. What kind of reach do newspapers have these days anyway?

"Those of us who worked with Allan knew him to be impatient, caustic, often correct, but not quite so often as he was convinced of being correct, funny, warm, encouraging, and intelligent, strong on intuition and, though he would deny it, empathy."

Uncle Charles was two years older than Allan M—, from the same pre-punk generation. In the photo on the desk, Charles has an arm around the neck of Robyn at eight, a cigarette to his lips. An Olympia beer is at close range. Charles had been dead thirty-plus years, taken by the scourge of his prime.

"Allan was born in British Columbia, Canada, a child of the late 1950s. As a boy, he moved with his family to the suburbs of Los Angeles, California. There is no indication that he distinguished himself in any documented way while a student at Covina High School or Mount San Antonio Community College. His career as a creative writing major at San Francisco State University is notable for being cut short. Allan quit his academic pursuits after his junior year, and never returned to the classroom.

"As detailed in his autobiographical books, *Punk Elegies* and *Prisoner of X*, Allan pursued a writer's life in the alleys of downtown Hollywood in the late 1970s and as an editor of pornographic magazines for twenty years ending in 2002. The final stages of his career played out sporadically on the World Wide Web, first as an editorial director at a celebrity gossip aggregator and later as the social justice editor at a site with an expressed business model of improving the world.

"Allan left this planet after what can only be described as a lifelong struggle with life on this planet. He leaves behind a wife, an ex-wife, and various far-flung acquaintances and friends who might be asking themselves what they knew of him, what attracted them to him, and what of him lasts with them."

"Maybe you have answers," types the last boss. "Maybe you have more questions. Please leave them in the comments thread."

Is that all too much? Robyn wonders. She balks at clicking "post." She'd like to submit this extensive downer to the review of some semi-objective person who has knowledge of Allan M—, and also emotional detachment. There is one person.

Boxer has driven with his wife to a doctor's appointment to check on the developing baby. The second-time parents are not getting along, and the problem appears to be chronic. Boxer's wife asks for the restroom key and leaves Boxer on his own in the waiting room. A phone call buzzes in. Boxer sees that the call is from Robyn. He expects his wife will be on the toilet for a quarter hour. The opportunity is here to take the call and connect, to open possibilities, to engage in superficial intimacy, and to explore the limits of propriety. Boxer holds the phone face up in his palm and counts rings until Robyn defaults to voice mail, a function he never checks.

9

THE DISPERSAL OF THE EARTHLY GOODS

ONE MAN'S ACCUMULATED GOODS, his enduring history of personal property, his earthly estate, dear possessions he has held as close as he has held his very life, every last bit goes on sale. All his treasures become the consolation prizes of some bargain hunter's scavenger crawl.

My clothes were what went first. It's not that Trina needed more closet space, as she explained on the phone to Paul. It's not that she intended to dramatically expand her current wardrobe. Most assuredly, she had no intention of introducing a new resident to the home habitat, especially not some person who would require a cleared section of closet. "I just want the option of spreading out my pieces so they hang with some breathing space between them."

"I totally get it," said Paul. "We want our garments arranged so they present themselves to us. We want enough room to set the stage for a display."

"Does that seem selfish?"

"Honey, it's been six months. I'll put together an event."

On the day of the clothing dispersal, Paul climbed the Hollywood Hills street maze in a car piloted by Gail. Mandy leaned forward from the backseat, panting. After finding parking, extracting themselves from the car, pulling their outfits together, and walking into the house, the three long, long-time friends were disappointed to discover that Trina had invited my twenty-four-year-old, one-hundred-pound niece, Zoey, to attend the event.

On pretense of needing the bathroom, Mandy pulls Gail aside: "I'm sure Allan's left absolutely nothing in Zoey's size."

"People seek closure in different ways," cautions Gail. "But it makes no sense for that child to be here."

"I heard that!" calls Trina, checking the diapers on her mother. Ruthie actively slumps on a sofa in a side room connected to the guest bathroom. "Maybe Zoey wants something like a jacket or a shirt that she can wear as an oversize keepsake."

"We might as well get started," says Gail, crossing Ruthie's sightline and exiting the room.

"Should we wait until everyone else is here?" asks Trina.

"It's just us three," answers Paul. "I didn't want a crazed mob scene up here. You know how grabby people get when it comes to clothes."

"Do I ever," says Trina, delivering the sarcasm with far less arch than it might have supported. Sharply, she asks, "And what about you Gail? And Mandy? Do you think Allan left something in your sizes?"

"Well he was putting on a lot of weight there at the end," says Mandy straight-faced.

"I had thought that they might find something for their husbands," says Paul. "Hello, Ruthie," he says to the wife's mom.

"Mm-hmm," agrees Ruthie.

Gail and Mandy steer Trina from the little side room toward the downstairs bedroom area, where the clothes closets are. "I hope it's not a sensitive topic," says Gail. "But Bradley is about the same age as Allan was, and not that far off in taste levels."

"And my Glen has always admired the way Allan dresses," says Mandy. "He's said it more than once."

"The way he *dressed*," corrects Trina.

Slacks, suits, fashion denim, and dressy and casual long-sleeved shirts are arrayed on hangers downstairs. A lifetime distillation of T-shirts is stacked on the bed. Casual, with no appearance of rushing, in a coordinated blocking maneuver, Mandy and Gail front on the T-shirts. Their bulk and oversized handbags bodily deny Zoey access.

Gail slips a vintage Birthday Party T, thin fine cotton imprinted with the unmistakable spike haired profile of young Nick Cave, into her massive purse. "Bradley would totally wear this onstage," she says. "It would be a totally unironic gesture."

Mandy makes a double-fisted grab of the Sid Vicious "Action Man" shirt and a Sonic Youth *Sister* crew neck given to me by Richard Kern twenty-five years earlier. "Glen is a big fan of the photographer who took this picture," explains Mandy. "Robert Kern."

Zoey moves forward, quietly insistent. Dislodging the hang of Gail and Mandy's paired handbags, she reaches out, stretching and flexing her fingers. The massive handbags regroup and push Zoey back. Gail attempts an unobtrusive fold on a faded-black Iggy Pop tour shirt that I'd filched off the merchandise table before the Idiot show at the Santa Monica Civic Auditorium, 1977.

"That shirt's kind of cool," says Zoey. "That's Iggy Pop, right?"

The faded-black Idiot shirt slips from sight into the black depths of Gail's bag. "Oh no, honey," says Gail. She waves a manicured hand as if a mosquito has landed on a wet nail. "This is an old people's garment. It's three generations outside your scope of interest."

"Are any of you interested in his shoes?" asks Trina.

Paul Smith, Prada, Dries Van Noten, John Varvatos, Church's, Armani, Gucci, some handcrafted French and Italian brands I never could pronounce, all lined up along the bedroom baseboards and stuffed with cedar shoe trees.

"Footwear is tough," says Paul. "It's not like you can put shoes in the laundry or send them to the dry cleaner. If you'd like, there's a men's recovery house I work with that could probably put these shoes back on the street again."

"Oh, wait," says Gail, latching onto a pair of tooled burgundy boots in a cowboy cut. "Bradley has been working on a record with John Doe, and it has a sort of country vibe. They may do some live sets…" She holds the boots up at eye level as if seeing them from the lip of a stage.

Gail's attention pans around to the garments on hangers: Prada, Armani Black Label, Dries Van Noten, Gucci. She allows the suits and jackets to raise an appearance of muted indifference. Paul stands back from the suits, slacks, and sport coats, lurking in the cut, a hand to his chin. Gail speaks first, as if forcing herself to be helpful. "We're obligated to attend the wedding of Bradley's cousin's kid," she says. "You know, this blue suit might just work on Bradley for that."

Zoey checks the label as the garment passes in front of her. "Armani."

"Allan bought it in Rome," says Trina. "Not long after we met."

"That is such a great story," says Mandy. "You know how Glen will not wear a color? Maybe I should take home this black corduroy jacket and pants. It's sort of very unique, don't you think? Glen likes things that are sort of very unique."

Mandy recedes with her prize, a vintage Dries Van Noten corduroy ensemble, and Paul steps forward.

"Now that I've had some time to process," says Paul. "I feel that some of these solitary jackets, and the suit jackets, will fit me, and some silhouettes will flatter Dieter. He wanted to come today, but there's an architect he needed to meet at the restaurant."

"It's taken you so long to admit that Allan had acceptable taste," says Trina. "Acceptable to the refined standards."

"His taste was acceptable enough to pick you," says Paul. His hands stroke the goods. "I'll grant him that."

"Which jackets caught your eye?" asks Trina. "I'm curious."

"Let me see…" Paul riffles through the richness of fabrics and cuts. "Where to start?"

Bickering whispers draw Trina out of the closet and into the downstairs hallway. Mandy works the knob of a closed door, at first without success.

"Let me try," says Gail. She shoulders Mandy aside. "See? It's easy if you go about it patiently."

Trina is there. "Patient Gail," she says, just above her breath. "That's what they call you."

"What's in this room?" asks Mandy. "Oh, this is where all the records are!"

"Nobody goes near the records," says Trina. She moves past Mandy and firmly shuts the door. "The room containing the records is off limits."

"Should we just look at them?" asks Gail. "He might have some items of great interest."

"I'm sure he did have some items of great interest," says the wife. "I've received detailed instructions about the dispersal of the records."

Mandy is reluctant to move away from the door to the records room. "But Zoey might have her heart set on taking home a record."

"I have no interest in the records," says Zoey. She had been interested in the T-shirts. Now that the T-shirt interest is removed, she has no interest whatsoever.

"Zoey's the only person who knew him who doesn't have an interest in the records," says Trina. "Do you know that guy Wiseman? The Lurker?"

Paul pauses with an armload of black shoes at the foot of the stairs. "Wiseman with the nineties ponytail and the pedophile shades? Does he ever work? I have never been to Stella when Wiseman was not at his corner table with his personal set of crayons, drawing on the butcher paper."

"That's the guy," says Trina. "I can't stop for my morning coffee. He jumps up and rushes into Intelligentsia. 'Are you ready to let go of Allan's records? Are you ready?'"

"I didn't realize Allan and Wiseman were close," says Gail.

"I didn't say they were. I'm guessing they were never in a car together. And Wiseman sure as fuck has never been over here where he would see that records existed."

"It must be quite a collection," muses Gail. "Its fame has trickled all the way down to Wiseman."

"Do you think Allan has any rare Zappa in there?" wonders Mandy. "Glen has an obsession with anything rare and Zappa."

"Colin Cowboy asked the same thing," says Trina.

"When is that Cowboy going to realize he's gay?" asks Paul starting up the stairs with a second haul of footwear. "In all seriousness."

Trina gazes on the diminished lineup of shoes as if suddenly realizing that an extension of her is being trimmed.

"Colin showed up at Moda Yoga," she says. "Completely awkward and sweating like a sprinkler. 'Oh, I come here all the time,' he tells me, like I wouldn't have noticed if he did or didn't. He actually had a list of records he wanted me to take home and look for. He said he would get the best prices."

"Why not take him up on it?" says Gail. "He handles estates all the time."

"Allan warned me something like this would happen. He said that if he ever died, someone would show up as a friend and offer to make the most possible money for me on the records."

Paul tromps down the stairs and scoops up the last of the shoes.

"Allan was talking to you about being dead? While he was still alive?" Paul wedges the heel of a Tod's driving loafer beneath his chin. "That's a pretty morbid bit of self referencing."

Trina turns away from the space where the shoes had been. *He will be someone who never liked me,* her husband had told her, *and he'll come after my records.*

"It wouldn't matter if Zoey did want records," says Trina, leading Mandy toward the stairs, pushing her friend toward the upper level and out of the house. "A vinyl executor has been designated."

Paul waits at the top of the stairs, out of breath from sudden exertions. Both arms are comically loaded with sport coats, suit jackets, slacks, shirting, leather jacketing, and designer-cut denim. Clothing hides his heaving chest, shoulders, face, and head.

"Zoey, honey," he calls. "Can I get a little help carrying these items out to the car?"

A few weeks later, Trina can no longer put off repainting the room that contains a wall of shelving stocked with records. It is time for those things to go.

She phones Nicolas Cockroach, the designated vinyl executor.

"I'm ready to move them out," she says.

Trina sets a date to sort through the vinyl, and Nicolas arrives precisely five minutes ahead of time. The dogs rush the front gate, and Trina buzzes Nicolas in. Bardot growls and backs away. Fangs glistening, she charges Nicolas, amplifies her growling, and backs away tail tucked. Bulger muscles through Bardot and jumps, placing his face level with Nicolas Cockroach's face.

"Don't jump, Bulger," says Trina, emphasizing the words *jump, Bulger.* She's comfortable with Nicolas being a little off balance.

"It's fine by me if the dog jumps," says Nicolas, ambling between leaping Bulger and lunging Bardot and across the front patio.

"You're early," says Trina. "I was just about to crate them."

Nicolas declines her offer of water or fruit. Bardot and Bulger circle him whether he's standing or moving. He follows the widow downstairs toward the record room, in a whirl of dogs. Once Cockroach stands in the room downstairs, breathing deeply and scanning the rows of records, Bulger and Bardot settle, bellies to the floor. Trina realizes that Nicolas knows about dogs.

"For your help brokering the records, Nicolas, Allan has left all the forty-five rpm seven-inches to you."

"This entire box?"

"Don't even look at them now," says Trina. "That's my stipulation. Just take them. Gloat on them when you get home."

Nicolas sees the Germs' first single haphazard in the box, and the second Germs single as well. He sees a clutch of Dangerhouse plastic. These are all exquisite treats. They could pay his rent for a month or two, if it ever came to that.

"If you want to keep a few of the albums," Trina is saying, "I guess my husband would have been okay with that as well. But not more than twenty or thirty."

She lays out a stack of cardboard flats bought ahead of time at the Box Store.

"I know the albums I want," says Nicolas Cockroach. Trina gives no indication of urging him to elaborate. She doesn't tell him not to either. "The Beach Boys' *Surf's Up*," Cockroach says from memory. "The Byrds' *Untitled*. Arthur Lee's *Vindicator*. Bob Dylan's *Planet Waves*."

"In your judgment," Trina says, "I should have played Allan's songs at the funeral?" She grips a cardboard flat and folds, bends, and links the material so it forms a record-size carton. Her movements are precise, slow, educational. Nicolas would do well to pay attention and take note.

Nicolas is embarrassed. "I hadn't expected you to make the connection."

"The note on the program at the memorial, listing the songs?" asks Trina. "That note was for your benefit, Nicolas. I knew he'd told you the songs he wanted."

A silence stretches out. Nicolas Cockroach has time to think over the situation and to concede. "Well, you gave him the photo booth.

You gave him the photo booth and the pool party. You gave him the young girls in bikinis. You gave him everything it would take to make a man happy."

"That's what I kept telling him," says Trina.

The awareness of being alone with Trina, close enough to touch one another, flushes through Nicolas. They are so close and so alone that accidental touch may be inevitable. He takes the risk of looking at her straight on and prolonged. She permits this boldness. He sees himself being sized up by a woman of ongoing refinement, in her taste levels, in her emotional depths. Complexity is key to her nature, as it was to her husband's. Nicolas is too simple for her, always was, but she doesn't resent that he has taken time to look.

"It's too bad he couldn't have stayed around longer," says Cockroach. "There is so much here to stay around for."

Nicolas slides a cardboard flat free from the stack and manipulates it into a cube-shaped container. He stands, leans back and pauses, gazing upon the full length and height of the record shelves. He pulls his phone from his pocket and takes a photo of the record wall.

"Do you plan to Instagram that shot, Nicolas?"

"Unless you prefer I don't."

"My guess is he was hoping you would show it all off."

Nicolas stares again at the wall of stacked sound, taking in the floor-to-ceiling tunes. He tries to open his senses to all the circling emotions in all those spiraling grooves. He reaches to the top row of shelving cubes and grasps two handfuls of albums furthest to the left. "I suppose I'll start here."

He places the albums in the cardboard box and flips through.

"Oh, you'll be interested to see this," Nicolas says, as if entertaining an audience. He pulls two LPs from the handful and slides their covers out of the clear protective plastic sleeves. *School's Out* with the panties, and *Killer* with the calendar intact. Some Alice Cooper fan somewhere will be made very happy by what you're doing here today, Trina."

Trina takes a seat in an oversized leather chair that dominates the background of the record room. She'd been trying to persuade Allan to sell the black behemoth since they'd moved in together. The chair didn't match any of the furniture they'd bought with her vision. It was huge and dominating. Before he'd met her, she knew, her husband had fucked girls bent over the padded arms of this chair, just as he'd fucked her on the chair once she'd come around.

Nicolas Cockroach reaches up to the high range of the record shelving and lifts out his second grab of LPs. "Badfinger, Syd Barrett, Captain Beafheart, and Big Star. He really was collecting to impress somebody. Himself, I guess."

"Your face is just like his face when he was looking at records: your eyes and mouth; your posture. The whole bit."

"Thanks."

"Is that a compliment in your world?"

"Belle and Sebastian?" says Cockroach. "What the hell is Belle and Sebastian doing here?" Nicolas reflexively slides the *Fold Your Hands, Child, You Walk Like a Peasant* disc from its cover. Two shiny squares of coated paper stock flutter to the floor from the sleeve. "*Oops*," Cockroach says. "What was that?"

"They sure look like Polaroid photos," says Trina.

Cockroach stoops, looks quickly at the photos and jams them back within the record cover. "Something like Polaroids," he says.

"Let me see. Give me the Belle and Sebastian."

The widow fishes out the pictures. The parked cars and the waistlines and the storefronts in these images indicate that the photos are decades old, from long before Trina met her dead husband.

"This looks like somewhere out on Melrose," says Trina. "Sometime late in the seventies."

"That's what I thought, too."

A young Viva is a center of attention in both snapshots. Young Allan joins her in one. The poses clearly predate the departed's years comingled with the wife. The pictures differ from the photos from the locked file cabinet in that Viva remains fully clothed, even after Allan joins her in the frame.

The visual mementos have surfaced an awkward moment in the room. The moment stretches into an awkward silence. The designated executor coughs modestly. The wife reviews her options: Embarrassed? Humiliated? Enraged? Indifferent? "You know what, Nicolas?" she says. Bulger and Bardot slink back. "I'm not up for this after all. Would you mind if we leave it for later?"

"Sure," says Nicolas. He disengages from the records and stands. "That's fine. It doesn't have to be today." Nicolas marches, at Trina's pace, up the stairs, to the front door, and out into the courtyard. The steel gate in the adobe patio wall, his quick hand discovers, is locked. Nicolas turns to face Trina. "I can always come back," he says.

The latch in the gate refuses to give. He can see in Trina's eyes that he will not come back. He cannot read whether or not she intends to unlatch the gate. Does she expect him to scale the wall?

"Wait," she commands. She goes back into the house and closes the door behind her, shutting the dogs outside. Alone in the front patio, in the limbo between the door to the house's interior and the gate to the road outside, the full weight of awkwardness slumps onto Nicolas's shoulders. Bardot and Bulger sit perfectly still and monitor his every twitch. To his credit, Nicolas is dutiful and hopeful and patient. Trina returns carrying a cardboard box and rewards all three of those virtues.

"Here, take these." She hands over the bin filled with forty-five rpm records. "It's the least you deserve. I'll give you those albums you wanted, but I can't be bothered to look for them now." She opens the gate, and Nicolas Cockroach makes his escape. Trina's urgent need to remodel the records room slinks out with him.

Trying to salvage a sorry weekend, Trina drives to meet a more recent friend, Janet, way out in Highland Park. The purpose of the trip is to look at a house to buy as an income property. Janet is a realtor. Janet has advised the wife to use Allan's retirement account as a down payment toward equity.

Stalled at the entrance of Café de Leche on York, Trina works her way through a cluster of hipster moms and douche dads. She scans the interior of the coffeehouse, not seeing what she's looking for. She stands near the front window, beside a table under the notice board: Rooms for let, dog walkers, reiki masters. Seated at that window table, Janet reaches out and touches Trina. "Honey, I'm sitting right here."

"Sorry, honey, I was soaking up the gentrification."

"You look disoriented," says Janet. "Or maybe I'm the one who's disoriented. It's weird seeing you in Highland Park."

Trina lowers into a chair across from Janet's.

"Would you like a coffee?" asks Janet. "Maybe a pastry?"

"You know what, Janet? I'm trying to decide how I feel about my dead husband keeping photos of a woman he knew when he was twenty-one. He kept these photos for more than thirty years after he lost contact with her."

"I told Gail I was meeting you out here. She couldn't picture you slumming it in Highland Park."

"Keeping sex photos I understand," says Trina. "These others, the clothed photos, and hiding them from me, it's confusing."

"Let's go look at the house?" suggests Janet the realtor.

Even while assessing the exterior appeal and interior advantages of the primary residential structure and the tenant-ready converted garage behind it, Trina's mind refuses to change the subject. She wonders what could be more clichéd than to marvel at having lived with the man for so many years and been in the dark about the contents of his mind. Beyond that insipid profundity crested a whole range of towering clichés. Who, really, could presume to know the motivations and aspirations of another human being?

Walking back toward their cars, the realtor points Trina toward a tiny vintage shop nestled on a spoke street off York. "Wait, T!" The realtor hesitates in view of the storefront display of clothing and furnishings. "Are you telling me you've never heard about this place?"

"I see a thrift store."

"It's curated vintage. Let's stop in. We don't need to buy anything."

"Really? I don't like stopping in at a store," says Trina, "unless I anticipate seeing something I need to buy."

Trina follows Janet in through the tinkling door. While Janet navigates the store's three tight aisles, Trina stands in the front, next to the cash register. She scans racks of clothing. Her gaze wanders to the wall space above the side racks. Premium collector garments are arrayed as decorative hangings. Three of these elevated items, illustrated T-shirts, make an impression on Trina: she's struck by the spike-haired profile of Nick Cave, and Sid Vicious heralded in Action Man mode, and Iggy Pop posing as a jazz-handing idiot.

"Just T-shirts," she says, to no one, hardly out loud.

Janet presents a Sonic Youth *Sister* graphic imprinted upon a Hanes Beefy-T. "Can you believe someone would pay three hundred and fifty dollars for an old piece of underwear?" says Janet.

"I'll believe just about anything," says Trina. Her attention circles a pair of burgundy Lucchese cowboy boots, rarely, if ever, worn, premium priced. Trina picks up and holds one boot by the toe as if weighing the destruction she might work by its heel.

"What are you seeing?" asks the realtor. "Allan wore boots like those?"

"Cowboy boots?" says Trina. "He might have bought something like this on his own, before he knew me."

"That boot's like something Colin Cowboy would show up in."

"I wonder where Colin is showing up these days?"

In fact, Colin has shown up at Pretty Marina's place. She fends him off at the couch and takes a seat in her living room's single chair. Marina says, "Someone told me you were getting back with your wife."

"Well, my girlfriend and I broke up; so the wife is back on the table."

"You said you would help me put up my shelves," insists Marina. "I thought that was why you came over here."

"It seems I don't have the right tools with me," says Colin, straightening the front of his western-cut Lee jeans. "I misunderstood."

Pretty Marina goes into tidy-up mode along the periphery of her living room. "My message was pretty straightforward."

"You literally invited me over here to install shelving?"

"I need these shelves."

"Why so urgent? Is Nicolas Cockroach buying your affections with a load of records he swindled off of Trina?"

"Nicolas is not the swindling type. Anyway, that whole deal fell through."

"Which deal? Between you and him? Or between him and Trina?"

"Something awkward went down when Nicolas met Trina. She kicked him out of her house. Without any of the records." Marina notices Colin's prey drive fully divert. He's done with objectifying her for now. His mind is on the hunt in some other locality.

For days on end, Colin's hunting mind returns to M—'s record room. Eventually, he devises the pretense of running into widow Trina by accident in the grains aisle at the Erewhon health-food store on Beverly.

"It's funny," Trina says, pushing her cart as if to roll around Colin, "I don't remember seeing you in this market before."

Colin pivots sideways and aligns his direction with Trina's cart. "I'm here every day." He proffers a bottle of cold-pressed juice as evidence of constant Erewhon patronage. "You've seen me here a dozen times. You see me here so often, you don't notice seeing me."

Trina replicates the laugh that comes out when someone has charmed her.

Colin sticks to Trina in line at the cash register. He presents himself as wanting to help. He asks for the opportunity to be of service.

"And what service do you feel I need?" says Trina, exhibiting zero trace of flirtation.

"I will transport the records to a reputable store approved by you and negotiate a strong price."

"Do I need to worry about your skim?"

"I'll give you an inventory," he says. "We'll count up how many records are there, and I'll procure a receipt for the quantity of records from the store that buys the lot."

The wife knows this as a pliable, permeable assurance. Trina pictures Viva dressed in a punk miniskirt and blouse leaning against the back of a Ford Maverick on Melrose Avenue. Trina disregards that image. It has no bearing on her process. Two facts—Colin's clear intent to steal records and departed Allan's clear antipathy toward Colin—cement the wife's decision.

"Okay," she says.

"Thank you for entrusting me with this legacy," says Colin.

"That's not the word I would use."

"But it is a legacy."

"*Entrust* is the word I would not use."

Again, Trina sets the date. Colin defines the appearance of punctual and dutiful, pressing the front gate buzzer at the appointed moment. He walks directly downstairs to the vinyl trove. The girl dog barks from her cage in the next room. The big dog watches Colin operate.

"Has he always been hung like that?" asks Colin.

"I could put Bulger in his crate," offers Trina.

"Why bother? I'm sure Bulger's a good boy, aren't you, Bulger?" Bulger edges closer to Colin. The dog's big, back feet are spring-loaded like a rabbit's. The dog remeasures the distance to Colin's neck.

"Are you a good boy, Bulger?" asks the wife. She and the dog lock a gaze. It's as if the big dog knows that Colin's fingers are the last thing the dog's departed master would have wanted manipulating his treasured material goods. The big dog breaks off eye contact with the widow and notices that Colin is filling two cartons at once. One carton fills much slower than the other. By the time this one special carton fills up, six regular cartons have filled.

Bulger stays on watch until the end of the records. Colin has filled five special cartons and more than thirty of the ordinary type. One at a time, Colin hefts each carton, lugs it up the stairs, carries it through the front courtyard, and slides it into the back of a borrowed van. The five special cartons are carried up the stairs and slid into the van last.

"Should I bring the money to you?"

"A check in the mail is fine." The wife shuts the iron gate.

The fully loaded van proves unwieldy to navigate. Colin wishes he had a copilot to guide him through the narrow twists of the hillside passages, but he can't have anyone observe what he's doing and demand a cut. He pulls the borrowed van into a subterranean parking structure halfway between the widow's house and the buying record store. His single-guy apartment, the one he is in the process of giving up, is an elevator ride above. His shoulders and back are strained and pained.

He opens a storage space in the parking basement and wheels out a hand dolly. He loads the five crates of special records from the van onto the hand dolly. The dolly is overloaded, but Colin wants to make the haul in a single trip. The amount of physical effort he's put into this day, he's earned his premium. Up in the apartment, the lease has all but expired. The contents of the flat are in boxes, packed and sealed and waiting for the movers. Colin slides the crates of albums he has appropriated off of the dolly. He shuffles on a corresponding quantity of crap records, records inherited from a roommate who proved to be temporary and to have bad taste and hoarder tendencies. Down in the underground parking level, he loads these castoff records into the borrowed van.

Colin maneuvers the borrowed van into the parking lot below a massive music store on Sunset Boulevard. He leaves his driver's license as collateral at the store's security booth and is allowed to use the store's hand dolly. After making three trips hand carting stacked boxes of records up to the store's main floor and power lifting the cartons up onto the trade counter, Colin wishes he had an assistant along to help with the brute labor. The store employees pointedly decline his invitations for eye contact. He makes half a dozen more runs down to the parking lot with an empty dolly and back up with a strenuous load. Finally, in Colin's mind, M—'s entire cargo has been transferred from the van. Colin leans upon the buy counter for support. "That's the last of it."

"This is going to take a while," says the buyer, digging into the first crate.

Colin wanders the store. He flips through half a thousand jazz albums in the basic bins, starting at the unsorted A titles and browsing into the unsorted Ks. He has trouble concentrating on the records flicking through his hands. Titles from the M— haul, stacked securely in the five cartons sitting in his packed up living quarters, run through Colin's mind: Original double-LP German pressings of *Tago Mago* by Can and Amon Düül II's *Yeti*. He'd counted four albums by Munich-based electro-folk hippies Popol Vuh. Colin can't recall specific titles. When he goes to sleep tonight, he will own four Popol Vuh albums, which is four more than when he woke up this morning. He's gained a few records on the green Brain label that he's tracked selling for obscene prices on the Internet markets. That Faust album, *So Far*, complete with the photographic prints that he'd heard of but never seen—it's his.

He's taken copies of both Gram Parsons' solo studio albums, although he already owned the second one. That first Velvet Underground album will look so cool on his shelves with the banana on the cover half peeled off and fingered back on. Colin pictures David Bowie's *The Man Who Sold the World* on Mercury Records—on the cover, a cartoon cowboy wields a gun. The cowpoke's open mouth connects to an empty voice bubble. Really, there is nothing to say other than that Colin Cowboy has landed a windfall of literally hundreds of fantasy finds, records that never show up in store bins anymore, that are sifted out for online auctions and stashed in deep-pocket collections. *Today*, Colin swells as he reflects, *has been a real world bonanza.*

He looks up from the merchandise and wanders the store, looking at girls, looking for approach lanes, presorting the attached girls from the girls on their own. He narrows down his potential start-ups. A Latin girl of about twenty-six is carrying a stack of glitter and glitter-adjacent used vinyl and a slight, delightful layer of baby fat. A blonde of indeterminate vintage, possibly a very youthful grandmother, studiously winnows through a selection of romance comedy DVDs. *Eeny meeny miny,* Colin thinks. He hears his name called over the store public address system and diverts directly to the trade counter.

"Cash or store credit?" asks the store buyer. M—'s albums are stacked higher than the buyer's head all up and down the counter.

Colin flexes his aching shoulders and licks a smashed finger. After trundling in forty unwieldy and weighty crates of records, why not skim off a layer of vigorish? "Can I get twenty-five percent in store credit," he asks, "and three quarters in cash?" It's not like Trina is counting on the money from these records to maintain her residence. Taking one-quarter of the haul won't violate the spirit of their agreement.

The store buyer is in accordance with Colin's reasoning. The buyer has a habit of his own. While grading and sorting, he has siphoned off a few gems overlooked by Colin, rarities so seldom-seen that to spirit them away without giving a first look to the store owners is to risk immediate dismissal. When break time rolls around, the buyer's selections will go directly into the trunk of the buyer's car. He can hardly believe that the sharpster who brought in this obviously picked-over haul had missed these gems.

The M— lot is transferred upstairs, where the store's online auction associate senses that the stash has been cut once heavily, and lightly again. He pulls Alice Cooper's *Killer*, with the perforated poster flap clean and intact, for the eBay feed. Belle and Sebastian's *Fold Your Hands, Child, You Walk Like a Peasant* is a stealth earner; he's seen it go for thirty and up.

The online auction associate can't begin to guess what titles the buyer deep-sixed from the bulk. He pulls three dozen more killer online goods to be marketed on the Web, and a clutch of personal favorites that are destined to disappear from the store as if into thin air. He is astounded that his personal picks had survived a pair of culls, but it's not like he and the store's buyer can talk it over.

At the next workstation in line, the store's brick-and-mortar pricing clerk is relatively new on the job. While assessing the resale value and pricing the towering M— stacks, she is aware that the goods have been dipped into and expects to come across nothing truly extraordinary. Her expectations are not failed. She does set aside a promo copy of Big Star's *#1 Record* on Ardent, hole punch. Her sense is the vinyl will play better than it looks, and she slides it into a sideline section of her workstation.

One of the store's job benefits is preferred choice and a hefty discount on used items that come into the store. The pricing clerk has one beef with that policy: she is not paid enough to take as much advantage of the price cut as she'd like to.

She and the bin clerk have commiserated with one another about seeing more to buy than they can afford. That conversation has not aged well. The bin clerk wordlessly picks up the cart of fresh discs to be distributed throughout the store. He wheels off in pensive silence. At the Bs, he is drawn from his inner reflections by a super-pristine original of the Beach Boys' *Surf's Up* record. He transfers the record to the back of the workload. *Surf's Up* will be exiting the sales floor when he does. By the time he finishes his cycle through the store, a small stack of holdbacks has accumulated in his cart. He squints toward the daylight glaring in through the glass double doors opening onto the Sunset Boulevard sidewalk. Skeevy Steve perches up there in the bag-check booth, alert and opportunistic like a big, bold house rodent. The Skeevy arrangement is twenty percent of sticker price, and Steve sees nothing. How else will a poor bin clerk be able to afford a record habit?

A *veterano vato*, one of the Monterey Park originals, has driven into Hollywood to show his two teen daughters around the city's biggest record store. The vato plucks a slightly battered but fully functional *Where Did Our Love Go* by the Supremes from the new arrivals bin. He loses sight of his daughters. The record is clean enough and in the nice-price range. He loses track of the urge to school his kids. He reads the back of the Supremes album aloud to anyone within earshot: "'Baby Love.' 'Come See About Me.' This is the shit." He returns to the new arrival bin, a bin enriched with a fresh flow of my everyday vinyl.

"Dad," say his girls an hour later, "what are you doing? When are we going?"

"Just hang out," he says to his daughters. "It'll be worth it when we get home."

One week after Colin Cowboy's transaction, Nicolas Cockroach comes into the store. Nicolas Cockroach is a good-faith record-store consumer in good standing. He gravitates to the Bob Dylan tag in the rock vinyl section. Nicolas holds a copy of Bob Dylan's *Planet Waves*. Two copies of that title are in the Dylan bin. Cockroach hums the parts everyone knows from "Forever Young." He wonders if one of these two copies of *Planet Waves* could be from the M— collection. If so, which one? The record he holds could have been traded in by anybody. It's a good record, even if it's not the copy that was in that downstairs room of floor-to-ceiling shelving. Nicolas hums a bit deeper into "Forever Young," skipping to the fast version that starts Side Two.

An unaccustomed feeling of worth and service overtakes Cockroach as he whisper sings Bob Dylan verses on the record store floor. Nicolas has the sense that he is keeping a tacit promise, that he has honored his side of an unspoken bargain. Nicolas Cockroach drops the record back into the bin and leaves the store empty handed, certain that one of those two Bob Dylan records had formerly belonged to M—, and reasonably sure that whoever takes it home will be a better person for doing so.

Nicolas Cockroach views the store as a heartbeat for the diffusion of dead men's records. The sounds encoded in the plastic grooves pulse out from the storefront, course along surface streets and freeways, reverberate beyond the furthest reaches of the city and the county, cross state lines, board airplanes and fly overseas to kingdoms never reached by their dead former owners. All these records are reborn and sounding off in some new situation, some distant capillary in a far, venous network.

An unfortunate fraction of his dead friend's albums, Nicolas knows, will be bought and filed away as part of a completion compulsion. These prizes will reside in the collection of an owner who has no intention of playing them. If these discs were sentient objects, they would be looking forward to that collector's death, biding their time until an estate sale hands them the possibility of playing at life again.

Frank McGovern is a guy from my demographic. He's living according to choices slightly different than the ones made by me. He married a woman twelve years younger. He and his wife have two daughters, seven and nine. Given a twenty-minute after-work window in the massive record store, he buys two albums he'd owned and lost during his youth.

Neil Young's *Everybody Knows This Is Nowhere* makes itself heard on Frank's hi-fi player while he prepares dinner for his two daughters. My initials inked on the Reprise Records label turn at thirty-three and a third revolutions per minute. The initials indicate that I had maintained ownership of this copy of *Everybody Knows This Is Nowhere* from my mid-teens all the way through my post-middle age and on until my expiration date. The record spins the life force forward, and the McGovern daughters sing along with the band: *"I want to be a cinnamon girl."*

The girls eat, reminded to chew slowly, and Neil Young sings "Round & Round (It Won't Be Long)" at a dirge pace, the vocal drawing out how slow the given days turn and how soon the whole spin will be over.

McGovern reflects on what's ahead for his daughters. He cannot know what that will be and he cannot stop it, and he has taken on the task of preparing the girls for whatever the future will bring. He starts the record over and puts his daughters to bed. Gentle and patient, he lulls the girls with a singsong lilt, Neil Young's lyrics evoking angel-toned cowgirls and warm sands and sweet, sweet smiles.

The second record of mine Frank bought is Bob Dylan's *Planet Waves*. He's never been sure of this album. Why is "Forever Young" on there twice? He checks that his daughters are asleep in their beds. He takes a seat in the small room that houses his desk and books, record player and his few albums. He hears his wife come in from her yoga class. He shuts the door and plays the Bob Dylan record and reads once more the opening sentence of a middle chapter in Malcolm Lowry's *Under the Volcano*, a novel he's been dragging himself through for weeks.

The words Bob Dylan is putting into Frank's ears—couplets built on solitude and debt and cost and payment—blur out the Lowry words in front of his eyes. McGovern puts down the book and picks up a pen. He writes, 1) Bob Dylan "Dirge" *Planet Waves*, on a pad of yellow paper. He scrawls FUNERAL SONGS across the top of the pad.

His wife stands in the open doorway to the room containing Frank's desk. "What are you doing in here all by yourself?" she asks. "Why haven't you come to bed?"

THE DISPERSAL OF THE ASHES

M Y MOTHER-IN-LAW WATCHES PIE-EYED in her wrinkles as her daughter packs the old lady's essential clothes and medications into a single piece of rolling luggage. "Where am I going?" Ruthie asks.

"You're going to stay with Mark, your son."

"Am I coming back?"

"Yes, Mom. I'm going away for a few days. Then I'll bring you back."

"When am I coming back?"

"In a couple of days. I'm taking the dogs on a little trip up the coast."

"I want to know when I'm coming back."

The two white dogs have watched the wife downstairs packing a piece of luggage on the bed in the half-vacant master bedroom. The dogs have followed the wife upstairs and watched her pack up the Birthgiver. They track the Birthgiver being led from the house and placed into an unknown car. They feel how the Birthgiver feels. They slump to the floor, resigned to being next in line for expulsion. Trina ignores the dogs and secures the house's doors and windows. For some reason, she checks the oven and stove more than once to ensure they are turned off.

Soon after Ruthie departs, Chase arrives lugging an oversized suitcase and a child's backpack. She wears cargo shorts and a muscle shirt with the sleeves rolled. Chase is not invited to bring her luggage in beyond the front patio. "We're good to go," says Trina. She reaches for the dog leashes, and the animals spin and leap and keep all eyes on her to be sure they have not misread her. She does not change her mind. She is taking them along!

The dogs leap into the backseat of the widow's Volvo. She leans into the rear of the car and places a streamlined metallic urn on the seat between the dogs. "That's where your father would want to ride," she tells the dogs.

Chase settles into the passenger seat. She mimics shifting her package. "What did you say?" she asks.

"Nothing."

"I didn't quite hear you."

"'Nothing,' I said." Trina takes the driver's seat. Her passenger buckles in, and the car glides down the hill. The dogs strain forward.

"Do you have directions printed out?" asks Chase, establishing conversational command.

"I know where we're going."

Chase adjusts her seat back and looks out the window. The car merges onto the 101 North, and Chase takes control of the radio.

"Plug in the iPod," says Trina. "It's programmed, I think from last time we went up there."

"You mean the last time you and he, the ex-husband, went up there?"

Trina nods confirmation, and her passenger suggests switching up the tunes. "You know, introduce new themes. Hit some higher high notes. Meld our voices in fresh harmonies." All this is said very lightly, veering toward the jocular.

Trina responds by drifting into a verbalized cataloging of various times she and her ex had taken this same highway north to their habitual beach-town destination, Cayucos. Chase senses that the couple's trips had driven toward a vista of diminishing returns. She suggests, mildly, that Trina might have been on the road with a less-than-perfect traveling partner. Trina flings the Volvo across two lanes of traffic. In the back, the morbid thermos full of the ex-husband's incinerated remains clunks to the floor. Trina turns up the music so abruptly it startles the dogs. Chase understands that portions of the ride north, this portion in particular, will be occasion for silent reflection.

Silence reigns for one hundred and more miles. Finally, Chase convinces herself that not speaking up is a moral failing. "I'm not alone in those feelings about your ex," ventures Chase. "Your friends, I'm sure you know how they talk about him. I've heard them. They don't hide it from you."

"I haven't heard anything."

"But your wedding. None of your oldest friends, the friends who are driving up to meet you in Cayucos right now, to give you support there, none of them were at your wedding."

"What makes you think that's true?"

"I heard Paul tell someone."

The widow lets Chase see that she is thinking this over. "Chase, there is something you need to understand about these people, these three friends."

"I understand that they have your best interests at heart."

"These three people, we've known each other since we were kids. Things like boundaries, we never really bothered with. Allan showed up in a situation that was all enmeshed and knotted up. We were entwined in each other's lives beyond what is exactly healthy. Less now, of course, but back when Allan and I met, there was a lot of possessiveness and interference, and he resented that."

"You know, it's hard for me to say this, but maybe all three of them— Paul and Mandy and Gail—were not wrong."

"Oh, believe me, Allan gave me dozens of reasons to think what you're saying here might be true. But, I mean, you've had trouble with Mandy and Paul and especially Gail, haven't you?"

"Every situation is different. A new person comes and naturally your friends want to see if the new person is cool."

"They've been borderline bitches to you, Chase. And you're not even a threat to them."

Bardot, following this exchange closely from the backseat while Bulger snores, maintains a poker face. Trina presents a profile of composure and confidence at the steering wheel. The Volvo glides along the freeway exit lane at San Luis Obispo and swings into the turn heading north along the shoreline highway toward Morro Bay and Hearst Castle.

"Our friends are our friends for a reason," explains Chase. "And our life lessons are learned so we can live in a manifestation of wisdom. Have you ever noticed how a group of penguins reacts when one of their friends becomes vulnerable?"

"I haven't noticed that," says Trina.

"First," says Chase, "and foremost: The healthy strong penguins all circle around the vulnerable penguin. The vulnerable penguin is shielded from the elements and protected from predators. Do you know what the ring of supportive penguins does next? Do you want me to tell you?"

The widow nods assent and remains silent, apparently listening to Chase, but inside remembering. Trina and the dead husband had been up to this little town with her mom, when her mom could still walk and eat in a restaurant without attracting pity. They'd had two robust dogs and old Ruthie. Allan had done all the driving. She'd seen him bite down on curse words and swallow them rather than spit them out, in deference to the wrinkled woman in the backseat with the dogs. There had been some snappiness during that trip, a few flared tempers and heated exchanges. That's all part of love as it plays out for the long run.

The Volvo accelerates past the massive Morro Bay rock. A few hundred yards to the left of the roadway, the flat, glimmering ocean laps up the shoreline in the expiring sunlight. Trina hears Chase say: "It's only a matter of time before your friends recognize me as a part of the integral circle."

"I can see that," answers Trina, looking off over the watery horizon.

"The penguins always recognize a likeminded penguin," says Chase, finishing up. She is pleased with the effect her words appear to be having on the subsurface of the widow's face.

Trina and Chase are splitting a shoreline motel room, the same pier-view unit of Trina's warm memories. As Chase stows the luggage and the dogs settle in, Trina wonders if this arrangement is such a great idea.

"Hungry?" asks Chase, hopefully.

"We have dinner reservations at the local rustic bistro." Trina goes about changing from her driving clothes into her dining clothes.

"All I brought were shorts," frets Chase. "And two down vests, this one and the nice one."

"Put on the nice one," Trina instructs her. "You'll be fine. It really is a rustic place."

Paul, Gail Campbell, and Mandy Gold stand on the plank sidewalk outside Hoppe's Bistro, clocking the approach and parking of Trina's Volvo. Paul and the two girls—all in their mid-fifties—are dressed conspicuously chic. Trina clambers out of the Volvo, pulling Bulger and Bardot. The dogs jerk at their leashes. Paul and Gail check their watches.

"We said six thirty," says Trina.

"Six fifteen," Paul and Gail say. Their tandem delivery betrays long practice.

"Same old Trina," says Mandy.

"Wow, you people all look so fabulous," observes Chase. "I feel like I'm auditioning."

"That's silly," says Gail Campbell. "We're all good friends here. So don't say anything like that again. I'm Gail."

"Oh, we met at the house," says Chase, pausing awkwardly. "After the funeral. You left with the dogs."

"This is Chase, everybody," puts in Paul. "Chase has been instrumental in doing the heavy lifting for Trina. I believe Chase has been especially effective with those dogs!"

"Not super effective," says Chase, reflexively rubbing scar tissue on the meaty portion of her right thumb.

"I'm sure you're very competent, Chase," says Mandy Gold, adjusting her bra beneath the straps of her retro-paisley shift dress. "But I'm leery about eating dinner with those two animals loose under the table while I have my Pepper in my lap."

"Don't be alarmist," snaps Trina.

"You keep pepper in your lap?" asks Chase, politely.

"Chase, dear," explains Paul, "Pepper is Mandy's sweet, diminutive, and delicate Pomeranian." A rust-colored ball of fur resting on Mandy's suede moccasin shows its teeth. The dog punctuates a prolonged snarl with rapid-fire yips.

"We picked Hoppe's because the outdoor tables accommodate dogs," says Trina.

"Honey," says Paul, "don't you think the dogs would be happier waiting in the car?"

Mandy takes the gum from her mouth and installs it beneath a wooden handrail enclosing Hoppe's porch. "Pepper can't relax with those dogs," she says.

"Then put Pepper in the car," suggests Trina.

"But it's not just my dog," says Mandy. "No dogs can relax around those dogs."

"My dogs are completely under my control. There will be no problem."

"Oh, come on, Trina," says Gail. "Admit it. You've never been able to handle both those dogs by yourself."

"Of course I have."

"Not both of them at once," say Gail and Mandy at once.

Chase projects a deeply slighted cough. "I can help contain the dogs," she says.

"That's right," drawls Gail. "We've forgotten your proven competency with these animals."

"What do you mean by that?" demands Chase.

"Simmer down." Paul cozies up to Chase like he would to a friend. "It's no knock on you that those particular dogs won't warm to you."

Bardot and Bulger make a concerted and vocal scramble to reach Pepper.

"It's not worth arguing about," says Trina, straining to pull her animals back. She settles the dogs within the car, cracks the back windows, and emerges clutching the streamlined urn containing the earthly remains of her late companion.

"The prudent move would be to leave the urn in the car with the dogs," says Gail. "It will be safe there. No one will try to break in with those beasts in the windows."

"But this dinner is due to Allan…"

"I just feel it, I mean the ashes, will be a morbid reminder at the dinner table," reasons Paul. "I thought we were using the word *festive*."

"Okay, okay, you win," says Trina.

"Your dogs will be allowed a few last moments with their departed master," intones Gail, nuzzling Mandy's nervous dog, Pepper.

"The urn will be in the car," says Trina. "I will put the urn back in the car."

"Some objects are conversation starters," starts Mandy. "Some objects are conversation killers. That object, honey, I hate to be the one to say it but—"

Trina interjects: "There's nothing more to discuss. I'll put him back in the car."

A clump of people trundling up the boardwalk to enter Hoppe's leaves behind a lone, neon-haired female figure. The woman's black-satin nightgown, defiantly young on her, is saved from utter indecency by flesh-colored pencil leggings under it. Paul moves in on Chase's ear, all companionable: "My grandmother wore those same leggings! To treat her varicose veins."

Chase perks up. "I know this hot mess," she says. "It's the old thing who was calling herself Viva at the funeral."

"Paul!" calls out Viva. "I made it! But traffic was way worse than you warned me it would be."

"I love your spirit," says Paul. "Come join us!"

"Well, Allan always made a point to say hello," answers Viva. "I'm sure *he* won't mind me being here to say bye-bye."

"Let me just drop these ashes back in the car," says Trina. "With the only dogs in town that aren't allowed into this restaurant."

While Trina locks up the Volvo, Paul holds back, manning Hoppe's door for her. "Inviting that bipolar crone and not telling me was a cunt move," says Trina.

"It's a free country," replies Paul. "There's no law against a deluded old thing eating in a super fancy restaurant."

Inside Hoppe's, Chase is shunted to the end of the communal table, sitting beside the outsider, Viva. Paul sits closest to Chase and Viva, with Gail and Mandy positioned as Trina's gatekeepers, cordoning off willfully strange Viva and overly familiar Chase.

The waiter singles out Viva. "We'll start with you," he says.

"Is the soup of the day by the bowl only, or can I order a cup?"

"We could do a cup."

"I'll take a cup."

"Really?" says Paul. "Hoppe's is the most elaborate dining experience on the entire Central Coast, and you're settling for a cup of vegan cream of asparagus?"

Viva pulls her slip tight around her waist. "My conscience won't allow me to think of this as an occasion for gluttony."

"Don't be silly," says Paul. "And don't hold back." He leans in and enters the zone of confidentiality. "This is my treat. Just between you and me, I'm insisting that everyone overdoes it."

"Well, if it makes you happy."

Viva turns to the waiter: "I'll have the tuna tartare tower and the abalone steak plate."

"And to drink?" asks the server.

Viva demurs. "Let's stick with water."

"Viva?" asks Paul. "Did I see you hesitate? You must want some wine! Will some wine help you tell us everything we don't know about Allan?"

"Get me started," suggests Viva.

Paul calls back the waiter. "We'd like some wine!" Paul indicates Viva and Chase as though they are a matched set. "For this end of the table."

The waiter finishes with the party's orders and leaves. Without him, the mood and conversation settle toward desultory.

"Attention everyone," announces Paul, calling over the flat affect, "this is Viva. She is here to tell us about Allan. Now, Viva, that's Trina, the wife Allan left behind, sitting at the head of the table looking for something in her purse. I believe she's already made your acquaintance. That's Mandy to Trina's left, and Gail is sitting across from Mandy."

Mandy and Gail squeeze their lips in pained smiles. "Hello, Viva," they say in tandem. Trina pulls a pair of eyeglasses from her purse, puts them on, and stares down the far end of the table.

Viva takes a swig of burgundy and tilts the goblet stem toward Chase at her side. "And who's this one?"

"I'm Chase, and I don't mind if I help myself to a little of that wine."

Viva refills her own glass and hands the bottle to Chase. "Keep it, honey, two's my limit."

Gail remarks: "That's certainly not what I would have expected."

"Let's see," responds Viva, "you two girls have both known the widow, what, I'd estimate close to thirty years or more. Starting when you were in your mid to late twenties. Gail, you're take charge, a little preemptive with your point of view. Bossy some might say. Ostentation is something you detest, but look at that ring! Where's the hubby? I mean right now. Why isn't your husband here tonight?"

"He's on tour. He's—"

"Middle-aged and in a band. Don't flinch! Don't feel defensive. You're a person of upstanding moral fiber—there's no fair fault to find with you. Your ethical superiority expresses itself in an ostentatious—here's that word again!—refusal to gossip. But, when prodded, you will sincerely diagnose needs for improvement and prescribe regimens for betterment. But only if the person you're talking about isn't here."

Gail flushes, surprised to feel more flattered than insulted by this detailed assessment: "Is this your roundabout way of asking for my advice, Viva?"

"Hardly. If you weren't so battened down, you might be sexy. A little sexy, but you wouldn't be leaking the stuff, not like this one. The one you all call Mandy."

Mandy knocks her bra strap off base, adjusts it, then shrugs her shoulders. The strap slips down over the meaty top of her arm. "My husband, if you must know," says Mandy, "is off with our twelve-year-old son."

"To free you up for this trip?" says Viva. "That is thoughtful. You're the plump one, not that I'm saying that as a criticism. I mean, look at me. Obviously curves are my preference.

"You haven't got as good a grip on your neurosis as the others do," observes Viva. "You're the one who's more apt to blurt out inappropriate judgment and slightly racist descriptions. You're more vulgar than you are sexy, but again, look at me!"

Gail tosses an eye roll. "I would say we've done just about enough looking at you," she says. "Oh, joy, here come the entrées."

"Just in time," observes Viva. "I'm famished."

"Eat up, honey," says Paul.

"You know I can talk with my mouth full," answers Viva.

"I'm picturing it."

"And you do interest me, Paul. But not as much as this abalone."

The guests eat. They groan. They yum. They savor with eyes closed and lips smacking. "This surf and turf is *so good*," says Chase. She places a piece of each in her mouth and grinds the combo. "Awesome!"

Mandy tongues sauce from her lips. "The pork belly was better last time. Remember when just the four of us came up last time?"

Gail pauses for a reasoned rumination. "I'm not sure the original owner is still here."

"Can we talk about something that's not the food?" asks the widow.

"Trina, here's the real deal," answers Paul. "We only came along for the food. And we wanted to support you, of course. The food, I must tell you, is more lacking than usual. And not for want of trying, I assure you. There's no shortage of trying here. It's not a case of a little something missing. The problem is there's a little something extra in every dish, a little something that shouldn't be there."

"Allan was never crazy about Hoppe's food either," says the widow. "Remember?"

"Wow, so you're telling me that he and I had more in common than I ever dreamed of."

"Paul?" asks Viva. "Shouldn't your tone be a little less bitchy? I'm not judging. I'm just curious. I mean with the purpose of this little trip…"

"The purpose of this little trip," lays down Chase, "is for old friends to gather for a fine dining experience, to refresh our roots, and grow together into the future."

"Oh," responds Viva, too agreeable for comfort. "I'll be the newcomer in your finicky little clique. But don't presume my history doesn't go back."

Pepper barks, a shrill and piercing report.

"Sharpened human voices make Pepper nervous," explains Gail.

"Then I'll be blunt," interjects Paul, "for Pepper's sake. Historically, Viva, the departed and I agreed on being disagreeable. I have always openly shared my feelings that this dead man had been an incorrect match for Trina."

"His passing," reiterates Gail, "is not to dominate the conversation at this celebratory meal, celebrating old friends."

Viva leans across the length of the table toward the widow. "Then why even bring the ashes, Trina?"

Trina digs in her purse again. Did she forget to pack some refuge in there? She speaks into the depths of the bag: "Who said I brought the ashes?"

"The ashes that you've left for safety in the car with the dogs?" suggests Viva.

"Here's the bigger question," retorts Trina. "Maybe it's one you've never asked yourself. What is the purpose of you being here? I mean, I can surmise that Paul invited you in hopes that you would luridly describe your past activities with my dead husband in a way that would relieve Paul of the need to besmirch him. Seriously though, what do *you* hope to gain from playing Paul's puppet?"

Viva gleams, pleased to have been spoken to directly and at such length.

"I have my reasons," she teases. "Do I need to announce them? Do you think I'm hiding something? I'm not about secret agendas and concealed motives. Paul made it sound like there would be a place for me here, and a chance to get what I want."

"This is a shared event," concedes Paul. "It has all the trappings of a shared event, I admit. But it also gives a unique opportunity for a private experience."

Chase takes a big swallow of alcoholic beverage. She takes a gobble of food. "Anyone who attends," explains Chase, "has the option to internalize and individualize and…" She searches for a meaningful word. "*Inculcate* a unique impression and memory." Chase detects that Paul's eyes have softened on her. Even Gail has relaxed the curled contempt of her lip. Progress is being made! Chase is excited. She gulps wine despite knowing she is cut out to be a sipper. She slathers peppercorn sauce on the landed portion of her surf and turf. She knows the sauce is too rich for her system. She splashes more wine into her goblet and tosses the red stuff in after the fatty steak.

Viva bats her lashes at Chase's excesses. "I am a past romantic interest to the departed," says Viva, "whether or not you believe me. That makes me an appropriate participant at the ashes party."

"Ashes party," intones Gail. "That is a mischaracterization."

"When I receive my portion of the ashes," says Viva, "there will be no mischaracterizing what I do with them."

"Let me catch up here," says Chase. She swallows quickly, twice. "You think you deserve some of these ashes? I mean, personally, I wouldn't mind if you take them all."

Gail and Mandy laugh heartily and briefly.

"I think," Paul thinks out loud, "Chase is showing her alcohol."

"I had a romantic connection with Allan M—," Viva insists. "Short-lived but long remembered, and documented in his book. Surely that entitles me to a portion of his remains. To disperse or to memorialize as I see fit."

"By that logic," reasons Gail, "his first wife should be sent a pill bottle full of—"

"I talked to the first wife," says Viva. "She washes her hands of him in any form."

"You tracked down his first wife?" exclaims Mandy. A gob of pork belly exits her lips. "That is perverse. Wait a minute! Don't I remember reading somewhere that you two went down on each other?"

"I mean, personally," blurts Chase, "I wouldn't mind if you went down on them all."

Mandy plucks a bacon-wrapped scallop off Paul's plate. "Chase loves a running gag," she says.

"We all love a running gag," agrees Paul.

Emboldened, Chase takes the brash and contrary action of helping herself to a third serving of the wine Paul had ordered for Viva, finishing off the bottle. Paul observes this excess darkly. "Maybe all the comic relief is too soon for Trina," he says. "She hasn't welcomed back her sense of humor yet."

"Trina, honey. You're so quiet," says Gail, also darkly. "You're playing the ominous card a little hard."

"It really hurts me to say it, T," says Mandy, "but what Paul says is true and fair. I feel that you're attaching too much dark drama. You're giving it power."

"I'm just sitting here wondering," says Trina, glaring toward the far end of the table, "when is she going to start in on me?"

"I have nothing to start on you for," says Viva, "even if you do decide to keep all that's left of him for yourself. How would Allan like it if I started in on you?"

"Okay," agrees Trina. "Then I guess it's time to order dessert and get this over with."

By now no one feels like sweets. Paul, Gail, and Mandy audit the check and assign Chase an amount to pay. Once outside, the group of friends and Chase and Viva amble toward Trina's Volvo. The two white dogs watch attentively against the windows.

"Do we still take the moonlight beach stroll to walk off dessert?" asks Chase. "Even though there was no dessert?"

Paul begs off. "I have a Skype date with Dieter."

Trina objects mildly: "You'll be with him back in LA for lunch tomorrow."

"Dieter really wants to talk tonight."

Mandy says, "I'm afraid Pepper has had enough excitement for one day."

"Pepper needs a pill," says Trina. "That dog is skittish because you keep coddling her."

"My dog is not skittish. She just doesn't want to go stumbling around in the dark."

Gail says simply, "I have business to take care of."

Trina turns her back to her friends and unlocks the Volvo. Bulger and Bardot bound out from their front-seat perch. These are eager animals. The rushing dogs put Trina's control to the test. Bulger takes a nip at the air between him and Chase, and lunges toward Mandy and Pepper the Pomeranian. Bardot growls and snaps at the Pomeranian and at Mandy in retreat.

"Your animals don't scare me," says Viva. "I could get along with these dogs. I feel very likeminded with them."

"If you're hinting around for an invitation to join us on the beach," says Chase, "it won't come."

Four car lengths up the sidewalk, two local community college dudes, Justin and Jason, and a chick they've known since grammar school lounge on the steps of a closed antiques shop. Casual and opportunistic, the locals keep watch on the weekenders, not fully interested. They see the short one with the red hair put a hand palm up to the butch lady's chest. If the locals moved a car length to the south, they might make out the short one's words.

"Can you excuse us a second, Chase?"

Pushing stalwart Chase back a step, the widow takes a private moment with Viva and the dogs. "You know already I won't give you any of his ashes," says Trina, quiet, mild, and firm in Viva's face.

"I suppose you're right," agrees Viva, equally mild. "I suppose you've guessed already that I'll be satisfied just to be present when you let him drift out to sea."

"Sure," says Trina, "and I trust you fully understand that when and if I decide to release the ashes, any company other than his dogs will be totally unacceptable to me."

Viva squats and looks Bulger's big head straight in the woeful, yearning eyes: "Well then, we are at an impasse."

NOW THAT I AM GONE

"I know a way to move beyond it."

Viva straightens slowly, showing strain, and braces as if against being physically shoved aside.

"Is everything okay over there?" calls Chase, ignored even by the trio of locals who are clocking every move as it plays out.

"Viva," says Trina, "or whatever name you want to choose, I found Polaroid photos of you. You're almost a child. In some of these pictures you're naked, fucking even."

"With him?"

Trina loosens the dogs' leads. The animals approach Viva and sniff her out.

"You look good," says Trina. "You both look good. It's easy to see why he kept them."

Viva lowers her guard, drops carefully to her knees, and the dogs nuzzle her face. Viva twists her mouth away from the two dog tongues. "It's almost as if you're about to offer me something of value," she says.

"It's something of him that will last, and he's with you. Think of it more as a gift rather than a trade."

"A meaningful memento. That's fair to you?"

"Text an address to Paul for me. Don't tell Paul what it's about. I'll send them to that address."

Viva stands, with pain, and steps back from the dogs. There's no call to shake Trina's hand or embrace. The touch with the dogs has been contact enough.

"By the way," says Trina, "you're going to see you were mistaken about that penis on your phone being his. The evidence is incontestable."

"I may have confused things. That's entirely likely."

The locals watch Viva detach herself from the other two women and walk off in a lone direction. There was a time, a number of years in a row for instance, when Viva was highly desirable. The locals can tell. Viva was a widely attractive woman. But the car she buckles herself into, which starts on the second try, communicates clearly that this lady's glory years have not paid off in a comfortable future.

"The punk rock lady is so much older than forty," says the local girl, taking a cigarette from the lips of one of the boys, Jason. "She's ruining that slip-as-a-dress look for the rest of us."

"Jealous much, Snake Hips?" asks Justin.

"Hey, I thought we weren't going to call her 'Snake Hips' anymore," says Jason.

With effort and using both hands, Trina wrangles Bulger and Bardot under control. She drops the key to her car. Jumpy and jerky, Chase is hyper vigilant at Trina's side, on the gallant lookout for an opportunity to be of use, to make her move toward indispensability. Trina's car key lands silently in a soft hump of sand beside the car's front tire. In her eagerness to assist with the dogs, Chase misses the key dropping. A casual observer would have seen the whole thing.

The local chick and Justin and Jason watch Trina and Chase walking the two dogs across the sand toward the waterline. Snake Hips says, "You guys both saw that key drop, didn't you?"

"Sure we did," say the two guys.

"But neither one of you ran up and said, 'Excuse me, miss! You've dropped your vehicle's key.'"

"I done my good deed for the day when I gave you that cigarette," says Jason.

"Look over there!" says Justin. "The big one is hitting on the little one."

"Nah," says Jason. "Those two ladies are arguing. The dogs are not into it."

Chase double-arm yanks Bardot's leash, and the locals feel the pronged collar bite into the dog's neck. Bardot digs her teeth into Chase's thigh.

"Wow, that's so cool," says Snake Hips.

Chase shouts: "I'm bleeding!"

Trina looks away. "It's nothing."

"This could be serious."

"You're making a big thing out of something that is almost nothing." Trina holds both dogs and looks out toward the deep water. Behind her, Chase vomits on the sand.

Chase fans sand over her bile and the chewed, undigested mass. "I ate too much rich food," she mumbles. Both dogs turn up their noses.

Snake Hips puts on her most reasonable face. "You guys should look in the car," she reasons. "See if there's anything good to steal. Maybe there are drugs. Or a gun."

"You're a dope, Snake Hips," says Justin.

On the beach, all focus and concentration is lost. Even the dogs aren't paying attention. "I'll leave the car parked where it is," says Trina. The motel lot is only twenty-five yards away.

The widow has lost her visualization of the urn containing the physical remains of her husband. The streamlined stainless object sits on the Volvo's backseat. The thing is not identifiable right away as the thing it is. It appears to be a valuable thing, a thing that would have great personal worth. Snake Hips immediately recognizes a precious quality intrinsic to the urn. She clutches the object beneath her windbreaker cool against her skin.

Trina places her shoulders under Chase's armpit, on the side of the thigh bite. The stricken woman breathes sharply and is delighted with the olfactory treats that inhalation carries with it. Chase savors Trina's scent and thinks: *Maybe this cloud has a silver lining.*

"Whenever things get this far down," she grumbles, "they start looking up again." Chase's bitten leg rubs against Trina's thigh with every step. They walk ribcage to ribcage.

"The important thing," says Trina, "is we need to get you back to the room. So you can clean yourself up." The room contains two beds separated by, Trina is happy to note, a space of floor covered in dog beds.

Snake Hips slinks away from the Volvo. The two local boys trail after. "What did you get?"

"Now you're curious. Now that the work is done."

Snake Hips ditches these guys. She takes the canister home. Her older sister is asleep and her mother is out. Snake Hips grabs her sister's car, a red Geo bought used, and drives a couple of small beach towns to the south, to Los Osos. Snake Hips is looking for an acquaintance, Samson, an older dude who is more daring and more knowing than the hometown kids she has so rapidly outgrown.

Samson can often be found holding court to an imaginary friend or two on the bus bench outside the Merrimaker bar. That's where Snake Hips finds him. His most distinguishing feature is a pair of dark, square sunglasses that fit on his face like a viewfinder. Snake Hips lowers the Geo's window and calls out above the cover band music leaking from the Merrimaker: "Hey, Samson! I got something here. You might be interested in it."

"Chick, I had what you got so many times, I can't imagine what you might do to make me interested again." But Samson has lifted himself from the wooden bench and ambled the few yards to the idling Geo. He leans on the Geo's roof. Snake Hips flashes the cylinder at the car window line and sees it reflect like a blunted artillery shell in Samson's viewfinder shades. "Wanna play with toys?"

"Let me see that tube," says Samson. He hefts the polished steel. "Whoever made this," he assesses, "was serious about it coming out well, and that's a good sign."

"How come?"

"Because, darling, this is a smuggling device. And the better made it is, the better the quality of the goods being smuggled."

"Used for smuggling what?" asks Snake Hips. "I'm not fully convinced."

"All we need to do is break the seal and I'll prove it to you."

Snake Hips drives with Samson slouched in the Geo's passenger seat. Samson holds his cigarette out the open passenger window. He directs Snake Hips to pull into a Los Osos alley. "Park it here. By the trash cans behind that burned house."

"Isn't that the house where—" begins Snake Hips.

"That's the house," says adventurous Samson. "As soon as we see what we own, we can knock on the back door and trade up. Leave your car lights on."

In the glow of the Geo, Samson and Snake Hips squat in the rutted alley. Samson extracts a thick folding knife from his pants and uses its serrated edge to pry open the seal on the modernist, streamlined urn. He dips a finger into the opening, places the ashen fingerprint to his tongue and tastes. Snake Hips watches Samson's viewfinder shades closely. Nothing happens. The daring, knowing dude tastes again: chalky and dusty, flaky and sandy.

A full and fully awake intelligence lights up what Snake Hips can see of Samson's face. "Oh my God. I know what this stuff is."

"What is it?" asks Snake Hips. She has suspicions.

"This is ash. They use ash to smuggle jewels. Like loose diamonds mostly, sometimes emeralds. Very rarely pearls."

Samson sifts through the ashes and finds no gems sticking to the narrowly separated digits of his empty, grasping hands. A stray breeze scatters the ashes in the alley behind the burned house.

"I was really hoping to be high by now," says Snake Hips.

"I'm pretty sure we can trade this casing for a hit. It could be repurposed."

"Or melted down," says Snake Hips.

There is no real wind to mention. The ashes lift for a moment, slanting skyward as if the ground beneath them had exhaled. The moment stalls, and the movement of the ashes in the breeze stalls. It's as if the packed dirt on the surface is sucking air back in, a long, slow inward rasp. The airborne particles filter down and settle among the alley debris, clumping up, adhering to the damp matter, caught in the muddy tracks.

In the lapse between moments, in the time it takes for Samson's sunglasses to come off and for his pupils to recoil from the Geo lights, my remains are absorbed by the muck and turned into grime.

11

SOME THINGS I DON'T MIND NEVER KNOWING AGAIN

I WAS IN A hospital. I wasn't really there for my own benefit. Conflict and tension informed my every interaction with the staff. I'd accompanied a poorly feeling friend. Not a friend, exactly, a very close acquaintance who was scheduled for an invasive diagnostic procedure that required a full-body anesthetic. The waiting area was a densely populated spread of uncomfortable chairs peopled by complaint and pained endurance. An afflicted individual deserving of gentle care could easily be lost in there.

Somebody unhealthy did something rude and pushy and was unattractive and gave off an odor and coughed and sneezed without doing anything to diminish the dispersion of their condition. There were no open windows only ventilation ducts recycling everything we were all exhaling. The staff expected me to stay for more of this treatment. I wheeled my comatose friend out of the recuperative setting without telling anyone I was leaving. My reasoning behind my actions was direct and to my mind self-evident: "I don't mind if I never see this place again," I explained. "Or any of these people either. Never again."

Against medical advisement, we trundled my patient into the car and shifted the transmission into drive. Traffic bunched up immediately outside the hospital driveway. Stifling quantities of all sorts of cars pressed nose to tailpipe. The vehicular chain of stalled souls; that's one more earthly connection I will not mind severing. Not one bit.

Ultimately, I'm in the car driving, thinking about myself quietly. No words come out. Really, what is there to say? The person in the passenger seat has just undergone a medical procedure disruptive enough to be placed in the custody of an able driver. As an able driver, I have nothing to say to the experience of a disruptive medical procedure. My passenger seems to notice nothing. I've turned left from Los Feliz Boulevard onto Fern Dell Drive, heading up into Griffith Park. I'm loaded down with this invalid who gives me no hope of finding anything good playing on the radio. I might as well be driving alone.

So I'm entertaining myself with freeing notions. For instance, I picture the hospital and the people in it as the tip of an iceberg of people and things I will not mind never seeing again. That cools me as I navigate the access road into Griffith Park, looking for a place to stop the car, ticking off parking spot after parking spot filled with annoying cars that are not mine.

Be patient and your reward will appear. You catch sight of an open slot, swing in, and slam on brakes. The car skids and jolts. You have avoided running over a grimly smug young biddy standing deep in the otherwise empty parking stall, arms crossed. Your car rocks back and its motion stills. The woman standing between the yellow diagonal parking lines extends one hand the full length of her arm, palm up. "This spot is taken," she shouts into your windshield. She recrosses her arms.

High on the tip of that iceberg of people and things I will not mind never seeing again? A person who stands in a parking spot to claim it for an automobile that is not present. My patient stricken beyond recuperation stirs in the passenger seat. "So, to summarize," sums up the invalid, "you're behind the wheel in a car. She is a person standing in a spot reserved for cars, not set aside for standing persons."

Convention and municipal codes obligate you to abandon this contested position and drive on. Don't lower your window and reason with the human pylon. Do not put the vehicle into park and shut it off.

Never get out of the car and escalate the discussion to the level of heated argument. Move along. Keep your eyes out of the rearview mirror. You need never again see this flesh-and-hubris obstacle to shutting off your motor and easing your ailing passenger to an upright position and communing at a snail's pace beneath the Griffith Park tree canopy for what might conceivably be one last time.

Forget your nature stroll. Look forward, up the road to where all future parking places are occupied. What do you see? You see that your only visible chance to pull off the pavement is at your side right now, and a smirking trespasser showing you the palm of her hand has thwarted that parking opportunity. Do not validate her presence with a second thought.

That last thought leads to another, which is what thoughts do, until finally they don't: Your life's trajectory, you think, is on a one-way streak. You are rolling on fast tracks into a cul-de-sac. You are speeding head on into a dead end. You will crash straight through. You are beyond medical intervention. You are about to enter that region of no return on the far side of the dead end. You will occupy an outland. You'll never encounter anyone on this side ever again. The facts of departure have been determined. You won't be coming back. The tipping point has tumbled. It's just this one last time. Go ahead. Let the confrontation in the park play out. Give yourself permission to run over the entitled placeholder.

You hit the accelerator, twist the wheel, and feel her legs fold under your bumper. Her body crumples beneath your auto carriage. Your tires bounce, and you hear bones crunch. Your senses are alive with the truth: this parking spot is yours.

So-called reasonable people might condemn your actions. Who are these monsters? I won't mention any names. It behooves no one to speak ill of the living. But let me hand out some general identifiers. You may not be able to place the names to the faces, but it's helpful to be able to spot these limiting, censorious, self-serving, falsely magnanimous prigs as soon as they've targeted you, before they've asserted their prerogative to be helpful:

An empty-eyed smiling goblin, insultingly robust, leads me to a rigid, comfortable, form-fitting chair. I could almost fall asleep. I almost relax. An arc light descends, obliterating the horizon. I take a deep breath and pretend I am dead. My mouth is stretched open and probed and drilled. I have not once wished a trip to the dentist could happen again. I will never miss seeing the last of that trade's tools and trappings.

At the auto mechanic's waiting area, the smells are toxic. The shop TV is always broadcasting some disheartening thing. Why must cars break down? Why are automobiles not better designed than human teeth? I don't mind missing out on car breakdowns. I don't mind missing breakdowns in the teeth. I don't mind doing without breakdowns.

Photos of cruelty to animals are evidence of another thing I won't mind never seeing again. I don't mind never seeing another person who is cruel or indifferent to the lesser (sic) beasts, and I won't miss the hateful humanitarians who insert these heinous images onto my screens.

I've also stomached more than I could ever wish to swallow again of the public big mouth, the high-volume intellectual braggart lecturing a clerk or a mute date or some other unwitting accomplice in the bookstore or record shop, holding the innocent, mild customers hostage with half-shouted esoteric cultural observations intended to establish his loud aesthetic superiority. Big mouth has contacts and does not mind dropping their names. He has discussed inside baseball, you and everyone else in the premises should know, with real established baseball insiders.

The public big mouth trumpets his empty breath and obliterates your peace of mind. He wants to fill the quiet space with nonstop language that indicates he is the keeper of special secrets. But no one so loud has ever kept a secret. This guy—he's almost always a guy—is probably not a college professor. Maybe he plays one in the recesses of his imagination. He is impervious to the reality that no one in this enclosed public space has signed up for his lecture. And here I am, lurking at the back of class, wondering why I didn't have the foresight to ditch it so I could go on listening to myself undisturbed, and, *Oh, wait! This guy up front, the one I'm complaining about with the big, empty voice, that guy is me!*

What a relief to know that I won't miss him when I am me no more.

A therapist's office is a place I don't mind never resorting to again. I signed up for the guided and mindful exploration of emotional complexities. I gamely talked through the ungainly topics and wrote the checks to become a better person. I wanted less anguish to be produced during my interactions with other people. My hope, my suspicion, was that other people could do better. My big unanswered—repeatedly asked—question about psychotherapy is, "How do I get other people to do better?"

"But people don't change," explained my therapist. "That's the secret you must grasp."

I got it, right away. "No amount of money and emotional investment can purchase an improved personality?" I said this in an accusatory tone, one that I won't mind never hearing out of my mouth again. "I have put in so much effort and money trying to bring about the impossibility of changing who I am," I said.

"Get your mind off yourself," said the therapist, as a parting shot. "Think about someone else once in a while during your life."

And here I am with my mind on someone else: my patient, the wheezing bundle of invalidated vitality in my passenger seat. I won't miss these declining days leading up to bidding that person good and final riddance. "Remember when you were young?" asks my passenger. "It was already too late. You're at the mall. You're at the middle school. You're in the Ivy League. You see brats marching along in their parents' image; cold eyes open to their own inherent, infallible, unchallenged excellence. Their parents could not be prouder."

No, I think, silently, in the car, *I will not miss the common parent*.

"The typical parent is by no means the worst parent," interjects my pained passenger. The patient's vigor is so last ditch it's obscene. "The super parent is the one to dread. The super parent imposes its will on a couple of kids and a spouse, and that domination only whets the super parent's appetite for control. The super parent needs to subjugate a bunch of us, as many of us as can be bent and broken."

The time in the hospital seems like it was from another lifetime. The morning is gone. Those waiting room hours do in fact belong to another lifetime. My passenger makes a face to illustrate a shift in shape. "Not all super parents have kids. A super parent's biological imperative is to discipline everyone else. These are the ambitious individuals who rise and thrive, like sociopaths, like politicians. Are you listening to me?"

I'm wedging the overheating car into a makeshift spot on the furthest, least-convenient reaches of Fern Dell, at the fringes of the dry city oasis that is Griffith Park. "I'm paying attention," I say.

"Why do the pricks keep pricking?" demands my fading charge from the passenger seat. "The House of Prick has won. The Family Prick has taken all the good stuff and claimed all the desirable places. Isn't that prize enough? The vast supermajority of us is made up of thoroughly beaten losers. What greater satisfactions do super prick Mom and Dad need?"

The car is finally parked. "Some malignant life force pushes the victors on and on and on. They need to be exceptional. They need to trample. These marauders raise their families to steadfastly maraud on, to extend the tradition of domination, to strengthen the elite position."

Did you really believe I had run over a human being for a parking spot? While a patient convalesced in my passenger seat? Swift retribution is tempting, but I'm headed for the long haul, the forever trip. I've done the right thing, and I'm paying for it once again. My passenger is peckish. "I can't believe you are making me walk so far. Do you have children? You behave like a person who has children."

"Maybe a snack and a beverage will help," I suggest.

"Sure. A coffee and a cake before I go."

Griffith Park has an on-premises café, a shed at the low hub of trailheads rising into the hills. Plying sustainable and organic foodstuffs, the café is called Trails, short for Trails Café. Parents who are very taken with being parents flock to Trails, along with their defining accessories, the kids. Many of the kids really are creeps already.

One of these parents is Colin Cowboy. Although he is impossible to miss or mistake in his always tasteful but incongruous tailored Western wear, Colin and I agree to pretend we don't know one another. Our current worlds share no tenable point of intersection. I could feel slighted, but I am happy to shield the company I'm keeping from Cowboy's kid, a sullen boy who exhibits signs of doom, and Colin's wife, the kid's mom, who displays signs of humble brag work talk.

Colin's wife is trim and proudly self-denying. In some bodily aspect that is impossible to pinpoint by inspecting her physical self, Colin's wife is excellent. Her costume is frumpy but costly, loose and forgiving other than in the area of her painstakingly sculpted buttocks. She proudly bemoans how excessively over budget the remodel of their meditation room has gone. "But the husband is into it…"

"Now that he's come home again," says a sotto voice friend.

"He's not home that much," confides the wife. "He's working on a big movie."

The patient, the one I've taxied from the hospital to the park for the healing shade of the tree canopy, has something more to say. When a fading acquaintance wants to put words into their last wheeze, who am I to say save it for later? "I don't mind never seeing a big movie again," says the patient, my designated passenger. "The big movies are bad idea movies—big bad loud ideas. They are so earnest and so condescending and delivered at such a surplus of decibels. The only thing you wonder while you watch is could no one turn that noise down, step up to the ham in charge and say, 'By the way, this is turning out dreadful, and we should have seen it coming'?

"You can't dash the ham in charge's dreams. You can't rain on the ham's Oscar contention parade. A lot of people get paid to march in that parade."

The patient has Trails Café food at hand, a quiche, a jar of granola-infused yogurt, a hot dog, a piece of pie. The patient cannot eat. The patient places the food in the center of the picnic table and takes up a cup of coffee. The patient blows on the milky dark fluid. "The big idea is to line their pockets with ungodly gains while giving the masses a gross unwatchable falsehood. The movie world's greatest contributions to society are income inequality, pessimism, and mass-scale social retardation. Establishing a buffered so-called creative class whose elitism is based on degrading the national narrative—let's put on an entire season of awards shows for that.

"These people should shoot themselves in the wincing face. This rancid shit they smear on the screen pays for their wives' meditation-room redesigns. The wife can enthrone and light one of her curated turds as if it's incense. I see her now, meditating on her stench and praising that particulate reek as if her shit is a big-idea, big-movie too. These people are leeches." The patient puts the coffee to the table, pushes it aside. None of that coffee has been sipped or swallowed.

"Think of all the movies we enjoyed together," I remind the patient, gently. "Remember how we bonded watching characters who showed us who we could be? How we should act?"

The patient gives the coffee another try and spits out what he tastes. "Look where that's landed us."

"But sitting in a dark enclosure full of other people, each of you totally alone and secondary to projected lives none of you can really touch, hasn't that experience given some preparation for what's happening to you now?"

"Clearly, you are not on my side." The patient pushes all the Trails Café snacks across the tabletop to me, as if they might be poisoned. No, it's like they are his last stacks of poker chips, and he's going all in. "From now on, until the end, I will close only one eye at a time."

"You look super attentive squinted up like that. What are you listening for?"

"I hear a buzz."

Four or five years ago, swarms of seasonal bees attracted by littered pie plates and pastry crumbs overran the picnic area around Trails. Now, a lone wasp zipping along the condiments counter scatters screaming kids and activates the consciously parenting parents. The women blanket the children beneath protective layers of mom jackets and dad parkas. The men band together and chase away the insect.

"I do miss bees," muses the patient. "Do you remember the masses of bees? I miss buzzing and honey and hives. I miss pollinated flora. Even the bee stings are something I might miss. Bee stings usually happen to someone else. When that occurs, they pay out a high-value entertainment dividend."

Colin Cowboy is not entertained. He is the stung human, and he has a terrible allergy. His throat swells and constricts. He loses his ability to speak. Colin is afraid, clearly, but he remains still. Stillness is essential to his survival. His eyes and gestures communicate with ferocious silence that stillness is demanded from all in his vicinity.

This particular bee sting is a thing I would hate to have missed.

Colin's wife is calm. So calm that perhaps she is beyond emotional investment in her husband's survival. She activates her phone. She takes immediate actions. She pushes the correct code numbers. Colin's kid had been quiet and sullen and is being a voluble asshole as a siren rises, approaches, and whirs into nothing. Men wearing threadbare uniforms and latex gloves settle Colin upon a stretcher and stuff him into an ambulance. Colin's wife stands at the ambulance doors, one hand on each latch, ready to slam them shut.

"Would you like to ride back here?" asks the ambulance attendant. "There's space."

Colin's eyes beg for company, and to hurry up about that decision. Colin's wife deliberates. She looks at the kid. She looks at her Trails Café parent friends.

"I'll be happy to hang on to the boy for a few hours," offers my passenger, "if that will help."

"I guess I'll take my child and follow along in our car," says Colin's wife.

The ambulance does not wait for Colin's wife. She collects her belongings and walks her child to the family car, parked in a spot she had stood tall and firm to reserve. Colin's wife reasons with her child to fasten his seatbelt. She backs from the parking spot, reverses direction, and drives with deliberate caution. She has lost track of the emergency vehicle.

Inside the ambulance, a freckle-faced attendant delivers a shot and breaks the news to Colin. "Just breathe," she says. "You can relax now. The worst is over."

Colin believes her. Air comes easier into his lungs, and a new certainty has set up in his mind: he will go through with the divorce. Claxons chart the ambulance's progress through the streets of East Hollywood. The vehicle runs red lights, fights the flow on one-way blocks, and muscles to a stop against a priority curb directly in front of the doors to a medical trauma unit.

"Thank you," says Colin. *I am still young*, he thinks. He has another whole life ahead of him. A stretcher on spring loaded struts clatters from the ambulance's cargo bay. Colin hits the pavement rolling and is deposited inside of a hospital.

There is no pain in seeing Colin wheeled through those sliding glass doors and no point in following. The next time a hospital space will contain me is never again. I don't mind.

12

A DREADFUL AFTERLIFE

O H, HELL. IT'S MY birthday again. It seems to always and forever be my birthday. The birthday work shift will be particularly long and awkward, in part because my coworkers are all much younger than me, decades younger in fact.

Back-to-back meetings stretch a pall across the morning and forenoon office hours. Midlevel management weasels have impressions to make. The weasels make those impressions by droning on in snide and vague and pointed exhortations that are more accusatory than motivational.

Shoulder-to-shoulder, our hands motionless on the surface of a polished conference table, my coworkers and I listen with a mix of anxiety and torpor like incest victims at a family dinner. Email *pings* my work inbox, *pings* and *pings*. Every *ping* represents an incisive question from a covert threat that requires a considered response. In the meeting room, plans and strategy are being mapped out for an outward-facing rebranding and an internal restructuring. That's not my department. It's also not the department of my coworkers, who sit shoulder-to-shoulder, hands motionless on the polished conference table surface.

The management team responsible for scheduling all these overlapping meetings calls a time out. The bosses contract into a congratulatory huddle, and all my young colleagues invite me to join them for a quick off-campus lunch, my obligatory birthday lunch. "Wasn't my birthday lunch just yesterday?" I joke.

My shot at humor hits a blank spot. Youth regards me vacantly. "Yesterday was Sunday," they say. "Did you forget?"

Actually, now that I think about it, I do not remember Sunday as yesterday. In fact, no recent Sunday comes to mind. If the email inbox on my phone were to ever pause in its *ping*ing, I might find a moment to take a breath and realize that this absence of a memorable Sunday troubles me. I decide not to mention my lapse in Sunday recall. I'm afraid my coworkers will only mistake my worry for another misfired shot at humor.

A nearby restaurant that fits our budgets seats our group on the outdoor patio. My colleagues are all sun deprived. If someone has a tan, it's a faded tan. Pasty here, pale, papered. I take a chair on the outer rim of the restaurant's al fresco seating area. The patio backs up against the public sidewalk. Automobile traffic inches parallel to the sidewalk, jammed on the boulevard heading across town, stalled at my elbow. The day is warm and still and shimmering in exhaust. The obscure sun will never burn through again.

"If we were naked, the age discrepancy between Allan and everyone else would be even more grotesque," says someone at the table, not sure who. Could I have been thinking out loud?

I've jolted awake, as if I'd been sleeping while driving, but that cannot be. Don't ask me to pinpoint the last time I was able to sleep. I'm sitting in a meeting called by a midlevel manager who has no direct command over me. Zero windows open the conference room to the outside world. Along with ten employees twenty years my younger, my role in this meeting is to say nothing contradicting the misapprehensions, misdirection, and disinformation being white boarded by the midlevel manager.

The work email inbox *pings* again and again on my telephone in my pocket, directly above my heart. I think of my children. As always when I think of my children, I think: *Why did I have children?* The children are as blanched as the colleagues. The children are headed for more of the same of what I have failed to escape.

There *is* some consolation, so I have been told, and I share that opinion. The consolation is that I have begun this new job, a fantastic new job. I am very fortunate to have landed this wonderful opportunity. I am reminded of my good fortune in a text from one of my immediate superiors. I am not at liberty to reply to her text because I am stuck in crosstown traffic.

I may yet become an optimist, if time permits. The first step is recognizing I was not always so lucky. My boss, Robyn, is a spot of different in company cultures and office landscapes. Recently turned forty, only one-point-eight decades my younger, the boss is thin and yoga fit and on-point stylish with an edge. She is tall; her hair is short. Facially, her features are symmetrical, confident and direct. On the whole, my colleagues tend to be unfulfilled, a little mean, competitive, and dismissive. But we are all elite. "Only elite people work here," Robyn reminds me. "Here where it never sucks." I leave my boss's office feeling as though I have just been given a personal pep talk. That high doesn't last.

Defying all logic and decency, some employees at the new fantastic workplace operate with less than absolute gratitude. A minority woman who graduated from Yale has been pulled from her order-fulfillment job to clean out the employee refrigerator. Her expression, toiling over putrefied veggie wraps and a ferment of forgotten kombucha shakes, is openly critical of the industry we toil in. "I would like to thank the enlightened white man who invented cause marketing," she says.

We are in the closed kitchen area, me, her, and one other dark-skinned lady. "If there is a God," says the other lady, "why was there not a preemptive stroke before the 'corporate social responsibility' brainstorm?"

There is something familiar and disturbing about this grousing. I can't quite place where, but I have an uneasy sense of disgruntled voices in the background and below the surface noise at my previous new fantastic job. I'm in the conference room, on my own all alone. And I'm wondering: *Why did Robyn single me out for a pep talk? Do I seem like a person who needs extra help?*

The white board stands empty and blank and unattended. There's something I'm missing. I am not seeing what everybody else sees. My email inbox *pings* and *vibrates*, indicating exceptional urgency. Robyn has sent a text message. "Have you forgotten something?" I really want to be transparent and honest with her, but honestly where to begin? "Everyone is here in the downstairs war room," types Robyn, "except you."

Now I remember. The company's CEO has scheduled an all-hands meeting, mandatory for all employees, superseding all other meetings. I'm in the elevator, going down, and my email is always *ping*ing. The number of unopened emails is stacking higher and higher. It's almost like I am out of sight behind the stacked emails. No one admits to seeing me enter the downstairs war room.

The CEO stresses that this socially responsible cause-marketing company, the one that has extended my new amazing job to me, is a more ethical and fair and world-improving company than any company any of us have ever worked with before. "And yet I have heard negative chattering," he says. He stands silent. His lips purse in disapproval and disappointment, like a high school principal speaking to a disruptive advance-placement class. "Disgruntled voices are at odds with the culture here."

The CEO's tacit warning raises troubling musings. Will my attentive presence with the two dark-skinned women in the kitchen characterize me in the narratives of the CEO's snitches as an ingrate who complains as he butters his company-supplied breakfast toast? For whatever perceived faults, the new great job is much better than the previous great job. An awkward encounter slightly beyond my perception happens during the dispersal of the all-hands office function, and I end up in my boss's office.

"I've been told," says Robyn, "that you need to make small talk, to mingle and blend and bind."

"I've become almost chatty with two of the ladies who work in the kitchen."

"The implication is that you should aim up. Curry favor with the founder, with the investor, and with the men who run the place, not just with their secretaries and administrative assistants." My boss's eye contact demands that I acknowledge the severity of her messaging. In any other context imaginable, Robyn is very pretty. We are both late for our next meetings.

My hands are always motionless on the polished wood table surface. Work stacks up. *Ping. Ping. Ping.* "Wait, everyone, can we pause here?" asks my boss's direct boss. This boss is the only person who has been talking. "I want to find out what Allan thinks about all this."

What I'm thinking about is: *I can respond to my work emails when I get home. I will feed the dogs and put the kids to bed and kiss the wife goodnight and finally address my inbox.* I make this vow or a version of it several times each day, at my desk, at the conference table, in my car, but I never reach home.

My wife, I know by now, is not at the apartment waiting for me. The children's needs have not been tended to. My own dinner is something I could stop at a drive-thru and wait for on the route home, but the children's needs have not been tended to.

This is not the first fantastic new job opportunity that I have been very fortunate to land. I have been lucky before. That luck did not end well. A catastrophic turnabout had torpedoed the previous fantastic opportunity. The company had brought in a marketing strategist. Her name was Sandra Sands. Sandra's tenure began innocently enough. The usual contradictory proclamations, empty air theories, hollow fact-like pronouncements. The expected selecting of scapegoats who are subsequently driven to termination.

One day I inadvertently corrected a misapprehension expressed by marketing strategist Sandra Sands. The misapprehension had been all mine. I'd mistaken tactic for error. That's a fault I'd never recovered from, and the next time the need for a scapegoat arose, I was fitted to the role. Scapegoats do not have second acts. But life is good and makes good on dealing out redemptive second chances. Life had given me a new role at a new job!

I have been summoned to my boss Robyn's office again. The eyes and the hold of her mouth indicate she is a person who is not sleeping particularly well or long or trouble free. "They have hired someone to be on a parallel track with me without consulting me," says Robyn, my immediate and clear superior. "I think you have worked with *her* before."

Maintaining a fixed smile and eye contact with Robyn, I run a review of the great women I've worked with at previous golden opportunities. I visualize the joy of reuniting with each or any one of them.

"Her name," says Robyn, "is Sandra Sands."

Is this cruel symmetry? Or is it a vicious cycle? The previous great job, and then Sandra Sands arrived. The current great job, and now Sandra Sands arrives. On her first day at the new job, I greeted Sandra before anyone else did: "Welcome, Sandra. Congratulations. I predict you will really like it here."

"If you think that being grandfathered in at this company will protect you," she replied, "you are mistaken." No, wait. I may be conflating. That may be something she said to me at the first great job we worked together.

My coworkers and I settle in for another meeting. Sandra Sands is the person who has called the meeting. Before getting to business, Sandra and an ally talk about how much they love their children, how family comes first.

"Shouldn't Robyn be here?" asks someone, out of line, not me.

"Robyn has decided to spend more time with her family," says Sandra Sands.

The company that has extended my new awesome job releases a film that dramatizes the plight and struggle of domestic workers of color in the backward and repressive American South of the 1960s. The movie has a strong opening weekend. To celebrate the movie's profit forecast and the principles championed by it, a Monday breakfast event is staged in the office's executive kitchen.

"How was your weekend?" someone asks, and I grasp how fast it has gone, so fast that those two elapsed days would be illusory except that I know better.

The Yale graduate is among three people of color at the crowded breakfast event celebrating a film that champions civil rights triumphs. Each of these three people of color is either serving bagels to white people or cleaning up cream cheese spilled by white people. These circumstances and their observation would be forced and a cliché except they are so freely given. I think about this chromatic dissonance during the traffic jam toward work. I have not slept a night through since learning that Sandra Sands is on the way. Now, of course, she is here. A time when Sandra Sands was not on the scene no longer exists.

People sell things from the curbs and the street corners—foodstuffs, kitchen gadgets, novelty garments. These street vendors are often a darker color than I am. Nothing they are selling seems to be worth rolling down the car window to buy. They can't be making a living. My teeth hurt from having clenched them throughout the nights that I do not sleep away. The pain in my mouth is the only sensory evidence I have, really, of lying in bed. During the traffic jam on the way home from work, my children's faces come to me. "Do not lose your job, Daddy," pleads the youngest, innocent and fearful, filling my rearview mirror. "What will come of us if you bring us no money?"

"You are so old, Daddy," taunts the eldest, knowing and aggrieved, pushing the youngest from the mirror. "No one will hire you again." I've left the workplace late. Sandra Sands, my boss, had called me into her office. I replay the exchange: Sandra Sands told me that my previous boss's last day had been the day before.

"Ten hours a day?" says Sandra Sands. "Some people might feel ten hours a day is working hard. I don't want hard workers. I want passion. Passion does not stop at ten hours a day." How will I find time to visit a dentist? I am either in a meeting at work or jammed in traffic driving toward work or stalled in after-work gridlock headed toward home. My health insurance has a very high deductible and a stack of exclusions for dental procedures.

I'm in a long-term consumer-facing branding meeting. The work inbox on my phone cannot accept another incoming email. The human resources woman stands in the open doorway and uses a one-finger gesture to pull me out of the meeting. My young colleagues look toward places within the conference room that do not contain me.

The human resources woman points me to a chair, closes the door of her office, and presents a set of documents sealing the discontinuation of my employment at the fabulous, socially responsible corporation. "You don't have to sign these documents now," she says. "Take them home and study them. The company is granting a twenty-one-day review period."

Stripped of word traps, the documents state that in exchange for a set sum of money I will refrain from bringing a wrongful termination suit against the fabulous employer, now and in some enlightened future when I become aware of facts that prove I am being wrongfully terminated. Of all the days in the year, this is the day that has to be my birthday.

In a previous lifetime, I had recourse to a therapist. She had black hair and pale skin and brown eyes and she was about ten years older than me. If I'd seen her walking on the street, I would have been interested in her. Her office was muted and temperature controlled. The chair was soft, firm, and supportive. In a place of comfort and security, I would allow her voice to reach me. "Really, Allan, here and now. What are you afraid of? What possibly is there to be afraid of?"

Her voice is from a past that I haven't the concentration to recall with sufficient clarity to believe I have not invented it. In the awkward twist of the broken seat of my car, stuck in the unmoving clot of cars between the inhospitable apartment I live in and the warren of cubicles and glass front offices where my career goals go unmet and my efforts unappreciated, with the malfunctioning air conditioning and with traffic noises seeping in through the floorboards along with gases and detritus, of course there is something to be afraid of. I am afraid of the known. I am afraid of being fired again.

Sandra Sands sets up a mandatory exit debrief meeting. I sit across a conference table from Sandra and the human resources professional. "Well," says the human resources pro, "this is never easy."

"No one ever enjoys this part of the job," says Sandra Sands, holding in a laugh.

"I've brought the termination agreement," I say. "The documents are signed and ready."

"Oh, no," says the human resources professional, "those documents are nothing anymore. We'll shred those. We have new paperwork."

"But will I have twenty-one days to review the new documents?"

"You don't need twenty-one days," explains the human resources woman. "I'll tell you what's different. This paperwork includes a waiver of your right to sue for age discrimination."

"Even when I find out that I am being fired due to age discrimination?"

"Correct."

"This is a whole different agreement. The dollar sum should change."

"Seriously, Allan," says the human resources woman, "the company is under no obligation to extend any sum of money whatsoever. We can just rip this up right now, if that's what you'd prefer."

"I need to return to the living," says Sandra Sands. "So let me give my assessment, and I'll be on my way."

"That's fine," says the human resources woman.

"Allan," says Sandra Sands, smiling pleasantly, "I will not be surprised if you never work again. In my view, you are unhirable, and it's not just because you're old." One time, I dozed off in a meeting, only for a short duration. My children came to me in my sleep. They told me I am doomed and that their futures are shrouded in doom, my doom.

I have not mentioned it before, but there is a tunnel on my commute very close to the cut off for my home. Every time I approach this tunnel, it's as if I've never noticed the entrance before, but its shadows consume me upon entry, and the depths instantly seem very familiar. It's impossible to know how many times, even to roughly guess how many times, I've driven through this tunnel.

Driving into the tunnel, I console myself. I have been fired again by Sandra Sands. I have forfeited the three-week review period granted me in the termination agreement. I have signed away my option to argue age discrimination. I have forfeited the right to claim I have been wronged. But tonight, when my head thumps into a pillow, and an incoming email *pings* the work inbox, my livelihood, my self worth, the definition of my identity, my sense of purpose and belonging, my status, my very value and survival as a human entity will not depend on responding lucidly to that *ping*. I will have the luxury of sleeping through until the morning. I cannot begin to tell you when was the last time I waked with the morning. Where do I even imagine I would look for that information?

I am so tired that I feel it makes sense to rest my forehead on the top of my steering wheel. I bow my head, I close my eyes, and I misplace all sense of who I am. My head jolts on my neck. I'm hunched forward as my car emerges from the tunnel into diffused and tarnished sunlight. For a moment, I can't be certain if the day is beginning or winding down. I come alive into who I am, and I know that I am headed out for the day, but it feels as though I am on my way back in for the evening.

Against all odds, I have landed a refresher career. I have reinvented my workplace skill set in the employment of a fabulous forward-thinking company. My jaw aches and my teeth clench. The complaints of my children purr and throb with the sounds of the jammed traffic and my car's broken air-conditioning. I am well on the way to arriving late for the first day of work at my new great job.

Hope is alive again.

13

AN AFTERLIFE I COULD LIVE WITH

Traffic never snarls, and parking spots always land within a single circle of the block. My new car profiles like a lynx and snaps like a whip. All the same, thank you, I'll travel by foot. Warm after-rain breezes have swept the weather crystalline clear. Time is not pressing. My dog Mugger, the young, black-maw boxer, is here beside me on the rolling meadow pathways. The dog laps at droplets that bejewel the tufts of emerald grass. He's finally learned to walk along properly without a leash.

Lou Reed, the popular recording artist, cuts in front of me at the coffee counter, and I realize where I am. I'd lost track of myself again. It's as if when I'm strolling along with Mugger, misting units spray us with a cool, citrus essence. Our senses transport us into another world. We step into a slightly idealized upgrade of the existence I'd grown so familiar with. Attention naturally drifts away from you.

Lou Reed is looking young. I'm looking young. Reed is revisiting his peroxide ragamuffin look of the mid-1970s. My current presentation matches the best photos of myself from my early-twenties, except my skin has cleared up splendidly. The cruel glint and angry jaw have given way to hooded twinkle eyes and a half-ready smile. Snarl is still Lou Reed's defining lip-lock. He slides his steel-rim, black-lens shades up from his pinching nostrils and parks them above his knotted forehead. His hands slither out palms down on the countertop. Lou's shoulders hunch forward, and his sunken eyes drill into the defenseless skull of the soft-target barista.

I recognize the barista! Her name is Marina, the one called Pretty Marina. She's warm and centrally appealing. Her black hair is maybe not dyed, and her tattoos are colorful and tasteful. She's sly and sweet around her eyes; maybe ready to doze away, maybe ready to pop extra wide-awake, just like the last time I pictured her. On our first visit to this coffee stop, Mugger received a biscuit directly from Marina's lips to his. My regard for her has only grown ever since. "Marina's very nice," agrees Mugger. "She always has treats. She never makes us beg or perform silly tricks."

All the servers at this coffee bar are like Marina—friendly and very caring as a rule, always remembering to inquire about the wife, and swell dressers. They all carry ready treats for Mugger and never make him beg.

"I can see why you don't have a tip jar in this godforsaken way station," says Lou Reed. He's aiming for a snarl. It's coming out a whine. "Someone should tell you the customer is king. When the king walks into his domain, the king should be hailed."

Barista Marina sets Lou's drink on the bar. The brew wafts all aromatic and Arabic under his disdainful nose. "Here's your coffee," Marina says. "Your highness."

"Why should I accept what you decide to give me? I'm new here, but I will put on airs. I'm not afraid of being kicked out of this no-fuck dolt sanctuary."

Marina has a smile for making friends: "I look you over, your highness, and I see the king of chilled cappuccino."

"I'm just visiting; so you deny me the courtesy of hearing out my specific coffee requirements?"

"Milk to the bottom of the logo," says soft and gentle Marina, as if chanting a soothing spell. "Ice shaved not crushed, triple shot cold-brewed single-origin espresso, three levels of dry-chill foam layered on top."

Lou has staked out his high ground, and he's not coming down: "You people think you have a groovy thing going on here?" he says. "You're casting some kind of cool spell in some groovy kind of place?" Caustic enunciation aside, there's something to what Lou's saying. I, for instance, do seem to be under some cool kind of spell. The continuous emotional friction scratching out of me in all directions, the conflict points of quotidian existence, they all seem to have been abraded smooth, to have rubbed themselves into nothing. Fear, anxiety, anger, suspicion, envy, all scraped off my consciousness, rooted out of my subconscious, cleared from my viewfinder.

Marina slips me my coffee and waives my gesture toward the cash register. "Is this the day your wife's coming in?" she asks.

This question infuriates Lou Reed, and I restrict my answer to a smile of general affirmation. The wife's arrival time is the lone unknown variable. She and I have been apart for a bit, due to circumstances not choice. I'm looking forward to seeing her and touching her. My anticipations are high, apprehensions low.

I sip my double-shot Americano cut with a dollop of full-fat cream. Mugger licks biscuit crumbs from his fat smiling lips. We lounge in our favorite seats. Every seat in the place is our favorite. The expansive, panoramic vistas contain sea and tree, cloud-topped mountains, fauna of air and sod, nature all lush and sweet. Your senses can't help but drift off into the scenic distance. Don't ask me where those senses go. Every time I blink my eyes and find I've come back, I have no sense of where I have been.

In the absence of irritation, at times, more and more often it seems, I lose track. It's almost as if there is no me other than when I consciously will my separate individual to appear and be. The groovy part is that when he's here, when I appear to me, everyone—especially Mugger—acts as if I am making a special appearance. Everyone I run into knows the special thing about me: it's that everyone else I encounter is special as well, and I recognize that. Milling at the coffee bar, I hadn't pegged Lou Reed as the guy from the Velvet Underground. At first, I took him for just another special person.

Marina has come out from behind the counter and is humoring Lou: "You're in a chill zone, Lou," she says. "There are no celebrities in a chill zone."

"My week beats your year," answers Lou.

I'm getting an impression: Pretty Marina must have been a Lou Reed
fan in a past life. It's unusual to see anyone trying to explain the chill zone
to someone who rejects what chill is all about. If some new dude comes
in all chill-zone resistant, you let that person act out his own story. Marina
must have been a huge Lou Reed fan. "Let me explain it again, another
way," she says to Lou, with no diminishment of the full affection she'd
started with: "Celebrity has no chill value."

"Touchy and feely is something I'd rather do than talk about,"
answers Lou. He sips his iced cap and mimes swallowing it with effort.
"Just show me to the VIP rope."

At first glance, the buffet brunch pop-up at the coffee bar appears
to be a self-serve high tea. But you never have any real appetite until
you serve someone else. At your first brunch you see all these blissed-
out people super-stacking comestibles on their trays. They appear to be
hogging all the sweetest cakes. Marina places Lou Reed at a table with a
clear vantage of all the other tables. Lou watches the presumed cake hogs
handing off delicacies to newcomers and late arrivals.

"I see how it is," Lou Reed says. "It's cliques. Everybody looks out
for their friends, *friends* defined as some asshole who can do something
for you later."

"Amazing," agrees Marina, Lou's eternal fan, "you are exactly correct!
Except that *friend* is defined as 'any person who's in need and in range.'"

"Those pastry whores solely want to help a stranger in a crowd?" Lou
dismisses Marina's truth in the backwash of his cold cappuccino. "Bitches
just want to *share*? Naïveté, honey, it only goes so far. Beyond that, you are
truly, shockingly insulting me."

"What is it about sharing that hurts your feelings, Lou?"

A perfect stranger places a macrobiotic salad on the table, addressing
a craving Lou had yet to articulate. "So now we're on first-name basis?"
says Lou. "Here's what hurts my feelings. I'm not crazy about this salad.
I prefer a light dressing. They've given me hardly any. So now I send the
salad back, and I'm the one the blogs will say is the asshole."

"Lou, you haven't tasted the salad."

"No one gives a shit about the work anymore," he says.

"Lou Reed is not looking at the big picture," is Mugger's take on the
scene. "His early work was stellar, but he excreted a few schlock decades.

Several years of subpar output reliant on reputation and propped on crap attitude preceded his widely lamented end."

Reed moves his smirk closer to Marina's open, placid, blushing face. "You're telling me I'm in a place where if I throw a tantrum, my effort will all be pointless?"

"Lou, Lou, Lou." Marina sighs, humored. "I'm a person who believes Lou Reed has always been every bit as great as Lou Reed imagined Lou Reed might have been. Still, you're no big deal here. We have a chill vibe. Everybody chills in the vibe."

Lou Reed lifts his salad bowl. He pulls back his arm and poises the bowl against his ear. "I will throw the tantrum. I will toss the salad."

Marina backs away from the half-cocked salad: "Excuse me for trying to help you make the tough adjustment to a chill situation."

"You're frustrated," says Lou. He forks salad through his grim lips. "I can imagine you once had what you thought were dreams and ambitions. But a fantasy is not a plan, is it, honey? So you have me suffering for your frustrations."

No one Marina meets has any existential basis for frustration. If she mouths this truth and holds her position with Lou, green flecks of lettuce spit will dot her face. Even as Lou's ineffectual fan, Marina is not frustrated. She saunters over and accepts a sip from my coffee and says: "Lou's one of these guys who's forever wishing he could be in some other life."

"That's the last thing I want."

Mugger and I are at the dog park waiting for the wife. The lawns are speckled with shade and sun. Animals and humans play eye tag, flirt and sniff. Maybe the wife will show up, maybe she will not. Our plans are loosey-goosey. Mugger tumbles with several dogs and fights with none. Circumstances are fluid.

The other dog owners are very nice. People stroll, aimless and with purpose; they mill and they cluster. Some turn their backs on others, but nobody shuts anybody out, which is pleasant. Beyond pleasant, French porn starlet Tabatha Cash emerges from a circle of smokers. She shifts a cigarette side to side between her lips. Tabatha Cash comes to me across the grass, a sinuous and sophisticated embodiment of her 1990s prime. Poodles and Bichon Frise dart across her path. Tabatha's pet snake drapes across her bare shoulders like a shawl of exquisite price.

"We keep bumping into each other," she says. She bumps full frontally into me. By trying to reproduce it, I would malign her French accent. I'd fall into stereotype trying to describe the Polynesian accents of her high Parisian hauteur.

"These bumps are not random?" I say. "Are they?"

"I keep an eye open for you." Tabatha winks, a private message, a happy conspiracy, a promise, and a request.

"You're making my day again," I tell her. "You're wearing your happy reptile, your friendly snake." I fall in step with Tabatha, naturally. Who wouldn't? I hadn't even realized that we were walking, and we are isolated, close, intimate, trailed and shadowed by Mugger. "I have never seen such a happy snake," I say, and I'm telling the truth. "I've never seen so friendly a reptile."

"Aren't all snakes happy? Aren't reptiles always friendly?"

"I suppose they are. When they're draped around you."

Tabatha winds a bare arm toward my shoulder, casually placing her perfect skin next to my naked, youthful craving. Heat and coolness transfer in equal measures, and the snake is free to move between us. Our exchange is seamless, sweet, sensual. The only strange thing is that Tabatha and I don't spend more time together. I hadn't anticipated that she would be here. I thought she was in the other place, the busy world I'd left behind.

Tabatha may still be lording it in the dog parks of Paris. Presence has never been explained, at least not to my complete satisfaction. And what among even the simplest phenomena, really, is more than half explicable? Everything that exists, especially the things that are any good, is beyond comprehension, if you stop to think about it. Tabatha's sway leads me to the dog park parking lot, crowded *and* orderly, a testament to the cooperation of considerate drivers. Tabatha opens the door to her metallic gold Escalade. Her snake glides inside and wraps itself into a dangle from the rearview mirror. "Get in," says Tabatha. "I'll take you wherever you want to go!"

But everywhere is within walking distance for me. "Maybe next time," I say. "You know I'm waiting for my wife."

"Well, *chéri*, if her face does not show soon, her spell is broken. You will be up for grabs."

"I'm more than half-enchanted, Tabatha, but the sky is so bright and cool and clear. Mugger and I just want to ramble outside."

The heavenly spheres are aligned inexactly to what I'd grown accustomed to when I looked at the sky as a boy and a young and an aging man. The stars and the moon make themselves available to mingle with the sun from morning on through the night. The daily light is as natural as sunlight, as starlight, as moonlight. The jewels in the heavens are all sky gems I've seen before, and nothing spinning around up there is jolting to my sense of how things should be. Have I mentioned that Mugger can talk? He claims that he always could and I'd never given him the chance.

"And how is Amira?" is the first thing the dog asked me. Amira and I had been together when we rescued Mugger from the dog extermination camp. "You know how much I loved Amira. She missed me terribly when you two broke up. How is she?"

"Amira is fabulous. I have no doubt in my mind. And yes she did miss you terribly."

We gaze off openmouthed before us at a rolling oak tree meadow. Mugger is panting as if Amira might be the next person to stroll into sight over the nearest hillock. "You know the next woman to appear could easily be the wife," I tell the dog.

"I hope you're right," says Mugger, but I am wrong. A nubile, elfin Viva, plucked directly from our frightening and wonderful youthful indiscretions, pops out from behind a tree trunk, lit up and light stepping. She's picked up a dog along the way, a sleek female Dalmatian who prances at Viva's heels in a chic polka-dot coat and introduces herself as Kool-Aid.

Kool-Aid and Mugger say hello and step aside for a private conversation.

"What are you guys doing here?" asks Viva. Her words don't quite reach my mind.

One hand on a twisted hip, a knowing mysterious smile like a kiss on her lips, Viva stands in front of me, casting a solid shadow, like Tabatha Cash had cast while elevating her snake at my side. Going eye to eye, I lose myself for a bit in Viva's gaze. "Mugger and I are at the park waiting for my wife," I say.

Mugger lifts his nose from Kool-Aid's tail. "Not that there's any need to wait," he says conversationally. "Not here."

"You mean everyone catches up?" asks Viva. "Soon enough?"

"I mean everyone arrives with plenty of time to spare," clarifies Mugger.

"Great," says Viva. "No rush. We can relax and enjoy a soft drink and a stiff massage." On previous strolls, I'd noticed an open-air massage studio adjacent to the dog park. On my own, the shop's allure had been resistible, but I follow Viva's loping, side-to-side gait across a cinder lane bordering the dog park and up the stairs to the massage palace entrance.

My first wife, Tommie, not the wife I am waiting for and expecting, stands just inside the gate. That ungovernable halo of black hair; I should have recognized it a block away. "Hi, Allan," says Tommie. "Mugger! We've never met, but I feel I know all about you."

"Same here," says Mugger. "You're the girl, any dope who lost you, it would halfway kill him."

"That's all behind us," I say, anxious to cover up the dog's lack of tact. "It's great to see you, Tommie! Are you just leaving? We're just arriving."

"I'm hostessing," says Tommie.

"Great," blurts Viva, never one to settle into a background role. "We're on the watch for Allan's later wife to show up at the dog park. So could you position us so we can keep an eye on the puppies?"

Tommie puts a hand almost to my arm. "The one you call the wife loves a vigorous massage," she says. "She and I talked once, and the subject came up."

"Then I guess you two will be old friends when she shows."

"No doubt we will. As for now, I have just what you need—four open tables on the front rail."

The dog park is the primary view from the front rail. Tommie takes our drink orders, and Viva and I visit separate changing rooms and wrap massive warm towels around our bodies. We settle in belly down on the middle two of the four open tables. To switch things up, I have Kool-Aid on the table at my side; Viva takes Mugger beside her. "This is the first place to bring the wife," I confide to Kool-Aid, "for her first afternoon in the neighborhood, for our first public activity once we are reunited."

Lou Reed drags his feet along the cinder path bordering the dog park, visibly agitated behind his black-lens cop shades. He spots the massage palace sign and makes a bothered beeline to the reception desk. Pencil in hand, looking up from a schedule book, Tommie takes Lou fully in with her eyes and welcomes him with an unqualified smile.

"Are you working here?" Lou says. "Is anybody working here?" He digs his fingers into the back of his neck.

"We'll squeeze that agitation right out of you," says Tommie. "You're in the right place."

"We are far from any right place I've ever known," says Lou. "Dog shit all over that park. Disease flourishes where dog shit drops."

Of course there is no dog shit in the park. The shit-free reality is counterintuitive, yes. But I don't need to tell you twice: no dog shit. Tommie sets up Lou not far from us, and scampers to fetch his complex drink order. Lou scans the premises, holding warm, capacious towels in his hands and a practiced frown on his face. He spots me and Viva. His happiness diminishes to see us, but his full ire focuses on the dogs supine on the massage tables to either side of Viva and me. "There is no escaping these animals," he says.

"You know," whispers Viva, "I've really come to appreciate the whole chill aspect here. Let me chill out this fussy little man."

Rising on an elbow, flicking turquoise strands back from her pancake-powdered cheeks, Viva cranes to face Lou. Her towels, I don't mind noticing, artfully loosen and separate to create a voyeur's treasure trail. "Are you from New York?" chirps Viva. She flashes a Polaroid-ready smile. "I was once from New York."

Lou jolts to his full height. He glares at Viva. "You've got to be kidding. I am New York. You don't need to tell me you're from New York. We know our dog shit in New York. Don't we, honey?"

Viva sits up on her massage table and swivels toward Lou. Her legs spread open beneath terrycloth. She slouches the fabric below her shoulders and commands her posture to erect attention. "We New Yorkers do know our dog shit. And we know about chance encounters in faraway places. Remember how we can turn the most awkward meeting into an impromptu romance? We know how to have a real good time together, don't we?"

Lou is nonplussed. "Step back, sweetheart. Don't move any closer to me. I'm afraid I'll fall into your babbling brook." Lou flings his warm, commodious towel to the floor. He slips, regains his balance, and bolts into the sunny moonlight outside.

Tommie watches Lou kicking cinders along the path bordering the dog park. "I'm sure we can help that man," she says, sipping Lou's complex drink. "Is everybody ready?"

The massage is a lighter touch than my body has ever known. "I'm not sure the wife will go for this," I confide to Kool-Aid. "She has always preferred deep tissue disruption."

Passing moments flow around me in a refreshing and relaxing and buffeting stream of pleasure in all its physical and intellectual and spiritual forms. I'm immersed in desired sensations. Ultimately, there comes a sense that you've soaked up a happy surplus of good feeling. Saturated with delight, you shower and towel yourself off.

Robyn, my favorite boss ever, is waiting for me in the locker room. She's dressed for business: white blouse closed at the neck and fastened with a trim navy tie, navy pencil skirt, red-soled navy pumps just steep enough to betray the false-staid effect of the shirt and skirt. "No pressure," Robyn says, politely looking away as I pull on my clothes. "When you're ready, not a moment sooner, let's synchronize and reenter the workforce."

I'm dressing power-suit casual. There's no ebb in the saturation of delight within me. That delight surges at the backspin Robyn puts on the word *reenter*. I'm prepared for business and happy to be about it. "Now is not a moment too soon, Robyn. Your job offer has arrived at exactly the right time."

Robyn leads the way to our offices, set in a villa overlooking the dog park. The workplace is clear and bright. My first impression of the dozen varied people at drawing boards and display terminals and desktop workstations is that everyone along the spectrum is happy to see everyone else. The entire crew cries out as a team, "Hi, Robyn!"

"Good morning!" my old boss calls in response. Someone, I don't see who, hands us each a cup of coffee. "And here's Allan at last," announces Robyn.

"Welcome to your first day," calls the team.

"I predict you'll like it here," says Robyn.

The immediate sense is that you and your fast-forming colleagues have things to do, statements to make, changes to create, innovations that will quantifiably improve living conditions near and far. Because I have job history with Robyn, she opts to work as my lab partner. I look out through one of our shaded floor-to-ceiling windows for a few seconds, watching Mugger twinkling on his toes along with Viva and Kool-Aid, patrolling the cinder path around the park on the alert for the wife.

"Shall we start?" says Robyn. And that's how we will begin every workday, enthusiastic, focused, coordinated, an exercise in unity. Our work goal is simple. We are transferring good faith. We facilitate the spread of blessed fortune. We place glad tidings within the grasp of anyone who is willing to reach for them. The goals are serious; the work is fun. Leaving the office, refreshed and recharged and rejuvenated from putting in a full shift, I help Robyn into her jacket. "It's like we're having playdates every day," I say.

Robyn twists the heel of her pump to display the red sole. "With no parental supervision," she purrs.

"I still don't understand exactly what it is you do on your job," says Viva. Mugger and Kool-Aid walk shoulder to shoulder ahead of us, their tails swinging in the air.

"You're sure she wasn't here?" I ask, not with anxiety, just to cover the bases. "Maybe she didn't see me here; so she went to wait inside somewhere."

"Sorry, Charlie. Mugger never would have let her slip past. And you haven't answered me. What do you and Robyn do together that you and I don't do together?"

"Think of Robyn and me as creating distribution hubs for good intentions and better outcomes."

"Better outcomes for who?"

"For anyone who's seeking a better outcome. We send upgrades back to the places where we all came from."

"You're mouthing a company line."

"It is the company line! But it's true too. Our services extend to the most remote human outposts back where we used to live, and also to people here."

"Even to your wife?"

"Especially to my wife."

"That's amazing," admits Viva, "considering you don't know specifically where your wife is."

The truth is that I'm becoming nearer and closer to the wife through my day-to-day "grind" at the office. The technology that has made integral cogs of me and the rest of the team is difficult to explain, like presence itself. Suffice it to say that a proprietary process empowers our efforts. Our trick is that we have sourced a network that doesn't require a network. Nothing has to be plugged in. Everyone is already plugged in. Somebody who's interesting to you, and who's interested in you, is always plugged in. This core reality is our business model. Robyn breaks it down at an informal PowerPoint pep talk: "You are forever connected, no matter how far adrift you feel (emotion) or believe (intellect) yourself to be."

Robyn and I have convened for an offsite meeting at the massage palace, brainstorming on adjacent tables. We roadmap a series of delivery system fine-tunes. Then we step into the dry-heat sauna and plop down nearly on top of Marina and Lou Reed. Lou's proximity to Marina is so tight that anyone closer would be cuddling, or touching at least. The wife would be right at home here. She would be plugged in. What am I saying? She *is* plugged in, like we all are plugged in.

Marina, for instance, has always plugged in to finding lost causes she can help lead un-astray. Naturally, she plugged into Lou Reed. "My battery is charging," Lou says. "I feel better. I feel better than I have ever since, well, since I can remember."

The sauna is filling up with holiday types, day-trippers on a guided excursion. Lou leans forward, confidential like. He slides the black-lens, steel-frame shades up his nose and bores me with those eyes: "To tell the truth, I feel better than all these other sucks put together."

More people need to experience the blessing of meaningful labor. In what seems like a relatively short elapsed time, everything you'd hoped you might have the chance to accomplish during the course of an entire lifespan is done. You have filled your time with winning moments. You've taken the situation in hand. Your work is done. You and Robyn are heading out after your last day on the job. "I'm so excited and happy for you," she says, "for what's happening next."

A message has been forwarded through Robyn. The wife is scheduled to arrive, and you and Mugger, right on time, are at the airport to meet her flight. Lost in something beyond thought, you sit silent with your dog enjoying people watching from the airport coffee bar. Lou Reed's voice intrudes, in your head, saying, "Sure, I feel better than ever. That's just who I am. I will not miss this place one iota." You turn around to verify the voice's source. Lou it is. "When I am gone from here," he says, "I will never give this place the first infinitesimal fraction of a thought."

He's sitting at a table of likeminded suck-ups he has found—or recruited. "Congratulations, man," says one of Lou's companions, sucking up. "It sounds like you plan to not stick around."

"I'm at the airport, my bags are packed and checked in," says Lou Reed, a bit caustic. "I guess that visual *sounds* to you like I'm ready to get on with my life."

"Just checking."

"I've got things to do," says Lou. "Let's get back to it. Let's move forward."

I've strayed, I realize, to the departures lounge. "How did we get here?" I ask Mugger. "Is this where I belong?"

"I'm the dog," says Mugger. "You're asking the dog?"

Marina steps out from the coffee counter to bus Lou's table. "To be clear," she says to Lou, "you are expressing a desire to be alive again?"

"What nonsense now?" asks Lou. "How can I desire what I already have?"

There is something to what Lou and Marina have said that bears deeper consideration, but a calm, knowing voice over the airport PA announces that a flight is landing. This landing very well may be the flight that brings the wife to me. Mugger and I rush to the arrivals pavilion. A full jetliner has just taxied in. The new arrivals straggle off. They look fatigued, as if they have come on a long, long-delayed trip. I watch them one by one, each and every worn one of them, from the first to the last, step through the gate and onto the carpet, blinking and failing to make full sense of where they find themselves.

Someone steps forward to greet each of the arriving passengers, not necessarily someone the passenger knows or expects to be waiting for them. This all seems familiar, but my only interest is in scanning the arrivals. I check them all off, from first passenger to last, and confirm with certainty: the wife is not among the tired souls on this flight.

"Mugger, am I forced to wait another day? Do I need to fly back and meet the wife where we were pronounced man and wife from this day forth, until…?"

"I'm a dog."

Tommie is in the information booth. Her face is filled with indications of assurance; all that assurance leaves no room for her signature smile.

"Tommie: How do I get to the departures ticketing area?"

Marina has joined Tommie in the information booth. "It's not as easy as you might think, Allan."

The fact that I am dead, that I am not dreaming this, moves to the forefront of my mind. "On the off chance that I am mistaken…" I say. "Let me ask you…"

"Oh, no," says Marina gently and warmly, "you are not wrong."

"Just checking," I say.

"Your time has elapsed," says Marina. Her small smile is pure kindness. "We're here to confirm that."

"It's not that I've had a realization exactly," I explain.

"Our policy is, we try to break it gently," explains Tommie.

"Of course I've known, maybe not all along."

Marina extends a hand as if to touch me. Her fingers never quite make contact. "We try to let the realization filter in by degrees."

"Naturally, I have caught on." Really, I have known the score from the start. Still, the outcome unsettles me, and I am happy to drift.

When I return from my drift, I'm on my feet, in the park where the dogs frolic. I wake to the fresh realization that I'm dead. There's no going back from that. Mugger thinks he has spotted Kool-Aid behind a clump of scrub. He trots off on his own and I walk with the sense that someone is pacing me at my side. Of course, I look over there. I can't see anyone. Nothing. Maybe my companion is just some other facet of me, or some invisible friend I've conjured up, or me idealized as I've imagined me to be. "I've just noticed," I say, halting in my tracks and turning in a full circle for emphasis, "that stopping to consider that you may have passed into a time when you are gone triggers the realization that really, truly you are gone."

"You've been leaving all along. You're conceived, and life is behind you."

You could never paint a picture of who or what I'm speaking with. Nevertheless, I have conversed. I have communed. I put a foot in front of the other. I walk strictly in line. I've strayed off the trail. I've strayed beyond where any path can reach. I've wandered to where every path ultimately jumps the trail. I lie back at rest on a sandy beach hearing the ocean surge.

I've been here at this shore before. We've all been on this shore. A deep, open secret floats directly in front of my eyes: the clouds above me move on different levels at different speeds passing in different directions. I crave a companion. I want to show someone that the clouds are drifting at different heights above us, in opposing directions, some faster, others slower.

The wife sits in the warm sand at my side. I find that the she is unavailable. We are as close and consciously present with one another as any human beings in our situation can be. Coarse granules sift between her fingers. Sand falls like planets dusted from the hands of some indifferent creator. I tell the wife, "Look at what the clouds are doing in the sky."

"I know. I was telling you about that."

Her shallow breath blows away my words. She sees beyond my observations. She's smiling. Sun glints from her eyes. Sitting with me and fully clear from me on the warm, glistening shore, Trina's features are indistinct within a hot glowing sphere. I know she's there. I see her outline flaming in the center of that blur of brilliance. I am drawn to look directly in. Life's mystery and miracles burn right in front of my eyes. The unknown is a given; the beyond is at hand. I own nothing now; the great, infinite, ineffable nothing is all mine. Nothing has always belonged to me. That possession should be taken on faith with every breath—from the first suck of air to the last expiration.

What I've learned in the spaces between these shifting clouds, the forever-transitory truth perceived flat on my back from that sleepy beach, is that the sun burns through. No cloud covering separates me; no swaddling mist protects me from that life-giving and all-extinguishing ray. Now evaporates, and this light becomes me.

ACKNOWLEDGMENTS

DEEPEST THANKS TO ALEX Maslansky, Cali Thornhill DeWitt, Rare Bird Books, and every person I've ever met. No confession this awkward could have been preserved without all of you.